Half a Can
of Tomato Paste
and Other
Culinary
Dilemmas

Also by Jean Anderson

The Art of American Indian Cooking
(with Yeffe Kimball)

Food Is More Than Cooking

Henry the Navigator, Prince of Portugal

The Haunting of America

The Family Circle Cookbook
(with the Food Editors of Family Circle)

The Doubleday Cookbook *(with Elaine Hanna)*

Recipes from America's Restored Villages

The Green Thumb Preserving Guide

The Grass Roots Cookbook

Jean Anderson's Processor Cooking

Half a Can of Tomato Paste and Other Culinary Dilemmas

A COOKBOOK BY

Jean Anderson

AND

Ruth Buchan

HARPER & ROW, PUBLISHERS

NEW YORK

Cambridge London
Hagerstown Mexico City
Philadelphia São Paulo
San Francisco 1817 Sydney

FIRST EDITION

Designer: Suzanne Haldane

Library of Congress Cataloging in Publication Data

Anderson, Jean, date
  Half a can of tomato paste and other culinary dilemmas.
  Includes index.
  1. Cookery (Leftovers)   I. Buchan, Ruth,
joint author.   II. Title.
TX740.A67 1980   641.5   79–3385
ISBN 0–06–010147–4

---

80 81 82 83 84 10 9 8 7 6 5 4 3 2 1

CONTENTS

Introduction

There have been cookbooks devoted to leftovers, it's true, but to our knowledge none that has dealt effectively (or, for that matter, specifically) with those partly used packaged foods that clutter refrigerator and cupboard.

The trouble is, most foods today are packaged in such a way that we must buy more of them than we need for a particular recipe, indeed more than we are apt to use within a reasonable period of time. And this holds as true for such perishables as bananas, green peppers, and fresh parsley, which we must buy by the bunch or piece or Pliofilm-sealed supermarket package, as it does for boxed, bagged, bottled, and canned foods.

Have a look in your refrigerator. Any half-empty tins of tomato paste there? Any partially squeezed-out tubes of anchovy paste? Any halves or quarters of green pepper gathering mold? A not-quite-empty carton of cream going sour? More than likely.

These are the problem leftovers that come immediately to mind. And yet so many of the staples that we consider nonperishable (corn meal, cornstarch, brown sugar, dates, and raisins, for example) do in the end become nonpalatable and nonusable if not actually spoiled. Because time so easily eludes us, we should all develop the habit of dating packaged foods—particularly the nonperishables—on the day of purchase, so we have some notion as to their age, so we can be thinking how we will ultimately use them, be it in six days or six months (some staples are long-term leftovers), and, most important, so we will know when we should begin using them up in earnest, before they reach the point of no return (become rancid or buggy or so stale that no amount of seasoning can camouflage their elderliness).

Too often, either because we lack the time to search through our collection of recipes for solutions or because we haven't the foggiest notion where to look to find easy, practical, and appealing ways of using up these leftover "staples," we end up throwing them out. Most cookbooks, as a matter of fact, aren't much help—even those devoted to leftovers concern themselves almost totally with leftover cooked meats, fish, fowl, and vegetables.

Too frequently, moreover, we are put off trying an interesting new recipe—or even preparing an old favorite—simply because it calls for an ingredient we don't have, one that we must buy in too large a quantity: 2 tablespoons of minced preserved ginger, for example, which must be bought in an 8-ounce jar; or ½ cup of sour cream, which comes in either an 8-ounce (1 cup) or 16-ounce (2 cup) carton. Even such staples as corn syrup, molasses, and buttermilk must be bought in outsize portions. Most buttermilk cakes or breads, for example, call for only 1 to 1½ cups of buttermilk, and unless there are buttermilk lovers around, the balance will merely appropriate refrigerator space until it spoils. All because there is no single, handy source that tells what to do with the leftovers.

We hope that this lexicon of leftovers will be that source, that it will provide, via quick tips and recipes, ideas for dealing imaginatively with leftovers. We have tried, quite simply, to avoid the dreary dishes that fairly scream "leftover"—the quickie casseroles held together with canned creamed soups, the "shelf-magic" skillet scrambles that taste as blah as they look. You may be surprised to discover that among our leftover recipes there are a few that call for fresh fish or shellfish or perhaps a fairly exotic flavoring.

And why not? Our aim is to demonstrate that leftovers mustn't forever be considered second-class family fare, that they can, indeed should, be used as ingredients in impressive party dishes that take advantage of the local catch, of the seasonal fruits and vegetables— indeed, of the fascinating foreign foods now sold by so many specialty shops across the country. We don't expect every recipe to appeal to every reader, but we trust that everyone will find something of value among them as well as in the basic information on the use, care, and keeping of staples that begins each section.

What we have done is to list—alphabetically—some fifty of the most commonly used ingredients that must be bought in larger-than-needed quantities, thereby qualifying as troublesome leftovers. If, for example, you've a couple of egg yolks (or whites) to use up, all you have to do is look up "Eggs" in the pages that follow. There you will find, not only ways of using up the leftover yolks and whites, but also information on how (and how *long*) each may safely be stored, directions for freezing them, a description of their roles in cooking, and suggestions as to where among your files and favorite cookbooks you may find dishes made with egg yolks or whites should our recipes not suit your needs of the moment.

We have discussed each potentially troublesome leftover individually, in alphabetical order, then followed with recipes that will show how to use up anywhere from the smallest amounts (1 to 2 tablespoons) to, as in the case of buttermilk or cloudy vinegar, fairly substantial quantities (2 to 3 cups).

We have tried, too, to avoid the sort of catch-22 situation with leftovers that beset one young bride. In order to make her mother's marvelous four-layer devil's food cake, she bought a quart of buttermilk, to use only 1½ cups of it. Her mother suggested that she bake the balance into her very special buttermilk pie, which, alas, also called for 1 cup of raisins. Applesauce cookies, the mother promised, would take care of the rest of the raisins. They did, but they also required a cup of rolled oats. The leftover rolled oats? "Well," the mother said, "why don't you make that meat loaf of mine you always loved so?" The daughter did, only to discover that she had a half a tin of tomato paste left over. And so it went.

There is always a danger of creating new leftovers at the same time that you are using up old ones. To minimize this risk, we have developed recipes in which any number of substitutions can be made and optional ingredients used without courting disaster. We have also shown, wherever practical, how recipes may be frozen—often in quantities for one, two, four, or more so that you can prolong the life of perishables as much as a hundredfold.

It is our hope that this lexicon will become a valuable kitchen reference, a problem-solving dictionary of leftovers that will encourage you to improvise and economize. The recipes, we believe, are imaginative, they are practical, and—more important—they are *flexible,* demonstrating that an extra tablespoon or two of tomato paste, for example, may even improve a recipe that calls for just 1 tablespoon.

Our list of leftovers is based upon our own personal experiences, of course, and may not solve some of the special problems you have encountered. Still, we hope that once you become accustomed to using this book, you will discover that its principles carry over and that you are coping—and cooking—creatively with *every* leftover.

JEAN ANDERSON
RUTH BUCHAN

New York

Anchovies

(Anchovy Fillets, Anchovy Paste)

These minnow-sized, Mediterranean members of the herring family have long been a European favorite for enlivening bland dishes such as stuffed hard-cooked eggs. Anchovies are oily, and like most other oily fish, powerhouses of flavor. For that reason, they must be used sparingly, which inevitably means leftovers whether you are dealing with anchovy fillets or with the paste.

ANCHOVY FILLETS

These are imported, for the most part from Portugal and Spain, and packed, 10 to 14 together, in flat, 2-ounce tins. The anchovy fillets may be rolled around a caper (perfect for garnishing canapés) or they may be packed flat in any of these ways: in vinegar (pickled), in salt (brined) or—and this is far and away the most popular—in olive oil and salt.

N O T E *Always taste a newly opened can of anchovies before using the anchovies in a recipe. If they are unduly salty, rinse the fillets well in tepid water, then pat very dry on paper toweling. And, of course, the oil in which the anchovies were packed should be discarded unless a recipe specifies otherwise. It will be too fishy and salty to use in the majority of recipes.*

Best Way to Store Once a tin of anchovies is opened, remove all fillets and wrap whatever you will not be using right away in foil or plastic food wrap, then store in the refrigerator in a conspicuous spot where the packet will not become lost or forgotten.

Maximum Storage Time Because anchovies are so heavily brined, spoilage is not a problem (salt, by the way, is one of the earliest preservatives known to man). But leftover anchovies *are* a bother, and no matter how well you wrap them, they are likely to smell up the refrigerator. So use them up within a week or two if possible (you'll find plenty of ideas in the pages that follow).

Roles in Cooking   For flavor and decoration. A crosshatch design of anchovies is what "makes" a steak Mirabeau, and a tiny fillet, coiled around a single caper, will nudge even the simplest canapé toward elegance.

Recipe Uses   Anchovies are integral to so many recipes: fish puddings, sauces, dips, flavored butters, even salad dressings (such as the classic Green Goddess dressing) and scalloped potatoes (such as Sweden's popular Jansson's Temptation).

Special Comments   Can anchovy fillets and anchovy paste be used interchangeably? Yes, in recipes where their appearance isn't important (dips and spreads, salad dressings, sauces, and the like). As for equivalents: 1 finely minced large anchovy fillet = 1 level teaspoon anchovy paste.

ANCHOVY PASTE

This is nothing more than anchovy fillets ground to paste, then blended with salt and a small amount of sugar (to mellow the flavor). Anchovy paste is packed in 2-ounce tubes, which is to say about the size of a small tube of toothpaste (this amount equals about 4 tablespoons, or ¼ cup). Like anchovy fillets, anchovy paste should be kept under refrigeration once it's opened, and although it will keep well for several months, it, too, is the sort of small, pesky leftover that is likely to clutter up refrigerator shelves or, worse yet, become lost.

Best Way to Store   Stand the tube of anchovy paste in a small, slim glass in the refrigerator (this way it won't skitter about the shelves and out of sight). Also make certain that the cap is screwed down tight.

Roles in Cooking   For flavor and, to some extent, to help thicken a sauce, gravy, or dressing. Anchovy paste has no thickening power, as does flour or cornstarch, yet it is such a heavy mixture that it will slightly thicken whatever liquid it is mixed with in a physical rather than a chemical sense.

Recipe Uses   Primarily for sauces, gravies, dressings, and so forth, where smoothness of texture is important. Anchovy paste blends with liquids more uniformly than finely minced anchovies ever can (see the recipe for Jansson's Temptation that follows).

How to Use Very Small Amounts   If you are as Scottish as we are, you hate to throw out a tube of anchovy paste even though it's all but squeezed down to the end. But what can you do with a couple of teaspoons of anchovy paste? Well, you can add anywhere from ½ teaspoon to 1 tablespoon to any seafood sauce or chowder (but do reduce the amount of salt in the recipe accordingly). You can smooth a dab into cheese, egg, or fish dips and spreads; you can add up to a tablespoon of anchovy paste to a tuna, chicken, or egg salad. You can even smooth a tablespoon or so into a potato soup or casserole, into baked stuffed or mashed potatoes. Anchovy paste is a far more versatile ingredient than we give it credit for, and it takes well to improvisation.

N O T E   *For additional recipes, included elsewhere in this book, that call for varying amounts of anchovy fillets and paste, see the Appendix.*

ANCHOVY-STUFFED EGGS

4 to 6 servings

Do not use more than 3 teaspoons (1 tablespoon) anchovy paste in preparing this recipe or the eggs will be too salty. If you use the capers, reduce the amount of anchovy paste to 2 teaspoons, for the capers, too, are salty.

    8 hard-cooked eggs, peeled, chilled well, and halved lengthwise
    1 tablespoon finely minced onion
    1 tablespoon minced fresh parsley
    ½ teaspoon dill weed
    1 to 3 teaspoons anchovy paste
    3 tablespoons mayonnaise
    ⅛ teaspoon freshly ground black pepper
    2 tablespoons tiny capers, drained well (optional)

Scoop the egg yolks into a mixing bowl, add all the remaining ingredients except the capers and the egg whites, and beat hard with a fork or whisk until creamy. Add the capers, if you like, then spoon the yolk mixture back into the whites, mounding it up slightly in the center.

Serve at once (the yolk mixture tends to darken on standing).

GREEN GODDESS DRESSING

About 2 cups

Here's a flexible recipe that enables you to use up as much as 4 teaspoons of leftover anchovy paste or 4 anchovy fillets. Use to dress crisp green salads. This dressing, by the way, is an American classic invented years ago by the chef of San Francisco's Palace Hotel in honor of George Arliss, who was starring in a play called *The Green Goddess.* The play has long been forgotten, but not the salad dressing.

Double the recipe, if you like, and store in the refrigerator in a tightly covered jar. The dressing will keep about 1 week.

1 large clove garlic, peeled and quartered
¼ cup minced fresh tarragon
¼ cup minced fresh parsley
¼ cup minced fresh chives
2 teaspoons minced shallots or scallions
2 to 4 teaspoons anchovy paste or 3 to 4 anchovy fillets, rinsed and minced fine
1 cup mayonnaise
1 cup sour cream
¼ cup tarragon vinegar
Pinch of freshly ground black pepper

Rub a small mixing bowl well with the garlic quarters, then discard the garlic. Add all the remaining ingredients to the bowl and whisk briskly to combine. Cover and refrigerate for several hours, whisking vigorously again before using.

ANCHOVY BUTTER

About ¾ cup

The beauty of this butter—in addition to the fact that it uses up 3 to 4 teaspoons anchovy paste or 3 to 5 anchovy fillets—is that you can shape it into a log, foil-wrap it and freeze it, then slice off individual pats as you need them. The anchovy butter will keep well for 3 to 4 months in the freezer, for about 10 days in the refrigerator. Spread on broiled steaks or chops, or on broiled salmon, tuna, or swordfish. Or do as the British do and spread it on toast.

> ¾ cup (1½ sticks) *unsalted* butter, at room temperature
> 3 to 4 teaspoons anchovy paste or 3 to 5 anchovy fillets, rinsed well and minced as fine as possible
> ⅛ teaspoon cayenne pepper
> 1 teaspoon lemon juice

Cream all the ingredients together until absolutely homogeneous, then cover and store in the refrigerator. Or chill the butter until firm enough to shape, roll into a log about 1½ inches in diameter, wrap in foil, and freeze.

JANSSON'S TEMPTATION

6 servings

This classic Swedish dish is traditionally made with minced anchovy fillets, but we prefer the following version for several reasons. First of all, by using anchovy paste and blending it with the cream, the fish flavor more evenly pervades the potatoes (anchovy fillets, no matter how finely minced, always seem to clump). Second, this recipe is a superb way to use up leftover anchovy paste—anywhere from 1 to 3 tablespoons of it. If you use the full 3 tablespoons, you probably will not need to add any salt to the recipe, but if you use less, you may. Taste the anchovy-cream mixture *before* pouring it into the casserole, and add salt if needed.

> 4 medium yellow onions, peeled and sliced quite thin (about ⅛ inch thick)
> 3 tablespoons butter
> 6 large baking potatoes, peeled and sliced ⅛ inch thick
> Freshly ground black pepper
> 1 to 3 tablespoons anchovy paste
> 2 cups light cream
> Salt, if needed, to taste

Preheat the oven to hot (400°F.).
Sauté the onions in the butter in a large, heavy skillet over moderate

heat for 8 to 10 minutes, until limp and golden but not brown. Now layer the onions and potatoes in a well-buttered 2½-quart casserole as follows, sprinkling with freshly ground pepper as you go: one-third of the potatoes, one-half of the sautéed onions, another third of the potatoes, the remaining onions, and, finally, the remaining potatoes.

Whisk the anchovy paste vigorously with about ½ cup of the cream until uniformly blended (or, if you prefer, beat with a rotary beater), then combine with the remaining 1½ cups of cream. Taste the mixture, and if it is not salty enough to suit you, add salt. Pour the anchovy mixture evenly over the top layer of potatoes (it will not cover them) and bake, uncovered, in the preheated oven for 1½ to 2 hours, or until the casserole is richly browned and the potatoes are tender.

Serve at once.

VISBY FISH PUDDING

6 servings

Visby is a delightful medieval walled town, all cobblestone streets and half-timbered houses, on the Swedish island of Gotland. This mousse-light fish pudding, a great favorite of frugal Visby cooks, uses up a lot of the leftovers that tend to clutter our refrigerators and cupboards: anchovy paste, for example, cooked fish, even stale bread. It's a flexible recipe, moreover, in that you may also add as much as ½ cup grated Gruyère or Cheddar cheese or ¼ cup of grated Parmesan.

> 1 pound cooked fish, boned and flaked (any fish may be used, but such delicate white fish as flounder, haddock, or sea bass is especially good)
> 4 cups cooked rice
> 3 large eggs, beaten lightly
> 1 to 3 tablespoons anchovy paste
> 3 cups milk
> ½ cup grated Gruyère or Cheddar cheese or ¼ cup grated Parmesan (optional)
> ½ teaspoon dill weed
> Pinch of grated nutmeg
> Pinch of freshly ground black pepper
> Salt, if needed, to taste

2 slices stale bread, buzzed to crumbs in a food processor or electric blender (or simply grated on the second coarsest side of a four-sided grater)
1 tablespoon melted butter

Preheat the oven to moderate (350°F.).

Combine the flaked fish, rice, and eggs in a large bowl. In a small bowl, beat the anchovy paste with ½ cup of the milk until uniformly smooth (a whisk or rotary beater is the best implement to use). Add to the fish mixture along with the remaining 2½ cups of milk, the optional cheese, the dill weed, nutmeg, and pepper. Taste the mixture and add salt, if needed. Pour all into a well-buttered 3-quart casserole.

Combine the two topping ingredients, then scatter the buttered crumbs evenly on top of the casserole. Bake, uncovered, in the preheated oven for about 1 hour, or until the pudding is softly set—like a custard. Remove from the oven and cool for 15 minutes.

To serve, simply spoon up as you would any casserole.

Bananas

(Ripe)

It may seem out of place for us to include bananas in a lexicon that deals for the most part with packaged foods. But not really, when you consider that bananas must be bought by the package or bunch, which at the very least means three bananas. Those who live alone, or who do not fancy eating bananas out of hand, may indeed have difficulty using them before they spoil. The best plan, we've found, is to turn ripe bananas into something less perishable—an ice cream, for example, or a batch of muffins or cookies, which can then be frozen and kept for months.

Best Way to Store   Uncovered, at room temperature but away from direct sunlight. Once bananas are soft, refrigerate them to retard over-ripening. The skins will blacken, but the bananas will remain delicious.

Maximum Storage Time   So much depends upon the ripeness of the bananas at the time you buy them, also upon the weather. But you will be lucky to be able to hold ripe bananas longer than 5 days.

Roles in Cooking   To add flavor, primarily. But mashed bananas will help bind cake or torte layers together. And sliced bananas add a soft, textural counterpoint to the crispness of apples and pears in fruit salads and compotes. Bananas, by the way, are unusually high in potassium (an aid to circulation of the blood).

Recipe Uses   Look first to the salad and dessert sections of your favorite cookbooks for ways of using bananas, then to the quick breads and cookies. Bananas are also often broiled or sautéed and served as vegetables accompanying pork, poultry, ham, or seafood.

N O T E   *For additional recipes, included elsewhere in this book, that call for varying amounts of ripe bananas, see the Appendix.*

B A N A N A   Y O G U R T

2 Servings

Here's a delicious quickie—serve as a bracing midafternoon refresher or as dessert.

> **2 very ripe bananas, peeled and sliced**
> **2 containers (8 ounces each) plain or vanilla yogurt**
> **Ground cinnamon or grated nutmeg**

Buzz the bananas and yogurt up together in an electric blender or food processor until smooth. Spoon into dessert dishes and chill for 30 minutes. Dust lightly with cinnamon or nutmeg and enjoy.

BANANA-OATMEAL COOKIES

About 2½ dozen

These cookies are moist and they keep well, so utilize any overripe bananas you may have by making up a batch or two to have on hand. Freeze the cookies, if you like—simply bundle up in plastic bags, twist the tops into tight goosenecks, and secure with twist-bands. The frozen cookies will remain nice and "fresh" for several months.

1½ cups sifted all-purpose flour
½ teaspoon baking powder
1 teaspoon salt
¾ teaspoon ground cinnamon
¼ teaspoon grated nutmeg
1 cup firmly packed light brown sugar
¾ cup vegetable shortening
1 egg, beaten well
1 cup mashed ripe banana
1¾ cups rolled oats
½ cup coarsely chopped pecans, walnuts, or other nuts

Preheat the oven to moderate (350° F.).

Sift the flour, baking powder, salt, cinnamon, and nutmeg together into a mixing bowl; add the brown sugar and combine with the dry ingredients, pressing out any lumps. With a pastry blender, cut in the shortening until the mixture is crumbly. Add the egg, mashed banana, rolled oats, and nuts.

Drop the dough from a teaspoon onto ungreased baking sheets, spacing the cookies about 1½ inches apart. (The cookies do not spread out as they bake, so you may want to flatten them slightly with the back of your spoon as you drop them onto the baking sheets.) Bake in the preheated oven for about 15 minutes, or until the cookies have lost their wet look and are slightly brown.

Remove while warm to wire racks to cool.

FROZEN BANANA CREAM

6 servings

The beauty of this dessert, aside from the fact that it salvages 3 to 4 overripe bananas, is that it utilizes such pesky leftovers as honey or corn syrup and that it can be made with almost any combination of milk, evaporated milk, or cream. The less heavy cream or evaporated milk you use, however, the harder you must beat the partially frozen mixture to achieve a smooth texture.

> **3 to 4 medium, very ripe bananas, peeled**
> **¼ cup lemon juice**
> **½ cup orange juice or a half-and-half mixture of orange and pineapple juice or orange juice and apricot or peach nectar (whatever you have on hand)**
> **½ cup honey or corn syrup (light or dark)**
> **2½ cups any milk-cream combination (but at least ¾ cup heavy cream or partially frozen evaporated milk), the cream or evaporated milk kept separate and whipped to stiff peaks (see note below)**

Purée the bananas with the lemon juice in a food processor fitted with the metal chopping blade or in an electric blender at low speed. (If you have neither processor nor blender, press the bananas through a food mill and combine at once with the lemon juice to prevent darkening.) Mix in the orange juice and honey, then the milk. Finally, fold in the whipped cream or whipped evaporated milk. Pour into a 9 × 5 × 3-inch loaf pan and freeze until mushy.

Scoop the mixture into your largest electric mixer bowl and beat at high speed until fluffy. Return the mixture to the loaf pan and freeze until firm.

Serve as is or topped with any sliced fresh or frozen fruit.

N O T E *If you are using ¾ cup or less of heavy cream or evaporated milk, once again freeze the mixture until mushy, then beat hard with the electric mixer until fluffy. Return to the pan and freeze until firm.*

Bouillons, Broths, and Consommés

(Canned)

These shouldn't be difficult leftovers to get rid of, and yet they often are—through either our own laziness or lack of imagination. Bouillons, broths, and consommés are most often packed in 10½- or 13¾-ounce cans (about 1¼ and 1¾ cups, respectively), which, unfortunately, rarely coincide with the quantities called for in recipes. So you are inevitably stuck with a cup or less—too skimpy a portion even for lunch on the run. Here, then, are some suggestions for using up small amounts of canned bouillons, broths, and consommés. But first, some clarification. Are these three items the same? Can they be used interchangeably? No, to the first question; yes, to the second. Bouillons and broths are essentially the same ("bouillon" is merely the French word, "broth" the English). But there is one qualification: bouillons are sometimes made with more than one meat—with beef and veal, for example—whereas broths are almost always made with one meat alone. And what about consommé? It is a richer meat or poultry broth that has been clarified (skimmed of all fat and sediment).

Best Way to Store   We like to pour the leftover broth or consommé into a clean jar and screw the lid down tight, instead of leaving it in its original can, before refrigerating, because we think the broth takes on a metallic taste. It's perfectly safe, however, to store leftover broths and consommés in their original cans in the refrigerator. Just be certain to cover the openings with foil or plastic food wrap to seal refrigerator odors out.

Maximum Storage Time   About 5 days.

Roles in Cooking   Bouillons, broths, and consommés all provide flavor, color, and an excellent source of protein—with practically no calories (about 35 per cup of chicken or beef broth, 60 per cup of beef consommé). All three are ideal liquids in which to cook vegetables, dumplings, and rice, and they are the very soul of soups and stews.

Recipe Uses   Sauces, gravies, casseroles, jellied meats, and aspics all rely—to greater or lesser degrees—upon bouillons, broths, and consommés, as do soups and stews. And French and Italian recipes are particularly lavish in their use of them.

How to Use Very Small Amounts   Broths and consommés make ideal moisteners of burgers and meat loaves (about ¼ to ⅓ cup per pound of meat, about twice that if you are also adding a moisture-absorbing filler like bread crumbs or oatmeal). Small amounts may be added to almost any soup, sauce, or gravy; they may be combined with tomato juice and drunk as an appetizer; they may even be used to dress green salads instead of the traditional vinaigrette (add a bit of lemon or vinegar for tartness along with the broth). This, by the way, is a marvelous way to cut calories (salad oils, we know, average about 100 calories per tablespoon vs. 4 to 7 per tablespoon for broths and consommés).

N O T E   *For additional recipes, included elsewhere in this book, that call for varying amounts of canned bouillons, broths, and consommés, see the Appendix.*

O N I O N - S M O T H E R E D   R O U N D   S T E A K

4 servings

This is one of those accommodating skillet dishes that you can more or less forget once the initial browning is done. It's a flexible recipe in that it enables you to use ½ to 1 cup of leftover beef or chicken broth and, optionally, ¼ to ½ cup of cream (light, heavy, or sour).

> 1½ **pounds top or bottom beef round, cut 1 inch thick**
> ¼ **cup unsifted all-purpose flour**
> 1 **teaspoon salt**
> ⅛ **teaspoon freshly ground black pepper**
> 2 **tablespoons beef or bacon drippings or cooking oil**
> 3 **large yellow onions, peeled and sliced thin**
> ½ **to 1 cup beef or chicken broth or water**
> ¼ **to ½ cup light, heavy, or sour cream (optional)**

Slash the fat edges of the steak every inch or so with a sharp knife so the steak will not curl or warp as it cooks. Mix the flour with the salt and pepper; sprinkle half of the mixture on one side of the steak and pound in well, using a meat mallet or the edge of a heavy saucer. Turn the steak and pound the flip side the same way with the remaining seasoned flour.

Brown the steak quickly on both sides in the drippings in a large, heavy skillet over moderately high heat, then remove from the skillet and set aside. Reduce the heat to moderate, add the onions, and stir-fry about 10 minutes in the drippings until limp and lightly touched with brown. Push the onions to one side of the skillet, return the steak to the skillet, then pile the onions on top of the steak. Pour in the broth and reduce the heat so that the broth ripples gently; cover and simmer for about 1 hour, or until the steak is very tender.

Remove the steak to a hot platter and keep warm. Boil the skillet liquids hard, uncovered, until reduced by about half—5 minutes. Smooth in the cream and heat and stir for 2 to 3 minutes longer (do not boil or the cream may curdle). Pour the skillet mixture over the steak and serve.

SAGEY MEATBALL CASSEROLE WITH APPLES

4 to 6 servings

Here's an easy oven dish that calls for a small amount of dry bread crumbs and up to 1 cup of leftover beef or chicken broth.

N O T E   *If you use less than 1 cup of broth, round out the measure with water; if you have no broth at all, use 1 beef or chicken bouillon cube or 1 envelope instant beef or chicken broth dissolved in 1 cup boiling water.*

    1 pound lean ground beef
    ½ pound pork sausage meat
    1 small yellow onion, peeled and minced
    ½ cup dry bread crumbs
    1 teaspoon crumbled leaf sage
    ¼ teaspoon crumbled leaf thyme
    Pinch of ground mace

C O N T I N U E D

    1 egg, lightly beaten
    1 teaspoon salt
    ¼ teaspoon freshly ground black pepper
    2 tablespoons bacon drippings or butter
    4 crisp, tart apples such as Winesaps, McIntoshes, or greenings, quartered and cored but not peeled
    ½ to 1 cup beef or chicken broth (see note above)

Preheat the oven to moderate (350° F.).

Mix the beef, sausage, onion, crumbs, sage, thyme, mace, egg, salt, and pepper together well and shape into 1-inch balls. Brown on all sides in the bacon drippings or butter in a medium-sized heavy skillet. With a slotted spoon, lift the meatballs from the skillet and arrange in a 1½-quart casserole with the apples.

Pour the broth into the skillet and bring to a boil, scraping up browned bits from the bottom of the skillet; pour over the meatballs and apples. Cover the casserole and bake in the preheated oven for 45 minutes, or until the meatballs are well done and the apples are tender.

Serve with mashed potatoes, noodles, or rice.

BAKED SQUASH AND TOMATO STRATA

4 servings

This recipe is best when made with a good strong beef broth or bouillon, but if chicken broth is what you have on hand, use that instead.

    1 medium yellow squash, washed, trimmed, and sliced thin
    1 medium zucchini, washed, trimmed, and sliced thin
    2 medium, vine-ripe tomatoes, peeled, cored, and sliced thin
    1 teaspoon salt
    ¼ teaspoon freshly ground black pepper
    1 cup strong beef or chicken broth, bouillon, or stock
    ¼ cup dry bread or cracker crumbs
    ¼ cup finely grated sharp Cheddar cheese or, if you prefer, Parmesan
    1 tablespoon butter

Preheat the oven to moderate (350° F.).

Layer the yellow squash, zucchini, and tomatoes in a buttered 6-cup casserole, sprinkling each layer with salt and pepper. Pour the broth over all; sprinkle the crumbs and cheese on top and dot with butter. Bake, uncovered, in the preheated oven for 45 minutes, or until browned and bubbling.

N O T E *If dinner must wait, this casserole can safely remain in the oven for an extra 15 or 20 minutes.*

O P E N - F A C E M E A T P I E

6 servings

With this recipe you can use up a cup of leftover beef or chicken broth or bouillon and, to give the pie a festive look, a couple of tablespoons of pimiento strips. Finally, you can add 1 to 3 hard-cooked eggs, if you should have them on hand.

1 medium yellow onion, peeled and chopped
1 medium sweet green or red pepper, cored, seeded, and chopped
3 tablespoons butter or margarine
1½ pounds lean ground beef chuck or lamb shoulder
½ teaspoon crumbled leaf oregano
½ teaspoon crumbled leaf rosemary
½ teaspoon crumbled leaf basil
½ teaspoon lemon pepper
¼ teaspoon salt
1 egg
1 to 3 hard-cooked eggs, peeled and minced (optional)
2 tablespoons all-purpose flour
1 cup beef or chicken broth or bouillon
1 baked 9-inch pie shell
1 to 2 tablespoons pimiento strips

Preheat the oven to moderate (350° F.).

Stir-fry the onion and sweet pepper in 1 tablespoon of the butter in a large, heavy skillet over moderate heat for 8 to 10 minutes—just until limp and golden but not brown. Transfer the sautéed vegetables to a mixing bowl, using a slotted spoon.

Stir-fry the meat in the skillet over moderate heat, breaking up large clumps, until no longer pink. Add to the bowl along with the herbs, lemon pepper, salt, raw egg, and, if you like, the hard-cooked eggs.

Melt the remaining 2 tablespoons of butter in a small saucepan. Blend in the flour, then add the broth and cook and stir over low heat until thickened and smooth—3 to 5 minutes. Add to the ingredients in the bowl and mix all together well.

Spoon this mixture into the pie shell and decorate the top with pimiento strips. Bake in the preheated oven for about 30 minutes, or until good and hot.

Cut into wedges and serve.

AUSTRIAN VEAL STEW

6 servings

This succulent stew is an uncommonly flexible dish in that the liquid used can be chicken and/or beef broth and/or dry red or white wine —just as long as the total quantity is 3½ cups, you can't go wrong. In addition, you may vary the amount of capers and sour cream in order to use what leftovers you may have—within reason, of course. Be guided by the proportions given below, but most of all by your own sense of taste.

Here is another recipe that freezes splendidly (directions follow).

> 8 slices bacon, cut crosswise in julienne strips
> 3 medium yellow onions, peeled and minced
> 1 clove garlic, peeled and minced
> 1 tablespoon paprika
> 1 to 3 tablespoons minced capers
> ⅛ teaspoon freshly ground black pepper
> 1 lemon, halved
> 2 pounds boned veal shoulder, cut in 1-inch cubes
> 3½ cups chicken or beef broth or a combination (include some dry red or white wine if you have either left over)
> 3 tablespoons all-purpose flour blended with ¼ cup cold water
> ½ to 1 cup sour cream, at room temperature

Brown the bacon in a large, heavy kettle over moderately high heat; remove the bacon to paper toweling to drain. Pour the drippings from the kettle, then spoon 4 tablespoons of them back into the kettle. Add the onions and garlic and stir-fry for 8 to 10 minutes, or until lightly browned. Blend in the paprika, capers, and pepper; drop in the lemon halves. Add the veal and stir-fry for 8 to 10 minutes, until no longer pink; remove the lemon. Add the broth (or liquid mixture), cover, and simmer slowly for 1½ hours, until the veal is tender.

Blend the flour-water paste into the kettle and heat, stirring, for 3 to 5 minutes, until thickened. Off the heat, blend in the sour cream and reserved bacon crumbles.

Serve over buttered wide noodles.

To Freeze Cool the finished stew, then ladle into individual-sized freezer containers (the half-pint size is perfect) or use pint cartons. Fill to within ½ inch of the tops, snap on lids, date, label, and quick-freeze at 0° F. Keeping time: 6 months.

Bread

(Stale)

You can, of course, quickly use up stale bread by buzzing it to crumbs (see pages 112–13). But there are other ways to deal with stale bread —as whole slices or as cubes.

Best Way to Store Tightly wrapped in the refrigerator. Refrigerating *fresh* bread is not a good idea because the cold actually accelerates the staling process. But once bread is stale, the point is merely to hold it for a day or so until it can be used.

Maximum Storage Time 3 to 4 days. After that the bread develops a noticeable stale flavor and begins to harden to the point of brittleness.

Roles in Cooking To form the basis of bread-cube stuffings (delicious with turkey and chicken), to provide the foundation of such economical classics as cheese strata and fruit Bettys. Stale bread is also ideal for making grilled cheese sandwiches and French toast.

Recipe Uses In addition to the suggestions that follow, your best bet for learning new ways to use stale bread would be to peruse the sections of your recipe files and cookbooks devoted to stuffings, bread sauces, and puddings. Have a look, too, at the sandwich chapters, paying particular attention to grilled sandwiches (the grilling takes the "curse" off stale bread).

Special Comments In making a Betty, try using stale raisin, whole-wheat, or protein bread instead of plain white bread—if that is indeed what you have left over. These same breads, when cubed, also make excellent poultry stuffings. For the record, 1 standard slice of bread = approximately 1 cup of ¼- to ½-inch bread cubes.

N O T E *For additional recipes, included elsewhere in this book, that call for varying amounts of stale bread, see the Appendix.*

CHEESE, BREAD, AND OYSTER BAKE

4 to 6 servings

Is it impractical—extravagant?—to buy a pint of oysters in order to use up six slices of stale bread? We don't think so, considering that none of us would hesitate to buy a pound of hamburger or a can of tuna for a pet leftover recipe. It's simply that for most of us oysters smack of the exotic—i.e., expensive. The truth is that, in season along much of the East and West coasts, they can be cheaper than ground chuck.

> 2 tablespoons butter or margarine, at room temperature
> 6 slices stale, firm-textured white or whole-wheat bread
> 6 sandwich-sized slices mild Cheddar or Swiss cheese
> 1 pint shucked oysters, drained but liquid reserved
> Enough evaporated milk, light cream, or milk to total 2½ cups when combined with the oyster liquid
> ¼ cup dry white wine or sherry
> 2 eggs, beaten lightly
> 2 tablespoons finely grated onion
> ½ teaspoon salt
> ¼ teaspoon liquid hot red pepper seasoning or ⅛ teaspoon cayenne pepper
> ⅛ teaspoon grated nutmeg or ground mace
> Paprika

Preheat the oven to moderately slow (325° F.).

Lightly butter one side of each slice of bread and cut into ½-inch cubes. Place half of the buttered bread cubes in a well-buttered 12 × 8 × 2-inch baking dish and top with the cheese slices. Arrange the oysters on top of the cheese and cover with the remaining buttered bread cubes.

Combine the oyster liquid–cream mixture with all the remaining ingredients except the paprika and pour evenly over the bread cubes. Sprinkle with paprika and bake, uncovered, in the preheated oven for 1 hour, or until a knife inserted in the center of the dish comes out clean.

O L D   S O U T H   S H R I M P   A N D   C H E E S E   P U D D I N G

4 to 6 servings

This recipe, like so many others in this book, is uncommonly flexible. The 2 cups milk called for, for example, need not be plain sweet milk; use part evaporated milk, should you have an opened can in the refrigerator, or use part light and/or heavy cream. As for the cheese, use whatever you have on hand—Cheddar, Swiss, jack, or a combination of them.

You can, if you like, freeze this recipe in individual-sized, freezer-to-oven ramekins or casseroles (directions follow the recipe).

6 slices stale bread (either white or whole wheat)
3 tablespoons butter or margarine, at room temperature
½ pound shelled and deveined cooked shrimp, coarsely chopped
1½ to 2 cups grated Cheddar, Swiss, or jack cheese
3 large eggs, beaten lightly
2 cups milk (or any milk and cream combination)
½ teaspoon salt
⅛ teaspoon cayenne pepper
⅛ teaspoon grated nutmeg or ground mace

Preheat the oven to moderate (350° F.).

Spread each slice of bread on one side with butter, then cut in ½-inch cubes. Place in a buttered 1½-quart baking dish along with the shrimp and cheese; toss lightly to mix. Combine all the remaining ingredients and pour into the casserole.

Set the casserole in a shallow baking pan and pour hot water into the baking pan to a depth of 1½ inches. Bake the casserole, uncovered, in the water bath in the preheated oven for about 1 hour, or until the mixture is set—until a silver knife inserted halfway between the rim and the center of the pudding comes out clean.

Serve straightaway.

To Freeze   To freeze this recipe in individual-sized, freezer-to-oven ramekins or casseroles, simply mix all the ingredients as directed in a large mixing bowl and spoon into four or six lightly buttered ramekins, filling each to within ½ inch of the top. Cover snugly with aluminum foil, then quick-freeze by setting directly on the freezing unit of a freezer set at 0° F. Once the casseroles are solidly frozen, overwrap in heavy-duty foil, date, and label. These will keep well at 0° for about 3 months.

To bake, let stand at room temperature for 30 minutes, then bake as directed but reduce the total cooking time to about 45 minutes.

BUTTERY BREAD AND BERRY PUDDING

6 to 8 servings

The best berries to use are blackberries, dewberries, loganberries, black raspberries, or dead-ripe blueberries. As for the bread, use firm-textured white or whole-wheat bread or a combination of the two.

> **8 slices firm-textured white or whole-wheat bread or, if you prefer, 4 slices of each**
> **¹/₃ cup (5¹/₃ tablespoons) butter or margarine, at room temperature**
> **1 quart fresh blackberries (or any of the other berries listed in the headnote above)**
> **1 cup granulated sugar mixed with a pinch each of ground cinnamon and mace**

Preheat the oven to moderate (350°F.).

Butter the slices of bread well (but on one side only), then arrange

4 slices one layer deep, buttered sides up, in a well-buttered 9 × 9 × 2-inch baking dish. Dump half the berries on top, sprinkle with half of the sugar mixture, then mash well with a potato masher so that the berry juices run down into the bread. Top with the remaining bread, buttered side up, then the remaining berries and sugar. Mash once again.

Bake, uncovered, in the preheated oven for 45 minutes, then remove the pan from oven and mash once again with the potato masher. Return to the oven and bake for 20 to 25 minutes longer, or until the juices are bubbling and syrupy. Remove the pudding from the oven and cool for 30 minutes before serving.

Spoon onto dessert plates and top each portion, if you like, with ice cream, whipped cream, or sour cream.

HOOTSLA (BREAD-CUBE OMELET)

6 servings

Here's an imaginative Scandinavian way to recycle stale bread.

  ¾ cup (1½ sticks) unsalted butter
  10 to 12 slices stale white and/or whole-wheat bread, crusts included,
    cut in ½-inch cubes
  5 eggs
  1 cup milk (use part evaporated milk, if you have it, or part light or
    heavy cream)
  ¾ teaspoon salt
  Several grindings of black pepper

Melt the butter in a large, heavy skillet over moderate heat; add the bread cubes and stir-fry for 5 minutes or so, until lightly browned.

Quickly beat the eggs with the milk, salt, and pepper. Pour into the skillet and cook for about 5 minutes over moderate heat, or just until the eggs are lightly browned underneath and softly set on top. As the eggs cook, lift the cooked portion around the edges, tilting the skillet so that the raw egg on top runs underneath to cook.

Cut into wedges or spoon out and serve.

BREAD CRUMBS: See **Crumbs.**

Brown Sugar

(Light or Dark)

Thanks to new and improved packaging (plastic soft-packs and boxes with airtight liners), light and dark brown sugars don't harden as fast as they once did. Still, you can't keep them ad infinitum and expect them to remain soft and manageable. They can—and will—become brick-hard if left on the shelf month after month.

Best Way to Store   Once any of the new plastic packages (or lined boxes) of brown sugar is opened, it can no longer be made airtight. And that's the problem, because the minute brown sugar is exposed to the air, it begins to dry (at least it will in all but the most humid weather). In keeping leftover brown sugar, your aim is to reseal the package as snugly as possible. Press out any air pockets as you smooth the wrapper around the remaining brown sugar, then fold the top tightly around the sugar and secure with a tight rubber band. Finally, pop the bag of sugar into an airtight canister or jar. (Friends report that they've had good luck storing the resealed box in the refrigerator. Try it if you have refrigerator space to spare.)

Maximum Storage Time   So much depends on weather. If you live in a humid area (or if the area where you live is having a wet season), the sugar will absorb moisture from the atmosphere and remain workably soft for some weeks or even months. But, when a dry spell comes (or when you turn the heat on in winter), the sugar can harden in a matter of days. However, if you wrap any leftovers carefully as directed above, the sugar should remain moist and soft for several weeks—even in the hottest, driest air.

How to Soften Hardened Brown Sugar It *can* be done more easily—and more ways—than you think. There's the old, tried-and-proved trick of tucking an apple quarter down in the sugar canister so that the sugar will absorb the apple's moisture (a slice of bread works almost as well). A friend of ours swears by her own slightly unorthodox method. She breaks the hardened sugar into clumps, dumps them into a large, shallow bowl, sets the bowl on the bathroom lavatory, then takes the longest, hottest shower she can stand with the bathroom door and windows shut tight (this sauna treatment works). Easier, perhaps, and possibly less damaging to the bathroom walls and ceiling, is this oven method:

Set a shallow pan of water on the floor of an oven set at 300° to 325° F. Break hardened brown sugar into lumps and spread out in a second large, shallow pan, then let stand, uncovered, on middle rack of the oven until the sugar absorbs the water and softens—usually within 30 to 60 minutes.

Finally, if you have a food processor, you can pulverize the hard sugar. But you must first break it into chunks of no more than 1 inch, then buzz them, a few at a time, with the metal chopping blade attachment (keep the pusher in the feed tube of the processor because the machine's action will raise a lot of filmy white sugar dust, and you should avoid breathing this). This pulverized sugar, by the way, has more the texture of the new granulated brown sugar and should not be used in cakes, cookies, or breads where exact measurements are crucial to the recipe's success. It's far better to use this sugar as a sweetener for sauces, fruit desserts, and custards.

Roles in Cooking Brown sugar's most important role is, quite simply, as a sweetener. But it also adds color, and in candies and preserves it is the thickening agent (you are dealing here with supersaturated sugar solutions that can be cooked to a soft ball for fudges and fondants, to hard crack for brittles, and, indeed, to any of the other candy-making stages in between—hard ball, thread, soft crack, etc.). Finally, brown sugar can be used to mellow the tartness of a food—a pasta sauce, for example, or a casserole or skillet dish in which you have used too-acid fresh tomatoes.

Recipe Uses Brown sugars are the very basis of ginger cookies and gingerbreads, not to mention dozens of cakes, candies, and confections —pralines and popcorn balls, for example, brown-sugar fudge, and brown-sugar pound cake. They are also integral to such savory American classics as Boston baked beans and barbecue.

Special Comments Can light and dark brown sugar be used interchangeably? Not completely. Dark brown sugar has a stronger molasses flavor—appropriate for baked beans and gingersnaps but overpowering, perhaps, for more delicate recipes (seafoam icing, caramel custard, etc.) where a butterscotch or caramel flavor is desired (light brown sugar is then the choice).

N O T E *For additional recipes, included elsewhere in this book, that call for varying amounts of brown sugar, see the Appendix.*

B U L G A R I A N   S W E E T - S O U R   B E A N   S O U P

6 servings

Although the purpose of this recipe is to use up odds and ends of brown sugar and vinegar, the soup is also an excellent place to recycle leftover vegetables (carrots, corn, green peas or beans, cauliflower or broccoli, cabbage)—let them simmer along with the beans, then purée all together. You can also add up to 4 tablespoons of tomato paste should you have a partially used can on hand, as well as up to 1 cup of leftover dry white wine. Simply improvise any way you like with the basic recipe below.

> 1 pound dried baby lima beans, washed and sorted
> 2 quarts cold water
> 1 large Spanish onion, peeled and coarsely chopped
> 1 large clove garlic, peeled and minced
> ¼ cup olive oil
> 2 medium ribs celery, washed, trimmed, and coarsely chopped
> 2 medium carrots, peeled and coarsely chopped
> ½ teaspoon crumbled leaf rosemary
> ¼ teaspoon crumbled leaf thyme
> ⅛ teaspoon freshly ground black pepper
> 2 to 4 tablespoons light or dark brown sugar
> ½ cup cider vinegar

⅓ cup minced fresh parsley (measure loosely packed)
1 teaspoon salt, or to taste
2 to 4 tablespoons tomato paste (optional)
1 cup dry white wine (optional)

Place the beans and water in a large, heavy kettle, bring to a boil, then boil for 10 minutes; turn the heat off, cover the pot, and let stand for 2 hours.

In a large, heavy skillet, stir-fry the onion and garlic in the olive oil over moderate heat for 10 minutes, or until touched with brown. Add the celery, carrots, rosemary, thyme, and black pepper and stir-fry for 10 minutes longer. Set aside for the time being.

When the beans have stood in the soaking water 2 hours, uncover the pot and mix in the sautéed onion mixture. Set over low heat, then cover and simmer for 2 to 3 hours, or until the beans are very tender. Purée the bean mixture, about 2 cups at a time, by buzzing in an electric blender or food processor fitted with the metal chopping blade; or put through a food mill. Return the bean mixture to kettle, stir in all the remaining ingredients, and simmer slowly, with the lid set on the kettle askew, for 20 to 30 minutes, or until the flavors are nicely mellowed. Taste for salt and add more, if necessary.

Serve in large soup bowls with chunks of crusty bread.

ANISE COOKIES

About 5 dozen

These cookies require ½ cup of molasses and ¼ cup of dark or light brown sugar, and may be made with either two leftover egg yolks or one white. They're dark and spicy, a delicious choice for Christmas. Best of all, the cookie dough keeps well for several weeks in the refrigerator, so you can roll and bake the cookies at your leisure.

3 cups sifted all-purpose flour
¼ teaspoon baking soda
1 teaspoon grated nutmeg
2 teaspoons ground cardamom
2 teaspoons ground anise

CONTINUED

¼ teaspoon salt
½ cup (1 stick) butter or margarine
½ cup vegetable shortening
¼ cup granulated sugar
¼ cup firmly packed dark or light brown sugar
½ cup molasses
2 egg yolks or 1 egg white, beaten lightly
2 teaspoons finely grated lemon rind

Sift the flour, soda, spices, and salt together onto a piece of wax paper and set aside. Cream the butter, shortening, and sugars until light and fluffy; add the molasses, egg yolks or white, and lemon rind and beat well. Slowly mix in the dry ingredients until well blended. Wrap the dough in foil or wax paper and chill overnight.

Preheat the oven to moderate (350°F.).

Using a small portion of dough at a time (keep the balance refrigerated), roll ⅛ inch thick on a lightly floured board and cut with decorative cutters. Space the cookies 2 inches apart on ungreased baking sheets and bake in the preheated oven for 10 minutes, until lightly browned.

Cool the cookies on baking sheets for 1 to 2 minutes, then transfer to wire racks. Store airtight.

KAUAI SWEET-SOUR SPARERIBS

4 to 6 servings

If your Scottish soul rebels against throwing away hardened brown sugar, here is a superb way to use ½ cup of it.

4 pounds lean spareribs, cut in serving-sized portions
1 can (13½ ounces) crushed pineapple (do not drain)
½ cup firmly packed dark or light brown sugar
½ cup cider vinegar
1 tablespoon finely minced fresh gingerroot or preserved or candied
    ginger, or 1 teaspoon ground ginger
1 teaspoon dry mustard
1 teaspoon Worcestershire sauce
1 tablespoon soy sauce

Preheat the oven to moderate (350°F.), then bake the ribs, uncovered, in a shallow roasting pan for 1 hour. Remove from the oven and drain off all the pan drippings.

Combine all the remaining ingredients, pour over the ribs, and bake, uncovered, for 1 hour longer, turning the ribs once and basting often with the glaze, until tender and glisteningly brown. (If the liquid in the pan cooks away as the ribs bake, simply add a little hot water to the roasting pan and use that for basting the ribs.)

Serve hot.

BUTTERMILK SPICE CAKE

Two 9-inch layers

This is a very simple way of using up an extra cup of buttermilk—as well as ¾ cup of light or dark brown sugar. The cake can be frozen and kept until you have another leftover—sour cream, perhaps—to use in a filling or frosting. Or you can use whipped cream and sliced bananas between the layers and top with plain whipped cream.

    2 cups sifted all-purpose flour
    1 cup granulated sugar
    1 teaspoon salt
    1 teaspoon baking powder
    ½ teaspoon baking soda
    1 teaspoon ground cinnamon
    ½ teaspoon ground cloves
    ¾ cup firmly packed light or dark brown sugar
    ½ cup vegetable shortening
    1 cup buttermilk or sour milk
    3 eggs

Preheat the oven to moderate (350°F.).

Sift together the flour, granulated sugar, salt, baking powder, soda, cinnamon, and cloves into a large mixing bowl. Add the brown sugar, shortening, and buttermilk and beat thoroughly (about 300 strokes by hand or 2 minutes with an electric mixer set at moderate speed). Add the eggs and beat well.

Divide the batter between two greased and floured 9-inch layer-cake pans and bake in the preheated oven for about 35 minutes, or until the layers pull from the sides of the pans and are springy to the touch.

Remove the layers from the oven and let cool upright in their pans on wire racks for 20 minutes, then loosen around the edges with a spatula and turn out. Cool thoroughly before filling and frosting.

EASY DATE-FILLED COOKIES

About 2½ dozen

These are sort of a "fig Newton" made with dates, shaped by spooning the date filling onto a brown-sugar drop cookie, then topping with a second drop cookie. The cookie dough is an excellent way to use up a cup of dark or light brown sugar; the date filling, half a package of pitted dates and odds and ends of nuts.

DATE FILLING

1 cup coarsely chopped, pitted dates
⅓ cup hot water
⅓ cup granulated sugar
1 teaspoon lemon juice
¼ cup finely chopped walnuts, pecans, or blanched almonds

COOKIE DOUGH

½ cup vegetable shortening
1 cup firmly packed light or dark brown sugar
2 small eggs
¼ cup water
½ teaspoon vanilla extract
2 cups sifted all-purpose flour
½ teaspoon baking soda
¼ teaspoon salt
⅛ teaspoon ground cinnamon

Make the date filling first. Simmer the dates, water, sugar, and lemon juice in a small, heavy saucepan over low heat for about 15 to 20 minutes, until quite thick, stirring frequently. Remove from the heat and mix in the nuts, then cool to room temperature.

Preheat the oven to moderately hot (375°F.).

Cream the shortening, sugar, and eggs until fluffy-light; mix in the water and vanilla. Combine the flour, soda, salt, and cinnamon and mix in to form a soft dough. Drop by teaspoonfuls onto ungreased baking sheets, spacing the cookies at least 2 inches apart. Top with ½ teaspoon date filling, then top with more cookie dough, again dropping from a teaspoon. Bake in the preheated oven for 10 to 12 minutes or until lightly browned.

Remove the cookies from the oven, let cool for 2 to 3 minutes, then transfer to wire racks to cool. Store in airtight canisters.

Bulgur and Kasha

These two names are often thought to be synonymous, possibly because much of the kasha marketed in this country *is* bulgur (cracked, roasted kernels of wheat, which are also known as "groats"). Originally, however, kasha meant *buckwheat* groats, made from a Siberian grain wholly unrelated to true wheat. Both bulgur and buckwheat are highly nutritious (especially in the B vitamins and in vegetable protein), and in the form of groats the two resemble one another so closely that they can be used interchangeably in recipes. Neither variety of groats is particularly perishable, but both are highly susceptible to insect attack.

Best Way to Store   Airtight in rustproof canisters or glass jars on a cool, dark, dry shelf.

Maximum Storage Time   About 6 months.

Roles in Cooking   Both bulgur and kasha can be used as extenders of meats; as thickeners of broths, soups, porridges, and puddings; as binders of meat loaves and croquettes. Both are served in much of the Middle East in lieu of rice or potatoes. Bulgur and kasha have a mellow, nutty flavor, an appetizing crunch, and a tweedy look—the perfect foil for spicy, colorful foods.

Recipe Uses   Thumb first through any Russian recipes you may have for ideas on using bulgur or kasha, then turn to any Balkan or Middle Eastern recipes, because it is in these regions that bulgur and kasha are the staffs of life. They are mixed into breads, dumplings, meat pies and loaves, even into salads. And they are simply delicious.

How to Use Very Small Amounts   A small handful (about ¼ to ⅓ cup) of bulgur or kasha may be stirred into a big pot of soup instead of rice or barley. And ½ cup or less, thoroughly softened in hot water, then drained, may be mixed with each pound of ground meat that is to be made into loaves or burgers (bulgur and kasha are especially good with ground lamb).

VEGETABLE-BULGUR PILAF

4 servings

Here's a quick and easy way to use up ¾ to 1 cup of bulgur or kasha that may have been sitting around on the cupboard shelf. Note that the recipe also enables you to utilize from 1 to 1¾ cups of beef or chicken broth or consommé.

> 1 medium yellow onion, peeled and minced
> 1 large carrot, peeled and minced
> 2 tablespoons butter or margarine
> ⅛ teaspoon ground coriander (optional)
> ¾ to 1 cup bulgur or kasha
> 1¾ cups beef or chicken broth or consommé (if you should have a smaller amount on hand, round the measure out with water)
> Salt and freshly ground black pepper to taste

Stir-fry the onion and carrot in the butter in a medium-sized heavy saucepan over moderate heat for 8 to 10 minutes, until golden; stir in the coriander and bulgur or kasha and stir-fry for 2 to 3 minutes, just until the grain is golden and begins to look translucent. Add the broth, bring to a gentle boil, and cook, uncovered, for about 20 minutes, or until all liquid is absorbed (the bulgur or kasha should be tender but with a certain amount of crunch, too).

Season to taste with salt and pepper and serve in place of potatoes or rice. Delicious with roast lamb or grilled lamb chops, as well as with roast beef, pork, or chicken.

TABBOULEH (ARABIC SALAD OF KASHA, TOMATO, ONION, AND MINT)

4 to 6 servings

An exotic salad, it's true, but an easy one as well. Use either kasha or bulgur (a splendid way to use up half a box that you've just had hanging around). *Tabbouleh* is also the perfect repository for any fresh parsley or mint you may have on hand. The classic *tabbouleh* always contains fresh mint; if you have none at hand, you can still make this recipe—it just won't be the traditional one.

¾ to 1 cup kasha or bulgur
2½ cups boiling water
¼ to ⅓ cup finely minced fresh parsley
2 to 4 tablespoons finely minced fresh mint (optional)
1 small Bermuda or Spanish onion, peeled and chopped
1 large, vine-ripe tomato, washed, cored, seeded, and coarsely chopped
3 to 4 tablespoons lemon juice
4 to 5 tablespoons best-quality olive oil
Salt and freshly ground black pepper to taste

Pour the boiling water over the kasha or bulgur and let stand for 20 minutes; drain very dry, then place in a clean, dry towel and squeeze out as much additional water as possible (this is important to keep the salad from being watery or mushy).

Transfer the grain to a large mixing bowl. Add all of the remaining ingredients (3 tablespoons of lemon juice to start and 4 tablespoons of oil), then toss lightly to mix. Taste and add more lemon juice, oil, and salt and pepper if needed. Cover and let marinate in the refrigerator a couple of hours before serving, then toss well again.

To dress up the *tabbouleh,* serve on a bed of crisp young romaine leaves.

B E E F   A N D   B U L G U R   L O A F

8 to 10 servings

With more and more people interested in preparing such Middle Eastern specialties as *kibbeh* (lamb and bulgur pie), bulgur is joining the ranks of problem leftovers, particularly since on long standing it becomes a favorite breeding ground of weevils and miller moths. One nutritious way to use it up quickly is by preparing this savory, meat-stretching loaf.

   1 cup bulgur
   2¼ cups water
   2 pounds ground beef chuck
   1 large yellow onion, peeled and minced
   ½ medium sweet red or green pepper, cored, seeded, and minced (optional)
   3 eggs
   1 cup beef or chicken broth, milk, or water (the broth and water will make for a softer, moister loaf than the milk, which coagulates as the meat loaf bakes)
   ¼ cup ketchup, tomato paste, or tomato sauce
   ¾ teaspoon salt
   ¼ teaspoon freshly ground pepper
   ¼ teaspoon crumbled leaf marjoram
   ¼ teaspoon crumbled leaf thyme

Preheat the oven to moderately slow (325° F.).

Boil the bulgur gently in the water in a covered saucepan for 20 to 25 minutes, until fluffy-tender. Cool for 15 minutes, then mix with all the remaining ingredients, using your hands. Pack into a well-greased 9 × 5 × 3-inch loaf pan and bake, uncovered, in the preheated oven for about 1½ hours, or until the loaf is nicely browned and pulls slightly from the sides of the pan.

Cool the loaf upright in its pan on a wire rack for 30 minutes, then turn out and serve.

Buttermilk and Sour Milk

Best Way to Store Both buttermilk and sour milk should be stored in the refrigerator in their own cartons, with the openings pinched tightly shut.

Maximum Storage Time A week to 10 days for buttermilk, 10 days to 2 weeks for sour milk.

N O T E *If sour milk should curd badly (separate into huge clumps), shake hard before using or pour the curds and whey into an electric blender or food processor and whir until fairly smooth. You can even break up the curds and reconstitute sour milk with an electric mixer set at high speed. The fact that sour milk is heavily curded doesn't mean that it's spoiled, just that it will be more difficult to measure accurately and to use in recipes.*

Roles in Cooking Both buttermilk and sour milk are used, first of all, for flavor. Their tartness teams well with salad greens, meats, and vegetables, and reduces the cloying quality of overrich sweets. The acidity of sour milk and buttermilk will also redden and enrich the color of anything made with chocolate, make for more tender-crumbed cakes and breads, and will even help tenderize sinewy cuts of meat (which is why marinades sometimes call for buttermilk or sour milk).

When combined with baking soda, both sour milk and buttermilk fizz and foam, producing carbon dioxide gas—an effective leavener of breads and cakes (¼ teaspoon of baking soda mixed with ½ cup of buttermilk or sour milk equals the leavening power of 1 teaspoon of baking powder). Finally, by substituting buttermilk for whole milk in sherbets and soups, you can dramatically reduce calories (1 cup of buttermilk contains approximately one-half the calories of 1 cup of whole milk).

Recipe Uses Buttermilk and sour milk can be used interchangeably in many recipes: pancakes, biscuits and other quick breads, cakes, cookies, salad dressings, and marinades. Sour milk should not, however, be substituted for buttermilk in soups, sauces, stews, and candies that require either high heat or prolonged heat (sour milk is an unstable mix and much more easily curdled than buttermilk). Finally, do not use sour milk in place of buttermilk for sherbets, ice creams, gelatin salads, and desserts where body or consistency is important. Cultured buttermilk has an almost creamlike smoothness and thickness that sour milk lacks.

Special Comments If you're in the middle of a recipe that calls for buttermilk or sour milk and discover that you have none, there's no need to dash out to the store. Here's a quick and easy way to sour sweet milk: To each 1 cup of milk add 1 tablespoon of vinegar or lemon juice; stir well, then set in a warm place (near a pilot light, for example) for about 30 minutes. The milk will sour right away.

N O T E *For additional recipes, included elsewhere in this book, that call for varying amounts of buttermilk or sour milk, see the Appendix.*

T A R R A G O N - B U T T E R M I L K   D R E S S I N G

About 1 ¾ cups

Good news for dieters! This dressing, which economically uses up ¾ to 1 cup of leftover buttermilk, is impressively low in calories—only 10 per tablespoon. If you have an almost empty jar of Parmesan on hand, add the cheese to the dressing—it will enrich the flavor but increase the calorie count only minimally. This dressing keeps well for about 1 week in the refrigerator. Use to dress crisp green salads.

> ¾ to 1 cup buttermilk
> ½ cup tarragon vinegar
> 1 tablespoon olive oil
> 2 tablespoons minced fresh chives or scallions
> ½ teaspoon crumbled leaf tarragon
> ¾ teaspoon salt
> ⅛ teaspoon freshly ground black pepper
> 1 to 3 tablespoons grated Parmesan cheese (optional)

Place all the ingredients in a 1-pint shaker jar, screw the lid down tight, and shake vigorously to blend. Let the dressing "season" in the refrigerator for several hours before using. Shake well again just before drizzling over a crisp green salad.

BUTTERMILK-HAM LOAF

8 to 10 servings

Few recipes are better repositories for leftovers than this ham loaf, which neatly accommodates the following: stale bread; leftover buttermilk (or sour milk or cream); tag ends of mustard, ketchup, or tomato paste; India relish; and capers. You can even use up ½ to 1 cup tart red jelly or ½ cup brown sugar by glazing the loaf.

1½ pounds ground smoked ham
1 pound lean ground pork shoulder
4 slices firm-textured white bread, buzzed to fine crumbs in an electric blender or processor (or simply break the bread into very small pieces)
2 medium yellow onions, peeled and minced
¼ cup minced fresh parsley
1 cup buttermilk, sour milk, or sour cream (or even sweet milk)
2 large eggs
1 to 3 tablespoons prepared mustard
1 to 2 tablespoons ketchup or tomato paste (optional)
1 to 2 tablespoons India relish
¼ to ½ cup capers (optional)
¼ teaspoon ground ginger
¼ teaspoon ground cloves
¼ teaspoon ground allspice
Pinch of grated nutmeg
⅛ teaspoon freshly ground black pepper
¾ teaspoon salt

OPTIONAL GLAZE

½ to 1 cup tart red jelly or ⅓ to ½ cup light or dark brown sugar (if hard and dry, break the sugar into small pieces by hammering with a rolling pin)

Preheat the oven to moderate (350° F.). Lightly grease a 9 × 5 × 3-inch loaf pan. (If you want to glaze the ham loaf, spoon the jelly or brown sugar into the pan and spread out so that the bottom of the pan is covered as evenly as possible.)

Mix all the meat loaf ingredients together well, using your hands. Pack the ham mixture firmly into the pan and bake, uncovered, in the preheated oven for 2 hours.

Remove the ham loaf from the oven and set on a wire rack. With a thin-bladed knife or small spatula, loosen the loaf around the edges of the pan, then let stand undisturbed until it reaches room temperature. Pour off the accumulated juices (save to make gravy, if you like), then turn the loaf out on a small platter.

Serve as is or accompany with the following sauce:

Sour Cream-Mustard Sauce

Whisk 2 cups sour cream with ¼ cup Dijon mustard. Add ⅓ cup drained capers, if you like, 1 tablespoon prepared horseradish, and 1 to 2 tablespoons minced fresh dill.

BUTTERMILK GAZPACHO

4 servings

Wonderfully quick, wonderfully cooling. And a most unusual way to use up 1 to 1½ cups of leftover buttermilk.

> 2 hard-cooked eggs, peeled and halved
> 1 can (12 ounces) vegetable juice
> 1 to 1½ cups buttermilk
> ½ cup chopped Spanish or Bermuda onion
> ½ cup diced celery
> ½ cup diced sweet green pepper
> ¼ teaspoon dill weed (optional) or 1 tablespoon minced fresh dill, if you are lucky enough to have it
> Freshly ground pepper to taste
> 1 lime, sliced thin

Sieve the egg yolks and place in a mixing bowl; add the vegetable juice, buttermilk, onion, celery, green pepper, and seasonings and stir to mix. Mince the egg whites, then wrap and refrigerate until ready to use. Also refrigerate the gazpacho for several hours—just long enough to blend the flavors.

To serve, spoon a little minced egg white into the bottoms of four soup cups, pour in the gazpacho, and garnish with lime slices.

BUTTERMILK POUND CAKE

One 10-inch tube cake

This old-fashioned pound cake, made with buttermilk and soda, has a dense texture but an unusually moist and tender crumb. To keep the cake fresh, store snugly wrapped.

> 1½ cups (3 sticks) butter, at room temperature
> 2½ cups granulated sugar
> 4 eggs
> 3½ cups sifted all-purpose flour
> ½ teaspoon baking soda
> ½ teaspoon salt
> 1 cup buttermilk or sour milk
> 1 teaspoon vanilla extract

Preheat the oven to moderate (350° F.).

Cream the butter until fluffy; gradually add the sugar, creaming all the while, then continue creaming until the mixture is very light and silvery—about 5 minutes with the electric mixer set at moderate speed. Beat in the eggs, one at a time.

Sift together the flour, soda, and salt and add to the creamed mixture alternately with the buttermilk, beginning and ending with the dry ingredients. Stir in the vanilla.

Pour the batter (it will be quite thick) into a well-greased and -floured 10-inch tube cake pan and bake in the preheated oven for about 1 hour 20 minutes, or until the cake is nicely browned on top and has pulled from the sides of the pan.

Cool the cake upright in its pan on a wire rack for 15 minutes (it will fall slightly at this point, which accounts for the cake's compact texture). Loosen the cake from the pan using a spatula, then turn the cake out on a wire rack and cool to room temperature before slicing.

NORWEGIAN
NUTMEG-BUTTERMILK COOKIES

6 to 6½ dozen

This recipe is more than a hundred years old and makes big, old-fashioned "munching" cookies, the kind that are not too sweet and thus good to have on hand. The dough freezes splendidly, and once the cookies have been baked, they will keep well for a week to 10 days if stored in an airtight canister.

> 1½ cups granulated sugar
> 1 cup (2 sticks) butter or lard (hog lard)
> 2 eggs
> 1 cup buttermilk
> 5 cups *unsifted* all-purpose flour
> 2 teaspoons baking powder
> 1 teaspoon baking soda
> 1 teaspoon salt
> 1¼ teaspoons grated nutmeg

Cream the sugar and butter until fluffy-light; beat in the eggs, then stir in the buttermilk. In a separate bowl, combine the flour, baking powder, soda, salt, and nutmeg and mix in, about 1 cup at a time, to make a soft dough. Divide the dough in four equal parts, wrap in foil, and chill overnight until firm enough to roll, or freeze and bake later.

Preheat the oven to moderately hot (375° F.).

Working with a small amount of dough at a time (about one-third of one of the foil-wrapped packages), roll about as thin as pie crust on a floured pastry cloth with a floured, stockinette-covered rolling pin. Keep the remaining dough chilled. (It's important not to roll too much dough at a time because it softens quickly, making it difficult to cut the cookies and transfer them to baking sheets.) With a floured 2½-inch round cutter (or fancy-shaped cutters, if you prefer), cut the cookies and space 1½ inches apart on very lightly greased baking sheets. Bake in the preheated oven for 8 to 10 minutes, or until the cookies are lightly browned.

Transfer at once to wire racks to cool. Store airtight.

B U T T E R M I L K   F U D G E

About 1 pound

This fudge *must* be cooked in a very large, heavy pan. We used an 8-quart (2-gallon) pan and needed every inch of it—at least at the outset, when the reaction of the soda, buttermilk, and heat made the mixture foam up alarmingly. It soon darkens and settles down to a simmer, however, and at this point you may transfer the candy to an easier-to-handle 4-quart saucepan. We cooked the candy from start to finish in the 8-quart pan and discovered that it cooked down below the bulb of the candy thermometer so that we could not get an accurate reading. We thus had to rely on the old-fashioned "soft-ball" test, that is, dropping a bit of the hot candy into a cup of cold water and taking it from the heat the minute it formed a soft, malleable ball that did not break apart in the cold water.

One additional note: this fudge "turns" quite fast as you beat it— and with almost no warning—so watch closely. The instant the candy begins to lose its sheen, pour at once into the buttered pan; otherwise it will harden in the saucepan and be impossible to remove. This may all seem a lot of bother, but if properly made the fudge is silky-smooth and absolutely delicious.

> 3 cups granulated sugar
> 1½ cups buttermilk
> 1½ teaspoons baking soda
> ½ cup (1 stick) butter
> 1 cup coarsely chopped walnuts or pecans
> 1 teaspoon vanilla extract

Place the sugar, buttermilk, soda, and butter in a very large (about 8-quart), heavy saucepan and set over moderate heat. Bring slowly to the soft-ball stage (236° to 238° F. on a candy thermometer) *without* stirring (stirring will make the fudge gritty). You'll find that it will take quite a while for the candy to reach the soft-ball stage—about 30 minutes. (You may also discover, as we did, that the syrup reaches the soft-ball stage before the candy thermometer registers 236° F., so rely on the "soft-ball" test described in the headnote above.) As soon as the candy forms a soft ball in cold water, remove from the heat and cool—again without stirring—until the candy thermometer registers 180° F.—about 10 minutes.

Meanwhile, butter well a 9 × 9 × 2-inch pan.

Add the nuts and vanilla to the fudge and beat hard for a few strokes, just until the fudge loses its sheen and begins to lighten. Pour at once into the well-buttered pan. Let harden, then cut into squares.

N O T E   *It's best to mark off the squares as soon as you pour the hot fudge into the pan—just score the top with a sharp knife—and then to cut into squares after the candy cools (this seems to reduce crumbling and make for neater squares).*

A N G E L   B I S C U I T S

About 2½ dozen

You will have to look long and hard to find a lighter, better biscuit than this one, which is an old Southern favorite. The recipe calls for 2 cups of buttermilk (but you can use 2 cups soured milk instead). It's also a good way to use up any packet of dry yeast that's nearing its expiration date. This biscuit dough, by the way, can be covered, refrigerated, and kept for about 1 week. Simply reach in and remove whatever amount of dough you'll need for one meal, then roll and bake the biscuits as directed.

> 1 package active dry yeast
> ¼ cup very warm water (105°–115° F.)
> 5 cups sifted all-purpose flour
> 1 tablespoon (3 teaspoons) baking powder
> 1 teaspoon baking soda
> ¼ cup granulated sugar
> 2 teaspoons salt
> 1 cup vegetable shortening
> 2 cups buttermilk or sour milk

Preheat the oven to hot (400° F.).

Dissolve the yeast in the warm water and set aside. Sift together the flour, baking powder, baking soda, sugar, and salt into a large mixing bowl. Using a pastry blender, cut in the shortening until the mixture has the texture of coarse meal. Pour in the buttermilk and yeast mixture and toss briskly with a fork just until the mixture holds together, forming a soft dough.

Turn out the dough on a well-floured pastry cloth, and with well-floured hands (this is a sticky dough), knead lightly for 1 minute. Roll the dough to a thickness of about ⅝ inch, then cut with a well-floured 2½-inch biscuit cutter. Bake on ungreased baking sheets in the pre-heated oven for about 15 minutes, or until the biscuits are nicely puffed and a pale tan on top.

Serve at once, with plenty of butter.

ORANGE BUTTERMILK PIE

One 9-inch pie

If you want to use a frozen, prepared pie shell for this recipe, be sure that you use the "deep-dish" size. The regular, shallow pie shell will only hold two-thirds of the filling and will make for a thin and skimpy pie.

N O T E   *To keep the bottom crust from becoming soggy, brush it well with lightly beaten egg white* before *you fill it—and be sure to let the egg white "air dry" about half an hour before adding the filling. It also helps to set the filled pie pan on a baking sheet that has preheated in the oven and to let it stand there throughout baking. For best results, bake the pie in the lower one-third of the oven.*

   1 orange
   1 cup granulated sugar
   3 tablespoons all-purpose flour
   ⅛ teaspoon salt
   3 eggs, separated
   2 cups buttermilk
   ½ cup (1 stick) butter, melted and cooled
   1 unbaked 9-inch pie shell

Preheat the oven to very hot (450° F.).

Using a swivel-bladed vegetable peeler, take the rind off half of the orange in long, thin strips—the *orange* part (zest) only, not the bitter white inner rind. Stack the rind strips together and cut crosswise into very thin slivers; set aside. Refrigerate the partially peeled orange to use another time.

Combine the sugar, flour, and salt in a mixing bowl; add the rind and toss well to mix. Stir in the egg yolks, buttermilk, and melted butter. Beat the whites to soft peaks and fold into the filling.

Pour into the unbaked pie shell and bake in the preheated oven for 5 minutes, then lower the temperature to moderate (350° F.) and bake the pie about 45 minutes longer, or until the filling is set like custard.

Remove the pie from the oven and cool to room temperature before cutting.

SPINACH-BUTTERMILK SOUP WITH VEAL AND PORK BALLS

6 to 8 servings

The beauty of this versatile recipe is that it neatly uses up a variety of leftovers—2 to 3 cups of buttermilk, 1 cup of bread crumbs, even tag ends of anchovy paste and/or grated Parmesan. The soup itself is tart—and hearty enough to serve as a main dish. You'll need only chunks of crusty bread to accompany, and for dessert a fresh fruit salad.

This soup freezes well, meatballs and all (directions follow the recipe).

VEAL AND PORK BALLS

½ pound lean ground pork shoulder or beef chuck
½ pound ground veal shoulder
1 cup soft, fine bread crumbs
1 small yellow onion, peeled and minced
1 large egg
Up to ¼ cup grated Parmesan cheese (optional)
Up to 3 tablespoons anchovy paste (optional)
2 tablespoons club soda (optional)
½ teaspoon salt (omit if using Parmesan and/or anchovy paste)
⅛ teaspoon freshly ground black pepper
Pinch of grated nutmeg

SPINACH - BUTTERMILK SOUP

2 large yellow onions, peeled and chopped fine
3 tablespoons butter
2 packages (10 ounces each) frozen leaf or chopped spinach
5¼ cups chicken broth (this is the amount contained in three 13¾-
    ounce cans)
2 to 3 cups buttermilk
⅛ teaspoon freshly ground black pepper
Pinch of grated nutmeg
Salt, if needed, to taste

Prepare the veal and pork balls first. Place all the ingredients in a large mixing bowl (omit both the Parmesan and anchovy paste, if you like, or use one or the other or both). Mix thoroughly with your hands, then shape into 1-inch balls and arrange one layer deep on a small tray; cover loosely and refrigerate for 2 to 3 hours, or until the meatballs have firmed up a bit.

Meanwhile, prepare the spinach-buttermilk soup. In a very large, heavy saucepan (a 4-quart size is a good one), sauté the onions in the butter over moderate heat for 12 to 15 minutes, until nicely browned. It is important that you brown the onions and the butter because they enrich the flavor of the soup. Add the solidly frozen blocks of spinach to the pan, cover, and cook over moderately low heat for about 30 minutes, or until the spinach is very soft.

Purée the mixture, about one-fourth of the total amount at a time, in a food processor fitted with the metal chopping blade, in an electric blender, or by pressing through a food mill. Return the spinach purée to the saucepan and add the chicken broth. At this point, turn the heat to its lowest point, cover the soup, and allow to mellow until the meatballs have chilled until firm.

Drop the meatballs into the soup, spacing them as evenly as possible. Adjust the burner heat so that the soup barely simmers, re-cover, and cook the meatballs slowly for 45 minutes, or until they are completely cooked through. Add the buttermilk, pepper, nutmeg, and, if needed, salt to taste.

Bring the soup just to serving temperature (do not allow it to boil, or it may curdle), then ladle into soup bowls and serve.

To Freeze   Cool and ladle into half-pint, pint, or quart freezer containers, to within ½ inch of the tops. Snap on the lids, date, label, and quick-freeze in a freezer set at 0° F. Keeping time: 3 to 4 months.

C A K E   C R U M B S : See **Crumbs.**

Candied (Glacéed) Fruits

We're most likely to be caught with an excess of candied cherries, citron, pineapple, and the like right after the holiday season—*just* when we're sated with fruit cakes, plum puddings, and other Christmas sweets. Luckily, candied fruits keep well—weather (either too dry or too moist) and insects are their biggest spoilers.

Best Way to Store Tightly wrapped in foil or plastic food wrap or, better yet, tightly capped in a glass jar. Leftover candied fruits should not be refrigerated (they may take on moisture). Simply tuck them away on any cool, dry, dark shelf.

Maximum Storage Time About 6 months—or until they harden and dry or, worse, absorb atmospheric moisture and become too gummy to use.

Roles in Cooking To add color, flavor, and texture. Candied fruits are also used to decorate a wide variety of festive holiday foods.

Recipe Uses Cookies, candies, cakes, sweet breads, puddings, frozen desserts, and dessert sauces are the foods in which candied fruits are most often used.

To Use Very Small Amounts Fold ½ cup or so of finely minced candied fruits into a pint of mushy vanilla ice cream, spike to taste with rum, then refreeze and serve as tutti-frutti. You can also approximate a Nesselrode sauce by stirring ¼ to ½ cup of finely minced candied fruits into 1 to 1½ cups of butterscotch or caramel sauce, then lacing lightly with rum. For a quick and easy dessert, combine equal quantities of crumbled macaroons and minced candied fruits with enough sherry or Port to bind them, and use to stuff peach or apricot halves or tuck into the hollow centers of cored apples just before you bake them.

SIMNEL CAKE

One 8-inch cake

Although this is a traditional Easter cake in England (the name "sim-nel" comes from the Latin *simnellus,* a Roman bread eaten during spring fertility rites), we think Christmas is an even better time to make it because that's the time you're apt to have leftover candied or glacéed fruits. It's also the time well-wishers are likely to drop in and welcome a bite of cake and cup of tea.

The recipe, you'll note, also calls for raisins; if yours happen to be old and dry, it's a good excuse to soak them in hot rum. They'll plump up if you let them soak for about 10 minutes.

CAKE BATTER

²/₃ cup granulated sugar
½ cup (1 stick) butter, cut into pats and brought to room temperature
3 eggs, well beaten
¾ cup raisins, coarsely chopped
½ cup mixed candied or glacéed fruits, coarsely chopped
1 cup *unsifted* all-purpose flour

FILLING

¾ cup granulated sugar
1 cup finely ground blanched almonds
1 egg
¼ teaspoon almond extract

Preheat the oven to moderate (350° F.).

To make the batter, cream the sugar and butter well, then stir in the eggs. Mix the raisins and candied fruits with the flour and fold into the egg mixture.

Combine all the filling ingredients and set aside for the time being.

Line an 8-inch spring-form pan with heavy brown paper, then grease and flour the paper well. Spread half of the cake batter into the pan. Draw an 8-inch circle on a piece of wax paper and spread the filling over it; using a pancake turner, lift up about one-third of the filling and gently invert it on one-third of the surface of the batter in the pan. Repeat in two more operations until the filling covers the layer of batter. (The idea is simply to add an even layer of filling, but because the filling is so thick and sticky and the batter so soft, it is impossible to spread the one on the other. The filling doesn't scatter well, either, so this technique of spreading it first on wax paper, then transferring in three more-or-less equal parts to the batter, seems best—but perhaps you can devise an even better system.)

Spoon the remaining batter on top of the filling, then bake the Simnel in the preheated oven for 1 to 1¼ hours, or until lightly browned.

Remove from the oven and cool to room temperature. Release the hinge on the spring-form pan, remove the cake from the pan, then cut into small wedges and serve (the cake is *very* rich).

B L U E   G R A S S   C H E S S   P I E

One 9-inch pie

This is one in the South's great repertoire of chess pies, and one of the easiest and most successful ways we know for using up leftover candied fruits.

   2 cups granulated sugar
   2 tablespoons white or yellow corn meal
   2 tablespoons all-purpose flour
   3 eggs, beaten lightly
   ½ cup (1 stick) butter, melted
   1 cup light cream
   1 tablespoon bourbon
   ½ to 1 cup chopped, mixed candied or glacéed fruits (or candied
      cherries or citron if they are what you have on hand)
   ¼ teaspoon salt
   1 unbaked 9-inch pie shell

Preheat the oven to hot (425° F.).

Combine the sugar, corn meal, and flour in a mixing bowl, then mix in the eggs. Stir in the remaining ingredients, one by one (except, of course, for the pie shell), and mix well after each addition.

Pour the filling into the unbaked pie shell and bake in the preheated oven for 15 minutes. Reduce the oven temperature to moderately hot (375° F.) and bake the pie for 45 to 50 minutes longer, or until puffy and golden.

Cool the pie to room temperature before serving. (You'll note that as the pie cools, the filling falls somewhat—but that is the nature of chess pies. They congeal into an almost jellylike curd as they cool.)

BOLO REI (KING'S CAKE)

4 small, round loaves

This traditional Portuguese Christmas bread is a marvelous way to utilize leftover glacéed fruits, raisins, and nuts. It is similar to the Italian *panettone,* but firmer in texture and not quite so sweet. The loaves freeze beautifully and are good any time of the year as a breakfast or tea bread. The ideal containers, by the way, for baking the loaves are 1-pound shortening tins.

  2 packages active dry yeast
  ¼ cup very warm water (105°–115° F.)
  ½ cup very warm milk (105°–115° F.)
  5 cups sifted all-purpose flour
  3 eggs
  ½ cup (1 stick) butter, at room temperature
  ⅔ cup granulated sugar
  ½ teaspoon salt
  3 tablespoons brandy
  ¾ cup finely chopped, mixed glacéed fruits
  ½ cup chopped pecans, walnuts, or blanched filberts or almonds
  ⅓ cup finely chopped seedless or sultana raisins

  TOPPING

  1 egg, beaten with 1 tablespoon cold water (glaze)
  ¼ cup coarsely chopped pignoli (pine nuts)
  ¼ cup crushed sugar cubes
  Red and/or green glacéed fruits (optional)

Sprinkle the yeast over the very warm water in a small bowl; stir until the yeast dissolves. Mix in the milk and 1 cup of the flour, then cover, set in a warm, draft-free spot, and let stand for 1 hour, or until the mixture forms a sponge that is about twice the volume of the original yeast mixture.

CONTINUED

Place the remaining 4 cups of flour in a large mixing bowl and make a deep well in the center. Add the eggs, butter, sugar, salt, and brandy and stir this mixture hard, disturbing the surrounding walls of flour as little as possible. Add the yeast sponge, glacéed fruits, nuts, and raisins and work the moist ingredients into the flour to form a soft, sticky dough. Transfer the dough to a well-greased bowl and brush the top of the dough lightly with oil; cover with a clean, dry cloth and let rise in a warm, draft-free spot until doubled in bulk—about 2 hours.

Punch the dough down and divide in four equal parts. Shape each into a ball with lightly floured hands and place in a very well greased 1-pound shortening tin. Cover the tins with a cloth and again let the dough rise in a warm spot until doubled in bulk—about 1 to 1½ hours.

Preheat the oven to hot (425° F.).

Brush the tops of the loaves lightly with the egg glaze, taking care that it does not run down the sides of the loaves into the shortening tins. Sprinkle the top of each loaf with chopped pignoli and crushed sugar, and, if you like, make fanciful designs out of the glacéed fruits. Bake the loaves in the preheated oven for 12 to 15 minutes, just until they are nicely browned and sound hollow when thumped with your fingers.

Cool the loaves upright in their pans on wire racks for 10 minutes, then run a thin-blade spatula around the edges of the loaves, remove from the pans, and cool upright on wire racks to room temperature before cutting.

Cheeses

(Soft, Semihard, and Hard)

In the interest of space, we will divide the kinds of cheeses that are most apt to clutter refrigerator shelves into three categories: soft cheeses (cottage, pot and ricotta cheeses, mozzarella, processed cheeses and cheese spreads, cream cheese); semihard cheeses (Cheddar, Swiss, Roquefort, blue, Monterey jack, etc.); and hard cheeses (Parmesan, Romano). This, to be sure, is a vastly oversimplified list from a cheese lover's view, but our arbitrary grouping will enable us to discuss the various cheeses, their keeping qualities, storage, and use more efficiently. It will also, we hope, indicate how cheeses of like character and hardness should be handled.

Best Ways to Store   All cheeses, from soft to hard, should be tightly wrapped, capped, or covered, then stored in the refrigerator. Spreads and cottage and ricotta cheeses can be stored in their original containers but the tops should be snapped or screwed down tight. Cream cheese, too, may be stored in its foil wrapper, provided it is not torn (if so, rewrap the cheese in aluminum foil). As for mozzarella and the semihard and hard cheeses, we prefer to rewrap them in double thicknesses of plastic food wrap, which seal out moisture and refrigerator odors but allow us to see what's inside each package.

Tip   If you lightly butter the cut edges of the semihard cheeses, they will be less likely to dry or mold.

Maximum Storage Time

Soft Cheeses   These are the most perishable of all and will keep fresh for only about 7 to 10 days. Pay particular attention to the dates stamped on the cartons of these cheeses and buy only those that have at least a week of shelf life left.

Semihard Cheeses   Under optimum conditions, these should last for 6 weeks to 2 months. The Cheddars may mold, but no harm done; simply trim off and discard any moldy portions (it's only penicillin).

Hard Cheeses   These are the best keepers, and if bought in large enough pieces (more than 1 pound), they should hold well for about 6 months. As for grated Parmesan, don't expect it to taste fresh after 4 to 6 weeks on the refrigerator shelf. As a matter of fact, we far prefer to buy Parmesan by the pound and to grate our own supply of it (a snap in a food processor). You will discover that the Parmesan you grate yourself, if stored in the refrigerator in a tightly capped jar, will taste fresher after 6 weeks than a commercially grated Parmesan will on the day of purchase.

Roles in Cooking   Next to eggs, cheeses are one of the most versatile of all foods. They are used for flavor, of course, and for color and food value (as a matter of fact, they are so rich in high-quality protein and in vitamins A and D that they are the perfect meat substitute). Cheeses are also used to thicken soups and sauces and to bind and fill a variety of foods; they are used as toppings (either solo or in tandem with crumbs); and, finally, they are used to decorate everything from soups to sweets.

Recipe Uses   Soups, sandwiches, cocktail dips and spreads, egg dishes, sauces, casseroles, quick breads and yeast breads, cheese pies —all rely upon one kind of cheese or another. So do dozens of French classics (hardly surprising when you consider that France produces hundreds of different cheeses), not to mention dozens of Swiss, Dutch, Scandinavian, Russian, British, and Balkan recipes.

How to Use Very Small Amounts   Snippets of soft or semihard cheeses can be melted into a variety of cream soups and sauces; they may be mixed into burgers or meat loaves, scattered over such cooked vegetables as broccoli, cauliflower, Brussels sprouts, zucchini, and asparagus. They may be folded into an omelet, scrambled into eggs, or tucked into Parker House rolls just before the second rising. Hard and semihard cheeses may be grated into crisp green salads, mixed with garlic butter (then spread onto garlic bread); they may be shredded and sprinkled into apple, peach, or pear pies and cobblers. They may be sprinkled over fresh fruit salads or compotes. And they may simply be strewn over buttered toast and browned under the broiler.

N O T E   *For additional recipes, included elsewhere in this book, that call for varying amounts of the different kinds of cheese, see the Appendix.*

Soft Cheeses

COTTAGE POTATOES

4 to 6 servings

A good and flexible recipe in which you can use up from ⅓ to ¾ cup of cottage cheese and ¾ to 1 cup of leftover evaporated milk or light or heavy cream, even yogurt or sour cream. You might also slip in as much as 1 cup of grated Cheddar, Swiss, or Monterey jack cheese. Improvise however you like, but taste as you add each ingredient.

4 large baking potatoes, scrubbed
¼ cup (½ stick) butter or margarine
1 teaspoon salt
¼ teaspoon freshly ground black pepper
¼ teaspoon ground mace or grated nutmeg
⅛ teaspoon ground cardamom
1 egg, beaten lightly
¾ to 1 cup evaporated milk, cream, (light, heavy, or sour), or yogurt
⅓ to ¾ cup cottage or ricotta cheese
1 cup grated Cheddar, Swiss, or Monterey jack cheese (optional)
¼ cup minced fresh or frozen chives (optional but a splendid addition)

Preheat the oven to hot (400° F.) and bake the potatoes in their skins for 1 hour, or until you can pierce them easily with a fork; remove from the oven (leaving the oven on at 400° F.).

Slit the potatoes open with a knife, then scoop the hot flesh into a mixing bowl and mash well with the butter, salt, pepper, mace, and cardamom. Mix in the egg, then all the remaining ingredients. Spoon lightly into a well-greased 6-cup casserole and bake, uncovered, in the hot oven for about 20 minutes, or until lightly browned.

Serve at once.

LOW-CALORIE COTTAGE CHEESE– CHIVE SALAD DRESSING

About 1½ cups

When you consider that mayonnaise contains 100 calories per table-spoon and a classic vinaigrette 95, this dressing, weighing in at approximately 12 calories per tablespoon, is indeed a boon to dieters. It's creamy and tart and a splendid way to utilize ⅔ to ¾ cup leftover cottage cheese. Stored tightly covered in the refrigerator, it will keep fresh for about 4 days.

⅔ to ¾ cup cottage cheese
1 tablespoon honey
1 teaspoon lemon juice
2 tablespoons minced fresh or frozen chives
1 scallion, washed, trimmed, and sliced thin
½ very small clove garlic, peeled
1 teaspoon salt
1 teaspoon paprika
⅛ teaspoon freshly ground black pepper
½ cup buttermilk, yogurt, or skim milk

Place all the ingredients in an electric blender cup or a food processor equipped with the metal chopping blade and buzz for about 1 minute nonstop, or until creamy-smooth. Use to dress crisp green salads.

CHINESE CHEESE PANCAKES

4 servings

A most unusual way to take care of ¾ cup of leftover cottage cheese. And an unusually good one, too. Serve as the main course of a light luncheon or supper.

4 scallions, washed, trimmed, and sliced very thin (include some green tops)
1 large rib celery, washed, trimmed, and sliced very thin
2 tablespoons peanut oil or butter
½ teaspoon salt
⅛ teaspoon freshly ground black pepper

½ cup finely minced leftover beef, lamb, pork, ham, chicken (or, if
   you like, substitute finely flaked tuna)
3 eggs, separated
¼ cup unsifted all-purpose flour
¾ cup cottage cheese

Stir-fry the scallions and celery in the peanut oil in a medium-sized
skillet over moderate heat for about 5 minutes, or until golden but not
brown. Mix in the salt, pepper, and meat and set aside for the time
being. Beat the egg whites to soft peaks and set aside also. Now beat
the yolks until frothy and blend in the flour and cottage cheese; fold
in the meat mixture and finally the beaten whites.

Drop the mixture by tablespoonfuls onto a hot, lightly greased
griddle set over moderately high heat. Flatten each pancake slightly
with the back of the spoon, then brown lightly on each side—about
2 minutes per side.

Serve immediately with melted butter and soy sauce, or, if you
prefer, with your own favorite mushroom sauce.

PROCESSOR PÂTÉ WITH COGNAC

About 1½ cups

You can make this pâté in less than 5 minutes and, at the same time,
use up half of a large package of cream cheese.

½ pound liverwurst, sliced, at room temperature
½ package (8-ounce size) cream cheese, at room temperature
1 small yellow onion, peeled and coarsely chopped
⅛ teaspoon ground cloves
⅛ teaspoon ground cinnamon
2 tablespoons Cognac or brandy
Salt and freshly ground black pepper to taste

Place all the ingredients except the salt and pepper in a processor
fitted with the metal chopping blade (or in an electric blender or
electric mixer bowl) and blend or beat hard for about 1 minute nonstop, or until smooth and creamy. Empty into a small bowl, taste, then
season as needed with salt and pepper. Cover the pâté and chill for
several hours, or until the flavors are well blended.

CONTINUED

Let the pâté stand at room temperature for about 20 to 30 minutes before serving so it softens into a good spreading consistency. Accompany with fresh Melba toast.

DEVILED HAM DIP WITH DILL

About 1½ cups

1 can (4½ ounces) deviled ham
½ package (8-ounce size) cream cheese, at room temperature
1 very small yellow onion, peeled and coarsely chopped
2 tablespoons Dijon or spicy brown mustard
½ cup sour cream or yogurt
½ teaspoon dill weed
2 tablespoons minced dill pickle

Place all the ingredients except the dill pickle in an electric blender or a food processor equipped with the metal chopping blade and buzz for about 1 minute nonstop, or until uniformly creamy. Empty into a small bowl and fold in the minced dill pickle. Cover and let stand in the refrigerator for about 2 hours, to allow the flavors of the dip to mingle.

Remove from the refrigerator, let stand at room temperature for 30 minutes, then serve with crisp crackers or potato or corn chips for dipping.

CREAM CHEESE AND ALMOND PINWHEELS

4 dozen

So many recipes call for 4 ounces of cream cheese, meaning that you are left with another 4 ounces—half of an 8-ounce bar. Next time it happens, we suggest that you try these unique cookies—provided you *also* have 2 egg whites to get rid of.

COOKIE DOUGH

1½ cups sifted all-purpose flour
2 tablespoons granulated sugar
½ teaspoon ground cinnamon
½ cup (1 stick) butter, at room temperature
½ package (8-ounce size) cream cheese, at room temperature, or 1
    package (3 ounces) cream cheese plus 1 tablespoon butter, at room
    temperature

FILLING

1½ cups finely ground blanched almonds
2 egg whites
⅓ cup granulated sugar
¼ teaspoon almond extract

Sift the flour with the sugar and cinnamon and set aside. Cream the
butter and cheese until fluffy, then stir in the flour mixture. Roll out
on lightly floured wax paper into a rectangle measuring about 13 ×
10 inches. If the kitchen is warm, slide the paper onto a baking sheet
and chill for 30 minutes or so—just until firm.

Mix all the filling ingredients together and spread on the dough,
leaving ¼-inch margins all around. Using the wax paper to ease the
dough over, roll up from the longest side, jelly-roll fashion. Wrap and
chill the dough for 12 hours.

Preheat the oven to moderate (350° F.).

Cut the roll of dough in ⅛- to ¼-inch slices and arrange 2 inches
apart on greased baking sheets. Bake for 12 minutes in the preheated
oven until firm but not brown.

Transfer at once to wire racks to cool.

CLASSIC CREAM CHEESE FROSTING

Enough to frost a two-layer 8- or 9-inch cake

This variation on old-fashioned butter frosting enables you to use up
from half to three-quarters of an 8-ounce package of cream cheese.
Note, too, the easy flavor variations.

CONTINUED

½ to ¾ package (8-ounce size) cream cheese, at room temperature
1 box (1 pound) confectioners sugar
1½ teaspoons vanilla extract
2 to 3 tablespoons cream (light, heavy, or sour; just enough to give the frosting a good spreading consistency)

Cream the cheese until light in an electric blender at high speed or in a food processor equipped with the metal chopping blade. Add the confectioners sugar slowly, beating all the while, then mix in the vanilla and just enough cream to make the frosting spreadable. Use to frost any favorite cake.

VARIATIONS

Coffee–Cream Cheese Frosting   Prepare as directed, but cream 2 tablespoons instant coffee powder along with the cheese.

Chocolate–Cream Cheese Frosting   Prepare as directed, but cream 2 ounces of melted unsweetened chocolate along with the cheese, or, if you prefer, beat in 3 tablespoons of cocoa. If you use the cocoa instead of the melted chocolate, you may have to increase slightly the amount of cream needed to make the frosting spreadable.

Orange– or Lemon–Cream Cheese Frosting   Cream the cheese with 1 tablespoon grated orange or lemon rind, then beat in the confectioners sugar. Omit the vanilla, but add cream as needed to thin the mixture.

Semihard Cheeses

ROQUEFORT-HORSERADISH SPREAD

About 1¼ cups

Note that this easy cocktail spread calls for 1 to 2 tablespoons tomato paste (an excellent way to use up tag ends). Serve as a spread for crisp crackers or as a topper for grilled hamburgers.

½ cup (1 stick) butter, at room temperature
1 teaspoon paprika
2 tablespoons finely minced onion
¼ cup prepared horseradish
¼ cup crumbled Roquefort or blue cheese, at room temperature
1 to 2 tablespoons tomato paste, chili sauce, or ketchup
Salt, if needed, to taste

Blend all the ingredients together well with a fork, then let stand for about 30 minutes at room temperature before serving so that the flavors will mellow and "get together."

NOTE *This spread will keep well in the refrigerator for about 2 weeks, if tightly covered.*

MUSTARD-CHEESE GLAZE FOR BROILED BURGERS, CHOPS, AND CHICKEN

Enough for 4 to 6 servings

An absolutely sensational way to rescue snippets of cheese, not to mention dribs of heavy or light cream or evaporated milk.

3 ounces (¼ to ⅓ cup) Gruyère or Cheddar cheese, very finely grated
3 tablespoons Dijon or spicy brown mustard
4 to 5 tablespoons cream (heavy or light) or evaporated milk
Pinch of crumbled leaf rosemary, thyme, or sage

Mix all the ingredients together with a fork, adding just enough cream or evaporated milk to give the glaze a good spreading consistency, then spread evenly over broiled chops (veal or lamb) or braised pork chops, or broiled chicken or burgers just before serving them. Return to the broiler, placing 3 to 4 inches from the heat, and broil for 2 to 3 minutes, or just until the glaze is flecked with brown.
Serve at once.

CRISP CHEDDAR, OLIVE, AND ONION CANAPÉS

About 4 dozen appetizers or 6 main-course servings

Cut small, these make excellent cocktail tidbits; cut larger, they can be served like pizza for a light lunch, supper, or snack.

PASTRY

¾ cup sifted all-purpose flour
¾ cup yellow corn meal
½ teaspoon salt
1 teaspoon paprika
¼ teaspoon crumbled leaf thyme
½ cup vegetable shortening
⅓ cup finely grated sharp Cheddar cheese
¼ cup cold water, or as needed

TOPPING

3 cups moderately coarsely chopped Spanish onions
3 tablespoons butter or margarine
¼ to ⅓ cup minced pimiento-stuffed olives
1 egg, beaten lightly
½ cup sour cream
1 teaspoon salt
⅛ teaspoon freshly ground black pepper
½ teaspoon paprika
¼ teaspoon crumbled leaf marjoram
1 cup moderately coarsely grated sharp Cheddar cheese

Preheat the oven to hot (400° F.).

Prepare the pastry first. Combine the flour, corn meal, salt, paprika, and thyme in a mixing bowl. Using a pastry blender, cut in the shortening until the mixture is crumbly and the texture of coarse meal; stir in the grated Cheddar. Drizzle water over surface, tossing briskly, just until the pastry holds together. Roll on a lightly floured board into a rectangle measuring about 9 × 13 inches. Lay the rolling pin across the center, lop half the pastry over the rolling pin, then ease onto an ungreased baking sheet and unfold. Bake, uncovered, in the preheated oven for 5 minutes. Remove from the oven and reserve. Lower the oven heat to moderate (350° F.).

To make the topping, stir-fry the onions in the butter in a large, heavy skillet over moderate heat for 5 to 8 minutes, just until lightly golden but still crisp. Spread the onions over the reserved pastry, then sprinkle the minced olives on top. Combine the egg, sour cream, salt, pepper, paprika, and marjoram and pour over the onions and olives. Bake, uncovered, in the moderate oven for 20 minutes, or until bubbling; remove from the oven and scatter the cheese on top, then return to the oven and bake for 5 minutes longer, or until the cheese is melted and touched with brown.

Cut into 1½-inch squares and serve as appetizers, or cut into larger squares and serve as you would pizza.

CORN AND PIMIENTO PUDDING

6 servings

Such an easy recipe! And one that will take care of ¾ cup leftover evaporated milk or cream, 1 cup bread or cracker crumbs, 3 to 4 tablespoons chopped pimiento, and 1 cup grated sharp Cheddar or American cheese.

> 1 medium yellow onion, peeled and chopped fine
> ¼ cup (½ stick) butter or margarine
> 1 can (1 pound, 4 ounces) cream-style corn
> ¾ cup milk, evaporated milk, or cream (light or heavy)
> 1 cup cracker crumbs or soft bread crumbs
> 3 to 4 tablespoons chopped pimiento
> 1 cup coarsely grated sharp Cheddar or American cheese
> ½ teaspoon salt
> Pinch of cayenne pepper

Preheat the oven to moderate (350° F.).

In a small skillet set over moderate heat, brown the onion lightly, in 2 tablespoons of the butter, for 8 to 10 minutes. Combine the onion with the corn, milk, crumbs, pimiento, cheese, salt, and pepper, then spoon into a buttered 6-cup casserole and dot with the remaining 2 tablespoons of butter. Bake, uncovered, in the preheated oven for about 30 minutes, or until lightly browned.

CHEESE AND SPINACH CUSTARD

6 servings

This recipe is particularly good if you use part evaporated milk—½ to 1 cup of it—and the rest plain milk. Note that you may also add 1 to 2 minced hard-cooked eggs and that you may substitute frozen chopped spinach for the fresh. Serve as a vegetable or light entrée.

> 1 very small yellow onion, peeled and minced
> ¼ cup (½ stick) butter or margarine
> ¼ cup unsifted all-purpose flour
> ⅛ teaspoon ground mace or grated nutmeg
> 2 cups milk (use part evaporated milk or light cream or half-and-half if you have leftovers of these)
> 1 cup coarsely grated sharp Cheddar cheese
> 1 to 2 hard-cooked eggs, peeled and minced (optional)
> 2 cups finely chopped, well-drained, cooked fresh spinach or 2 packages (10 ounces each) frozen chopped spinach, cooked according to package directions and drained very dry
> 2 eggs, beaten lightly
> 1 teaspoon salt
> ⅛ teaspoon freshly ground black pepper

Preheat the oven to moderate (350° F.).

Stir-fry the onion in the butter in a large, heavy saucepan over moderate heat for 10 to 12 minutes, or until the onion is nicely browned (the browning is important for flavor). Blend in the flour and mace, then add the milk and heat, stirring constantly, until thickened and smooth—about 5 minutes. Add the cheese, remove from the heat, and stir until melted. Mix in the hard-cooked eggs, if you like.

Combine the cheese sauce, spinach, lightly beaten eggs, salt, and pepper. Spoon into a buttered 8 × 8 × 2-inch baking dish, set in a shallow baking pan containing about 1 inch of hot water, and bake, uncovered, in the preheated oven for 30 to 45 minutes, or until set like custard.

Remove from the oven and cool for 10 minutes, then cut into squares and serve.

GOLDEN CHEDDAR AND CARROT SOUP

6 servings

If this is more soup than you can eat at one time, freeze the balance in individual-sized (half-pint) or pint containers so that you can enjoy it 3 to 4 months hence.

- 1 medium yellow onion, peeled and minced very fine
- 2 medium carrots, peeled and grated very fine
- 5 tablespoons butter or margarine
- Pinch of crumbled leaf rosemary
- 5 tablespoons all-purpose flour
- 2 cups any combination of milk and cream (milk, evaporated milk, light cream, heavy cream, half-and-half, etc.)
- 2 cups chicken or beef stock or broth (or use a smaller amount of stock if that is all you have and round the measure out with water)
- 1½ to 2 cups coarsely grated sharp Cheddar cheese
- Salt and freshly ground black pepper to season
- Minced fresh parsley, scallion, or chives (optional)

Stir-fry the onion and carrot in the butter over moderate heat for about 10 minutes, until limp and lightly browned. Blend in the rosemary, then reduce the heat to low, cover, and steam for 10 minutes, or until the carrot is tender. Blend in the flour.

Combine the milk and stock mixtures and add to the pan; heat, stirring constantly, until thickened and smooth—about 5 minutes. Turn the heat to its lowest point and allow the soup to mellow for about 10 minutes, or until no raw, floury taste remains. Remove the soup from the heat, add the cheese, and stir until melted.

Season to taste with salt and pepper and serve, garnished, if you like, with minced fresh parsley, scallions, or chives.

Hard Cheeses

ANATOLIAN
CHEESE-STUFFED PEPPERS

6 servings

For this recipe Turkish women would use a crumbly white goat cheese not unlike the Greek feta, but we have substituted the more universally available cottage cheese, with excellent results. This cheese stuffing is a handy place to use oddments of grated Parmesan, tomato paste, and cream (light, heavy, or sour), as well as stale bread.

> 6 small sweet green or red peppers (choose those that will stand securely)
> 2 tablespoons olive oil
> 1 large yellow onion, peeled and minced
> 1 medium clove garlic, peeled and minced
> ¼ teaspoon crumbled leaf rosemary
> Pinch of crumbled leaf thyme
> Pinch of grated nutmeg
> ¼ teaspoon salt
> ⅛ teaspoon freshly ground black pepper
> 1 pound cottage cheese
> 2 slices stale bread, broken or buzzed into fairly fine crumbs
> 2 to 3 tablespoons tomato paste
> ¼ to ½ cup grated Parmesan cheese
> 3 to 6 tablespoons cream (light, heavy, or sour)
> 4 large eggs, beaten lightly

Wash the peppers well; cut off the tops, then scoop out seeds and pith so the peppers are ready to stuff. Heat the olive oil in a large, heavy saucepan over moderate heat, then add the peppers and sauté gently for 3 to 4 minutes, just until they begin to glisten; reduce the heat to low, cover the peppers, and "steam" for 20 minutes, turning them now and then in the pan so that they cook evenly. Remove the peppers from the pan and drain upside down on several thicknesses of paper toweling.

Add the onion and garlic to the saucepan in which you sautéed the peppers and stir-fry over moderate heat for 8 to 10 minutes, until limp and golden; mix in the rosemary, thyme, nutmeg, salt, and pepper and stir-fry for 2 to 3 minutes longer. Remove from the heat. In a large mixing bowl place all of the remaining ingredients and stir to mix; add the onion mixture and stir well again.

Preheat the oven to moderate (350° F.).

Stand the peppers in a shallow ovenproof casserole so that they touch and support one another, then fill each with the cheese mixture. Bake, uncovered, in the preheated oven for about 30 minutes, or until the cheese filling is just set.

Remove the stuffed peppers from the oven and let cool for 15 minutes before serving.

PARMESAN-CRUMBED CHICKEN IN COGNAC-CREAM SAUCE

6 servings

This chicken spatters badly as you brown it, so use a deep Dutch oven instead of a shallow skillet for the frying. So you don't create leftovers when making this recipe, plan ahead carefully: you will need ½ to 1 cup of chicken broth, ½ to 1 cup of dry white wine, ⅓ to ⅔ cup light or heavy cream, and, finally, ½ to 1 cup *each* of soft bread crumbs and grated Parmesan (no, the discrepancies in measurements don't affect the finished dish).

The dish, by the way, is well worth the wait. It's one of the loveliest chicken dishes we have ever tasted, perfect for a small dinner party in that it can be prepared ahead of time—all but the finishing touches.

3 large whole chicken breasts, split
¼ cup olive oil
1 teaspoon salt
¼ teaspoon freshly ground black pepper
3 medium yellow onions, peeled and coarsely chopped
1 clove garlic, peeled and minced
½ to 1 cup chicken broth or stock
½ to 1 cup dry white wine
⅓ cup Cognac or brandy
⅓ to ⅔ cup cream (light, heavy, or half-and-half)

CONTINUED

TOPPING

½ to 1 cup soft bread crumbs
½ to 1 cup grated Parmesan cheese
¼ teaspoon crumbled leaf rosemary
Pinch of crumbled leaf thyme
1 to 2 tablespoons melted butter (use 2 tablespoons if you have as
    much as 1 cup of crumbs, otherwise use 1 tablespoon)

Brush each chicken breast liberally with the olive oil, then sprinkle
with the salt and pepper. Arrange in a shallow pan, pour in any
remaining oil, cover loosely, and marinate for 3 to 4 hours in the
refrigerator.

Drain the oil from the chicken into a large, heavy Dutch oven, then
brown the chicken breasts lightly in the oil; drain on paper toweling.
Stir-fry the onions and garlic in the same kettle over moderate heat for
8 to 10 minutes, until golden, then return the chicken breasts to the
kettle. Add the broth and wine, cover, and simmer slowly for about
45 minutes, until the chicken is very tender. Remove the chicken and
arrange in a large au gratin dish.

Boil the kettle liquids, uncovered, until reduced by about one-half
if you have used ¾ cup broth or more; until they have reduced by
one-fourth, if you have used less than ¾ cup broth. Add the Cognac
and again boil rapidly for 5 minutes. Blend in the cream and boil,
uncovered, for 3 to 5 minutes, just until the sauce has the consistency
of heavy cream. Pour the sauce evenly over the chicken.

NOTE   *You may prepare the recipe up to this point several hours ahead of time.
Cover and refrigerate until about 30 minutes before serving. To take the chill off the
chicken, warm the covered casserole in a moderately slow oven (325° F.) for 20
minutes, then remove from the oven, uncover, and proceed as follows.*

Preheat the broiler.
Toss all the topping ingredients together well, then scatter evenly
over the chicken (if you use the full amount of crumbs and cheese, you
will simply have twice as much crunchy crust, which most people like
immensely). Slide the casserole under the broiler, 6 inches from the
heat, and broil for 4 to 5 minutes, just until the mixture is bubbling
and touched with brown.

Coconut

(Flaked or Shredded)

Flaked coconut and shredded coconut (usually processed with both water and sugar to keep them moist, fluffy, and sweet) are available today in vacuum-packed cans (3½-, 4-, and 7-ounce sizes—1½, 1⅔, and 3 cups respectively, measured loosely, not packed down) and also in moistureproof plastic bags in a range of sizes from 4 to 16 ounces (about 1⅔ to 6⅔ cups respectively—again spooned loosely into the measuring cup). But no matter how small the can or bag, there somehow always seem to be leftovers because recipe quantities and package contents rarely gibe.

Best Way to Store   If the coconut was canned, wrap snugly in plastic food wrap and refrigerate; if packed in a plastic bag, reseal the bag as snugly as possible and refrigerate.

Maximum Storage Time   10 days to 2 weeks.

Roles in Cooking   Coconut is used primarily for flavor and texture, but because of its ability to absorb moisture it is also an effective thickener of stews and sauces. It also makes a decorative topping for cakes, cookies, candies, and pies.

Recipe Uses   We tend to equate coconut with sweets—candies, cakes, custards, and pies—and yet it is integral to dozens of savory dishes, too, particularly the curries of India and the stews of Latin America and the Caribbean. It can be baked into quick fruit-nut breads (simply stir anywhere from ¼ to ¾ cup grated or shredded coconut into the batter of your pet recipe along with the fruits and nuts), it can be sprinkled into fruit or mixed green salads, it can even be slipped into chicken, turkey, beef, or ham casseroles (usually ½ to 1 cup is about right, but if you should have a very small quantity—1 to 4 tablespoons —by all means stir that into your favorite casserole).

N O T E   *For additional recipes, included elsewhere in this book, that call for varying amounts of flaked or shredded coconut, see the Appendix.*

SPINACH-ENDIVE SALAD WITH COCONUT-BUTTERMILK DRESSING

6 to 8 servings

If you're down to ½ cup or less of flaked or shredded coconut and are too Scottish to throw it out, then try this unusual sweet-sour spinach salad. The dressing also frugally uses up from ½ to 1 cup of leftover buttermilk, keeps well in the refrigerator in a covered jar for about 10 days, and is, in fact, excellent over any crisp green salad.

DRESSING

2 tablespoons melted bacon drippings
3 tablespoons olive oil
1 tablespoon honey or light corn syrup
Juice of 1 lime
¼ cup tarragon vinegar
1 clove garlic, peeled and minced
½ teaspoon crumbled leaf tarragon
½ to 1 cup buttermilk (if you only have ½ cup buttermilk, use that plus ¼ cup milk or cream—light, heavy, sour, half-and-half, even evaporated milk—and the juice of 1 orange)
¼ to ½ cup shredded or flaked coconut
1 teaspoon Worcestershire sauce
1 teaspoon salt
⅛ teaspoon freshly ground black pepper
2 to 3 tablespoons minced fresh gingerroot (optional—use if you have ginger shriveling or going soft in the refrigerator)

SALAD

½ pound tender young leaf spinach, trimmed of coarse stems, washed well, and patted very dry on paper toweling
4 heads Belgian endive, trimmed and sliced thin
4 scallions, trimmed, washed, and sliced thin (include some green tops)

Prepare the dressing first. Place all the ingredients in a 1-quart shaker jar and shake vigorously to mix. Let season in the refrigerator for 3 to 4 hours before using. Shake well before each use.

Pile the spinach, endive, and scallions in a large salad bowl and drizzle in about ¼ cup of the dressing. Toss lightly, then add just enough additional dressing to coat each leaf lightly. Toss well again, taste for salt and pepper, and add more, if needed.

Toss once again and serve.

CURRIED COCONUT AND CABBAGE

6 servings

Shredded coconut always seems to be packaged in amounts larger than can be used in most cake, cookie, or candy recipes. One of our favorite ways to use up the balance is in this unusual cabbage dish, which we first tasted at a government lodge in Mahabalipuram in southern India. It is perfectly delicious, and so quickly made. Best of all, it never fails to impress.

  ¼ cup (½ stick) butter
  1 tablespoon mustard seeds
  1 medium yellow onion, peeled and coarsely chopped
  ¼ cup finely chopped sweet green pepper
  2 teaspoons curry powder
  1 medium cabbage, trimmed, quartered, cored, and sliced ¼ inch
    thick
  ½ to 1 cup flaked or shredded coconut
  ½ teaspoon salt
  ⅛ teaspoon freshly ground black pepper

Melt the butter in a very large, heavy skillet over moderate heat, add the mustard seeds, and heat for a minute or two until they begin to sputter. Add the onion and green pepper and stir-fry for 10 minutes, until limp and lightly touched with brown. Blend in the curry powder and let mellow for 2 to 3 minutes over moderate heat, then add the cabbage, coconut, salt, and pepper (simply pile all in the skillet). Cover and steam for about 5 minutes, until the cabbage begins to wilt. Toss all lightly with a fork, re-cover, and steam for about 10 minutes longer, or just until the cabbage is crisp-tender.

Toss well again and serve. This recipe is especially good with roast pork, lamb, or ham.

INDONESIAN CHICKEN WITH
COCONUT AND PEANUT SAUCE

6 servings

For such an easy recipe this is an uncommonly elegant way to use up
½ to 1 cup of flaked or shredded coconut and 1 to 1½ cups leftover
cocktail peanuts. We also like to use buttermilk in the sauce instead
of light cream, which the original recipe called for—it's significantly
lower in calories and adds a refreshing tartness to the dish. Perfect for
a small dinner party.

   3 whole chicken breasts, split in half
   ¾ cup unsifted all-purpose flour
   ¼ cup (½ stick) butter or margarine
   2 medium Spanish onions, peeled and chopped moderately fine
   1 medium clove garlic, peeled and crushed
   2 cubes (each 1 inch) fresh gingerroot, peeled and minced
   ½ teaspoon crumbled leaf thyme
   ½ teaspoon salt, or to taste
   ⅛ teaspoon freshly ground black pepper
   ⅛ teaspoon cayenne pepper
   ½ cup cream-style peanut butter
   2½ cups buttermilk
   ½ to 1 cup flaked or shredded coconut
   1 to 1½ cups coarsely chopped cocktail peanuts

Dredge the chicken breasts well in the flour, then brown in the
butter in a large, heavy skillet over moderately high heat. Transfer the
chicken to paper toweling to drain. Reduce the heat under the skillet
to moderate and add the onions, garlic, and ginger; stir-fry for 10 to
12 minutes, until lightly touched with brown. Mix in the thyme, salt,
black pepper, and cayenne and then stir-fry for about 2 minutes
longer.

Whisk the peanut butter into the buttermilk until smooth (a processor or blender buzzes the two to creamy smoothness in seconds) and
pour into the skillet. Return the chicken breasts to the pan, reduce the
heat so the mixture barely ripples, cover, and simmer for about 45
minutes, or until the chicken is tender. Mix in the coconut and peanuts
and simmer for 10 to 15 minutes longer, or until the sauce has thick-

ened slightly (do not allow the mixture to boil or it may curdle). Taste for salt and add more to taste, if needed.

Serve over fluffy boiled rice.

COCONUT-ALMOND COOKIES

About 20 cookies

You can use up old, dry coconut in these cookies if you just soak it in milk for half an hour or so (drain the coconut before using). You can also substitute flour for part of the cornstarch, but the cornstarch will make a more delicate cookie.

> 1 cup flaked or shredded coconut
> $1/_3$ cup chopped, toasted blanched almonds
> ¼ cup granulated sugar
> $1/_3$ cup unsifted cornstarch
> ¼ teaspoon almond extract
> 2 egg whites, beaten until stiff

Preheat the oven to moderate (350° F.).

Blend the coconut, almonds, sugar, cornstarch, and flavoring together. Fold in the stiffly beaten egg whites and drop the mixture by teaspoonfuls onto a greased, foil-lined baking sheet, spacing the cookies about 1 inch apart. Bake in the preheated oven for 15 to 20 minutes.

Cool the cookies before peeling off the foil.

Coffee

Leftovers are scarcely a problem with instant coffee, which you can stir up by the cup. But they *are* a problem with freshly brewed coffee because it's a rare pot that's emptied down to the last drop. Fortunately, there are more ways of using leftover coffee than most of us realize, which is what this section is all about.

Best Way to Store Coffee begins to stale the moment the grounds are exposed to the air and then again the moment it has been brewed. So the object is not to try to store the leftover breakfast or dinner coffee but to use it as soon as possible. (Does anything taste staler than a warmed-over cup of coffee?) Fortunately, leftover coffee used as an ingredient doesn't taste stale—at least it doesn't in the recipes that follow. Pour leftover coffee into a glass jar, screw the lid on, and refrigerate until ready to use.

Maximum Storage Time 12 hours, but if possible, use the coffee within 5 to 6 hours.

Roles in Cooking In addition to serving as a stimulant, coffee's greatest uses are to flavor foods and to add a warm amber hue.

Recipe Uses There are more of them than most people suspect. Coffee, for example, can be used as the liquid ingredient in many cakes, cookies, and confections (particularly those flavored with chocolate, spice, or ginger), it can be stirred into sauces both sweet and savory (½ cup or so of coffee makes a splendid addition to a rich brown meat gravy), it can be added to a pot of baked beans (up to 1 cup of strong coffee will immeasurably enrich the flavor and color).

How to Use Up Very Small Amounts Try substituting leftover coffee (½ cup or less) for part of the liquid called for in beef, veal, or lamb soups, stews, skillet dinners, and casseroles.

N O T E *For additional recipes, included elsewhere in this book, that call for varying amounts of leftover brewed coffee, see the Appendix.*

SWEDISH BROWN BEANS

6 servings

One of the traditional smorgasbord dishes, these richly spiced kidney beans bubble lazily in a molasses-sugar syrup laced with coffee (use what's left of the morning coffee instead of pitching it out). Anyone who likes Boston baked beans is sure to enjoy these, too.

    1 large yellow onion, peeled and moderately coarsely chopped
    1 large clove garlic, peeled and crushed
    3 tablespoons bacon drippings
    4 cans (20 ounces each) red kidney beans, drained thoroughly
    ⅓ cup firmly packed light brown sugar
    2 tablespoons cornstarch
    1 teaspoon dry mustard
    ½ teaspoon ground ginger
    ¼ teaspoon ground cloves
    ¼ teaspoon ground allspice
    ¼ teaspoon grated nutmeg
    ¼ teaspoon ground cardamom
    ½ to ¾ cup strong black coffee
    3 tablespoons molasses
    2 tablespoons cider vinegar
    ½ teaspoon salt
    ⅛ teaspoon freshly ground black pepper

Preheat the oven to hot (400° F.).

Sauté the onion and garlic in the bacon drippings over moderate heat for 10 to 12 minutes, until very lightly browned. Empty into a lightly greased 3-quart casserole, then add the beans.

In a small mixing bowl, combine the brown sugar, cornstarch, and all the spices, rubbing the mixture between your fingers to press out all lumps. Pour over the beans. Now combine the coffee, molasses, vinegar, salt, and pepper and pour into the casserole.

Toss all together thoroughly, then bake, uncovered, in the preheated oven for 2½ hours, stirring every 20 minutes or so, until the bean mixture has thickened and browned nicely on top.

FROSTED COFFEE-BRAN BARS

About 3 dozen

1½ cups sifted all-purpose flour
1½ teaspoons baking powder
¼ teaspoon baking soda
¼ teaspoon salt
½ teaspoon ground ginger
½ teaspoon ground cinnamon
¼ teaspoon ground cloves
¼ cup (½ stick) butter or margarine
⅓ cup firmly packed light or dark brown sugar
1 egg
½ cup molasses
½ cup cold leftover coffee
1 cup bran flakes cereal

FROSTING

2 cups sifted confectioners sugar
3 to 5 tablespoons milk
½ teaspoon vanilla extract

Preheat the oven to moderate (350° F.).

Sift the flour with the baking powder, soda, salt, and spices and set aside. Cream the butter and sugar until light; beat in the egg. Mix in the molasses, coffee, and bran flakes; add the sifted dry ingredients and mix well. Spread in a greased 13 × 9 × 2-inch baking pan and bake in the preheated oven for about 25 minutes, or until firm to the touch.

Meanwhile, beat all the frosting ingredients together until smooth. Frost the bars as soon as you take them from the oven. Cool before cutting.

GRANDMAMA'S SOFT MOLASSES COOKIES

About 5 dozen

Strong black coffee, used as the liquid ingredient in these dark, rich molasses cookies, seems both to mellow and enrich the flavor.

1 cup vegetable shortening
½ teaspoon salt
2 teaspoons baking soda
1 tablespoon ground ginger
2 teaspoons ground cinnamon
1 teaspoon ground cloves
1 cup granulated sugar
1 cup molasses
1 egg
4½ cups sifted all-purpose flour
⅔ cup strong black coffee (it may be warm but *not* piping hot)

Preheat the oven to moderate (350° F.).

Cream together until fluffy the shortening, salt, soda, ginger, cinnamon, and cloves. Beat the sugar in gradually, creaming all the while until light. Blend in the molasses, then beat in the egg. Add the flour alternately with the coffee, beginning and ending with the flour.

Drop the dough by teaspoonfuls onto greased baking sheets, spacing about 2 inches apart. Bake in the preheated oven for about 15 minutes, or until the cookies are crisp around the edges.

Transfer while warm to wire racks to cool.

THE VERY BEST DEVIL'S FOOD CAKE

Two 9-inch layers

This cake is a good choice for a birthday or special occasion, not only because of its flavor and tender crumb, but also because of its size. It's a tall cake, imposing and elegant when put together with a fudge filling and topped with a fluffy white icing such as Creamy Cornstarch Frosting (see page 93). By the way, if you have no sour milk or buttermilk on hand, you can quickly "sour" sweet milk by stirring in a tablespoon of lemon juice or vinegar. Try it.

> 1 cup granulated sugar
> 1 cup firmly packed light brown sugar
> 2 eggs
> 1 cup sour milk or buttermilk
> ²/₃ cup cocoa powder (not a mix)
> ½ cup (1 stick) butter, at room temperature, cut in 1-inch pats
> ½ cup vegetable shortening, at room temperature
> 2 teaspoons baking soda
> 2 teaspoons vanilla extract
> ¼ teaspoon salt
> 3 cups sifted cake flour
> 1 cup boiling strong black coffee

Preheat the oven to moderately slow (325° F.).

This is a "dump" cake. Simply add the ingredients to a large mixing bowl in the order listed and without stirring. When the last ingredient —boiling coffee—has been added, beat 1 minute with an electric mixer set at moderate speed or about 3 minutes by hand.

Grease two 9-inch layer cake pans well, then dust lightly with cocoa —the same way you would dust a pan with flour. Divide the batter evenly between the two pans and bake in the preheated oven for about 45 minutes, or until the layers are springy to the touch and have pulled from the sides of the pans.

Let the layers cool upright in the pans on wire racks for 20 minutes, then loosen around the edges and turn out. Cool completely before filling and frosting.

COFFEE-COCONUT SOFTIES

About 8 dozen cookies

The 2½ cups of raisins, nuts, and coconut called for in this recipe are entirely flexible. In other words, as long as the total remains 2½ cups, you can improvise with the individual amounts. Omit the coconut, if you like, or omit everything *but* the coconut. If your family likes raisins, use 2 cups of raisins and ½ cup of nuts. Play around with the combinations according to what you have on hand and what your family enjoys.

  1 cup vegetable shortening
  2 cups (1 pound) firmly packed light brown sugar
  2 eggs, lightly beaten
  1 cup hot black coffee
  3½ cups sifted all-purpose flour
  ½ teaspoon baking powder
  1 cup seedless raisins
  ½ cup flaked coconut
  1 cup coarsely chopped black walnuts, walnuts, or pecans
  1 teaspoon baking soda
  1 teaspoon vanilla extract

Preheat the oven to moderate (350° F.).

Cream the shortening and sugar until light, then beat in the eggs and ½ cup of the hot coffee. Sift the flour with the baking powder, then add the raisins, coconut, and nuts and toss well to dredge. Add all to the creamed mixture and stir well. Dissolve the soda in the remaining ½ cup of hot coffee and mix into the dough. Stir in the vanilla.

Drop the dough from a teaspoon onto lightly greased baking sheets, spacing the cookies 2 inches apart, and bake in the preheated oven for 10 to 15 minutes, or until the cookies are lightly browned.

Remove while warm to wire racks to cool.

ROAST LAMB BASTED WITH COFFEE

8 to 10 servings

Some ingenious Swedish woman invented this recipe, and a superbly simple one it is. All you do is use the leftover morning coffee to baste the lamb as it roasts—anywhere from 1½ to 3 cups of coffee. What could be easier?

  1 leg of lamb (about 6 pounds)
  ½ teaspoon salt
  ¼ teaspoon crumbled leaf rosemary

CONTINUED

¼ teaspoon ground mace
¼ teaspoon freshly ground black pepper
1½ to 3 cups leftover black coffee (do not use instant coffee, only that brewed from grounds)

Preheat the oven to hot (400° F.).

Rub the lamb well all over with the salt, rosemary, mace, and pepper and place, fat side up, on a rack in a large, shallow roasting pan. Insert a meat thermometer in the center of the meatiest muscle. Roast the lamb, uncovered, for 10 minutes in the hot oven, then lower the heat to moderately slow (325° F.) and roast, uncovered, as follows: 12 minutes per pound for rare (130° F. on a meat thermometer), 15 minutes per pound for medium rare (140° F. on a meat thermometer), 18 to 20 minutes per pound for medium (150° F.), and 22 to 25 minutes per pound for well done (160° F.).

As the lamb roasts, baste every 15 to 20 minutes with the coffee, and when all of that is used up, continue basting with the pan drippings, which will be richly coffee flavored.

When the roast is done the way you like it, remove from the oven and let stand at room temperature for 20 minutes before carving (this is to allow the meat to firm up and give the juices a chance to settle).

COFFEE-ORANGE GRANITÉ

4 to 6 servings

What a lovely way to rehabilitate the leftover morning coffee—*provided* the coffee has not boiled or stood on the heat and taken on a "stale" flavor.

1¼ cups granulated sugar
1 envelope unflavored gelatin
1½ cups water
2 to 2½ cups very strong black coffee (if the coffee is not particularly strong, stir in 1 to 2 teaspoons instant coffee powder or instant espresso)
Juice of 1 large orange, strained well

1 teaspoon very finely grated orange rind
¼ cup coffee liqueur such as Kahlúa or Tía María (optional, but a nice
  addition)

Combine the sugar and gelatin in a heavy saucepan, pressing out all lumps with a wooden spoon, then stir in the water. Set over moderate heat for 3 to 4 minutes, stirring often, until the sugar and gelatin are both dissolved.

Remove the syrup from the heat and cool to room temperature. Stir in all the remaining ingredients, pour into a 9 × 5 × 3-inch loaf pan, and freeze for several hours, or until mushy-firm.

Using an electric mixer set at high speed or a food processor equipped with the metal chopping blade, beat the partially frozen mixture until fluffy (if you're using the processor, you'll only be able to beat half of the mixture at a time). Return to the pan and freeze until firm. For a smoother consistency, beat hard once again as soon as the mixture is mushy, then return to the pan and freeze until firm.

To serve, scrape across the frozen mixture with a large metal spoon, shaving it up in fluffy crystals. Pile into stemmed goblets and serve at once.

C O O K I E   C R U M B S : See **Crumbs.**

Cooking Oils

(Plus Some Notes About Shortening)

We tend to consider these nonperishable—staples we can use from one year to the next. Not true. Cooking oils do go rancid after about six months on the shelf, so it's important to use them while they're fresh.

There are, of course, many different kinds of cooking oils: corn, peanut, olive, safflower, "vegetable" (which usually means a combination of oils such as cottonseed and soy). And, thanks to our increasing interest in foreign cuisines, exotic imports are becoming more readily available—sesame seed oil, walnut oil, and dendê, the thick, orange, highly aromatic oil of the Brazilian palm nut and the foundation of Bahian cooking.

As a general rule, the lighter an oil is in color, the milder it will be in flavor and the longer it will keep. The best keepers, then, are the oils with which we're most familiar—corn, peanut, vegetable, safflower. Being more flavorful, olive oil keeps less well, and the three exotics less well still.

Tip Buy the heavier, more highly flavored oils only when you need them for a special recipe, buy them in small quantities, and use them up as soon as possible.

Best Way to Store All oils should be stored, tightly capped or covered, in their own containers on a cool, *dark,* dry shelf. It's especially important that oils be kept away from the light, which will fade and stale them, also that they be kept tightly capped—exposure to air speeds rancidity. Do not refrigerate oils because the cold will cloud and "curd" them.

N O T E *As a deterrent to bugs and mice, wipe each can or bottle of oil well after each use. The wiping also keeps driblets of oil from running down onto your cabinet shelves and staining them, very possibly permanently.*

Maximum Storage Time About 6 months for corn, peanut, safflower, and "vegetable" oils; 3 to 4 months for olive oil; and about 1½ to 2 months for sesame, walnut, and dendê.

Roles in Cooking Oils serve as a medium for browning, frying, sautéing, and braising; they are the very foundation of a huge family of salad dressings and of such emulsified "egg" sauces as mayonnaise, *aïoli, tapenade,* and *pistou;* they may be used to shorten pastries, cakes, breads, and cookies (but don't try willy-nilly substitutions in your favorite recipes because oils have neither the same properties nor shortening power as butter, margarine, lard, or vegetable shortening; rely, instead, on recipes developed specifically for use with oils).

Because oils magically trap, hold, and mingle flavors, they are great unifiers for salads and cold marinated meats, fish, and vegetables, as well as for skillet dishes, casseroles, and stews. Oils also help to keep strands of pasta or grains of rice separate and distinct as they cook (just a drop of oil in a kettleful of water will do the trick). Rubbed onto a roasting bird, oils promote a rich, crisp brown finish; with a baking potato, their effect is precisely the opposite—they will soften the potato skin. Oils, of course, are also used to "grease" all manner of cooking utensils—cake pans, cookie sheets, pudding and gelatin molds —so the finished foods will slip right out or off. Olive oil, not to mention the more exotic imports, also contributes flavor and color.

And it goes without saying that all oils are high-energy sources. Calories vary slightly from oil to oil, but you can figure on about 115 to 125 calories per tablespoon vs. about 100 per tablespoon of butter or margarine and 110 per tablespoon of vegetable shortening. (Shortening, by the way, is far less likely to be a problem leftover—or, indeed, a leftover at all—because it is used more often than oil as a shortening in cakes, cookies, quick breads, and pastries. Its shelf life —if kept tightly covered in a cool, dark, dry place—is about 6 months.) As for the degree of saturation of the different cooking oils, it varies somewhat from type to type. The best advice we can offer is to scrutinize all labels before buying.

Recipe Uses Deep- and shallow-fried foods employ substantial amounts of oil (or shortening); marinades, salad dressings, and oil pastries rely upon oil, as do chiffon cakes. Peanut and sesame oils are *de rigueur* for Chinese stir-fried dishes, olive oil for Mediterranean and Middle Eastern classics, walnut oil for delicate European salads and desserts, and dendê for a wide variety of Brazilian meat, poultry, seafood, and vegetable dishes.

Special Comments Can oils that have been used for deep-fat frying be reused? Yes, they can, provided that they have not been used to fry seafood and that they *have* been properly filtered. The best oils for deep-fat frying, by the way, are the light, mild oils—vegetable, corn, and peanut. The heavier, stronger oils will smoke and scorch at temperatures far below those needed for successful deep-fat frying (350° F. and up). Here, then, is the way to filter and freshen oil that has been used for deep-fat frying:

Slice a peeled, raw potato into the hot oil and allow to crispen and brown; remove all the potato with a slotted spoon and discard (the potato absorbs flavors from the oil). Cool the oil almost to room temperature (this is simply to minimize the risk of mishap), then pour through a sieve lined with several thicknesses of clean, dry cheese-cloth. Pour the filtered oil into a clean glass jar or bottle, cover tight, and store in the refrigerator (it will keep fresh for about 1 month). If you intend to reuse the oil for deep-fat frying, refilter it the same way after each use. The minute the oil begins to lose color or to foam as it's heated, discard it—it is beginning to break down and become stale.

Tip Add 1 cup or so of fresh oil to recycled oil whenever you use it for deep-fat frying—it will lessen the oil's smoking and freshen its flavor.

You may be interested to know that solid shortenings may be recycled the same way—except that they should be filtered while they are still hot because they solidify upon cooling. They, too, should be refrigerated after they have been filtered. And kept tightly covered.

And, finally, a quick trick:

If you lightly oil a measuring cup or spoon in which you are going to measure molasses, honey, or syrup, you'll find that these sticky, viscous ingredients will slide right out, leaving almost no messy-to-clean residue and giving you a more accurate measurement.

N O T E *For additional recipes, included elsewhere in this book, that call for varying amounts of cooking oil, see the Appendix.*

CHUNKS OF CHICKEN IN SWEET-SOUR SAUCE

4 servings

Crispy, cornstarch-dredged morsels of chicken with carrots, pineapple, and peppers. Use light or dark brown sugar for the sweet-sour sauce if that is what you have on hand. Or substitute honey. They are equally delicious.

> 2 large whole chicken breasts, split in half, boned, skinned, and cut in bite-sized chunks
> 1 egg, beaten with 1 tablespoon milk and ½ teaspoon salt
> ¾ cup cornstarch
> 6 tablespoons peanut or vegetable oil
> 1 medium Spanish onion, peeled and cut in slim wedges

1 large sweet red or green pepper, cored, seeded, and cut in slim strips
2 medium carrots, peeled and sliced thin
½ cup firmly packed light or dark brown sugar or ⅓ cup honey
½ cup cider vinegar or rice vinegar
2 tablespoons ketchup
1 can (13¼ ounces) pineapple chunks (do not drain)
¼ cup dark soy sauce
¼ cup dry white wine or vermouth
⅛ teaspoon cayenne pepper
1 tablespoon cornstarch, blended with ¼ cup cold water

Dip the chicken chunks in the egg mixture, then in cornstarch; brown quickly in 4 tablespoons of the oil in a large, heavy skillet over moderately high heat; lift to paper toweling with a slotted spoon. Add the remaining oil to the skillet and stir-fry the onion, red or green pepper, and carrots over moderate heat for 10 to 12 minutes, until lightly browned. Add the sugar, vinegar, ketchup, pineapple, soy sauce, wine, and cayenne and simmer, uncovered, stirring occasionally, for 10 minutes.

Mix the cornstarch paste into the skillet and heat, stirring constantly, until thickened and clear—about 3 minutes. Return the chicken to the skillet and heat and stir for 3 to 5 minutes.

Serve over boiled rice.

SALSA VERDE (GREEN SAUCE)

About 1 cup

This nippy sauce is delicious served with cold roast beef or veal or baked ham. It can also be used to dress crisp green salads. What's best about it, however, is that it helps clean up odds and ends that may be preempting refrigerator space—anchovy paste, capers, green olives.

1 medium clove garlic, peeled and crushed
1 slice firm-textured white bread, trimmed of crusts
¼ teaspoon dry mustard
¼ teaspoon paprika

CONTINUED

½ to 2 teaspoons anchovy paste
½ cup olive oil
¼ cup red wine vinegar
½ cup minced fresh parsley
¼ cup minced, pitted or pimiento-stuffed green olives and/or small
    capers, drained (optional)
Salt, if needed, to taste
1 to 2 tablespoons water or dry white wine, if needed to thin the sauce

Mash the garlic, bread, mustard, paprika, and anchovy paste together in a bowl. Add the oil and vinegar alternately, beating constantly until slightly thickened. Stir in the remaining ingredients.

Let stand at room temperature for 30 minutes, then beat well again just before serving.

Corn Meal and Grits

Southerners are partial to white corn meal (as are New Englanders for certain recipes), but Middle Westerners favor the yellow. Southerners also like their corn meal "water" or "stone" ground because it has a finer, more floury texture and makes for lighter breads. The more granular, mass-produced corn meal may be acceptable to some folks, but a true Southerner won't give it house room, preferring to patronize some creaky local mill.

He is almost as persnickety about his grits, which are ground from dried hominy. In case you don't know what hominy is, it is corn that has been puffed in a lye solution (in the old days, plantation women made lye with wood ashes—a trick passed along by southern Indian tribes).

Best Way to Store The biggest problem in storing corn meal and grits is to keep bugs from them, so we advocate rustproof, airtight canisters or, failing that, large, wide-mouthed preserving jars with vacuum-seal lids (these are available in handy half-gallon sizes). Store the canisters or jars on a cool, dark, dry shelf.

Maximum Storage Time About 3 months.

Roles in Cooking To form the framework of breads, gruels, puddings, etc.; to thicken stews and sauces; to bread foods to be fried; to provide flavor, color, substance, or body and nutritive value (most corn meals and grits are now enriched, meaning that their vitamin and mineral content equals that of whole corn).

Recipe Uses Southern (i.e., from the South) American, northern Italian, Mexican, and Latin American recipes rely heavily on corn meal and grits, particularly for breads, dumplings, casserole toppings, dressings, and stuffings, even pastries and pie crusts. And, of course, that old New England classic, Indian pudding, is made with corn meal.

How to Use Very Small Amounts Small amounts ($\frac{1}{3}$ cup or less) of corn meal or grits may be mixed into meat loaves containing at least 2 cups of ground meat; 2 to 3 tablespoons may be stirred into soupy stews or skillet dishes (they thicken them right up). Corn meal can also be sprinkled over ready-to-bake yeast breads, scones, or biscuits that have been lightly brushed with butter or egg-white glaze (1 egg white, beaten until frothy with 1 tablespoon of cold water). The meal will give the baked bread a richly browned, nicely textural finish.

N O T E *For additional recipes, included elsewhere in this book, that include varying amounts of corn meal, see the Appendix.*

CORN DOGS

6 servings

It was in New Orleans' French Quarter that we first tasted these batter-fried franks—hot off a pushcart. We have since learned to make them at home and have discovered that, in addition to being delicious, they accommodatingly use up ½ cup of corn meal.

　½ cup corn meal
　½ cup sifted all-purpose flour
　1 tablespoon granulated sugar
　1 teaspoon salt
　⅛ teaspoon freshly ground black pepper
　⅛ teaspoon cayenne pepper
　1 egg, beaten lightly
　½ cup milk, evaporated milk, or light or heavy cream (whatever you have on hand)
　2 tablespoons cooking oil or melted bacon drippings
　12 frankfurters (the fully cooked variety)
　Vegetable shortening or cooking oil for deep-fat frying (about 2 pounds or 2 quarts)

Combine the corn meal, flour, sugar, salt, and black and cayenne peppers. In a separate bowl, combine the egg with the milk and the 2 tablespoons cooking oil or bacon drippings. Make a well in the dry ingredients, then pour in the combined liquids and beat until smooth.

Dip the frankfurters into the batter, letting the excess drain off, then deep-fry, about three at a time, in hot fat (375° F.) for 2 to 3 minutes, or until richly golden brown. Drain on paper toweling and serve.

N O T E　*Try to keep the temperature of the fat as nearly at 375° F. as possible by raising and lowering the burner heat as needed.*

O W E N D A W

8 servings

This is an old North Carolina recipe, a type of spoon bread made with both grits and corn meal and a perfectly delicious way to use up odds and ends of each.

　2½ cups water mixed with 1 teaspoon salt
　½ cup grits (not the quick-cooking kind)
　3 tablespoons butter or margarine
　4 eggs, beaten until frothy

2 cups milk (or any combination of cream and milk that will enable you to use up leftovers)

¾ cup corn meal

⅛ teaspoon freshly ground black pepper

Bring the water to a boil in a medium-sized heavy saucepan over moderate heat, then very gradually stir in the grits. Reduce the heat so the mixture bubbles gently, cover, and cook slowly for 25 to 30 minutes, stirring frequently, until the mixture is thick and the grits no longer taste of raw starch. Remove from the heat and mix in the butter. Cool for about 5 minutes, stirring often.

Preheat the oven to moderate (350° F.).

Mix the eggs into the partially cooled grits mixture. Add the milk gradually, then the corn meal, stirring all the while. Season with pepper, then pour into a well-buttered 2½- or 3-quart soufflé dish or deep casserole and bake, uncovered, in the preheated oven about 35 to 40 minutes or until lightly browned and set.

Serve straightaway, with plenty of butter (simply spoon out as you would any casserole mixture).

GRITS AND CHEDDAR CASSEROLE

6 servings

Here's an easy, economical recipe that is rich enough to serve as a main dish. You need only a crisp green salad and a fruit dessert to round out the menu.

5 cups water mixed with 1 teaspoon salt

1 cup grits (not the quick-cooking variety)

¼ teaspoon crumbled leaf thyme

⅛ teaspoon grated nutmeg

⅛ teaspoon cayenne pepper

½ pound sharp Cheddar cheese, coarsely grated (or a combination of Swiss and/or jack and Cheddar—whatever you have on hand)

½ cup milk, evaporated milk, or cream (light or heavy)

½ cup dry bread crumbs (or 1 cup soft bread crumbs), tossed with 1 tablespoon melted butter or margarine

Bring the salted water to a boil in a heavy, medium-sized saucepan over moderate heat. Gradually stir in the grits, then add the thyme, nutmeg, and cayenne. Lower the burner heat so the grits mixture barely ripples, then cover and cook for 25 to 30 minutes, stirring frequently, until the grits are thick and no longer taste of raw starch. Toward the end of the cooking time, preheat the oven to moderately hot (375° F.).

Layer the grits in a well-buttered 1½-quart casserole with the cheese, beginning and ending with the grits. Pour the milk evenly over all. Top with the buttered crumbs, then bake in the preheated oven for 20 minutes, or until lightly browned.

VARIATION

Ham and Grits au Gratin   Prepare as directed above, but use a 2-quart instead of a 1½-quart casserole and layer into it 1½ to 2 cups of diced, cooked ham (or roast pork, beef, or lamb) along with the grits and grated cheese. Top with the buttered crumbs and bake as directed.

OLD SOUTHERN BATTER BREAD

4 to 6 servings

This custardy corn meal pudding calls for a full cup of corn meal and it makes an excellent potato substitute. Batter bread (also known as "spoon bread") can be made with yellow corn meal, but Southerners insist on the stone- or water-ground white meal.

> 1 cup water
> 1¼ cups milk (if you have leftover evaporated milk or light cream, use that, then round the measure out with plain milk)
> 2 tablespoons granulated sugar
> 2 tablespoons butter or margarine
> 1 teaspoon salt
> 1 cup corn meal, preferably stone-ground white meal
> 3 eggs, separated
> 1 teaspoon baking powder

Preheat the oven to moderately hot (375° F.).

Heat the water, milk, sugar, butter, and salt in a heavy, uncovered saucepan over moderately high heat until scalding. Off the heat, mix in the corn meal briskly, a little at a time so there are no lumps.

Beat the egg yolks lightly and blend with the baking powder. Stir a little of the hot mixture into the yolks, then stir the yolks into the saucepan and mix well. Beat the whites until soft peaks form and fold into the corn meal mixture, then bake, uncovered, in a buttered 2-quart casserole or soufflé dish in the preheated oven for 30 to 35 minutes, or until puffy and lightly browned.

Serve at once, with lots of butter.

VARIATION

Rice Batter Bread Prepare as directed, but just before folding in the beaten egg whites, mix in 1 to 1½ cups leftover cooked rice. Fold in the egg whites, then bake as directed.

RHODE ISLAND JONNYCAKES

6 servings

These should be almost as thin as crêpes.

1½ cups stone- or water-ground white corn meal
1½ teaspoons salt
2 teaspoons granulated sugar
1½ cups boiling water
¾ cup milk (or substitute part light cream or evaporated milk if you have leftovers of either)
5 to 6 tablespoons bacon drippings or melted lard or shortening

Combine the corn meal, salt, sugar, and water, beating until smooth; let stand, uncovered, at room temperature for 10 minutes. Stir in the milk.

Heat about 2 tablespoons of the drippings on a large, heavy griddle set over moderate heat, and as soon as a drop of water dances and skitters across the griddle, drop the batter by rounded tablespoonfuls onto the griddle, spreading it into thin circles. Brown the jonnycakes slowly, allowing about 5 minutes on a side, or until they are golden brown. As soon as the jonnycakes brown, lift to paper toweling and keep warm while frying the remainder. Add fresh drippings to the griddle each time you fry a new batch of jonnycakes.

Serve hot, just as you would pancakes—spread with butter and drizzled with maple syrup.

Cornstarch

This fine white starch, ground from the hearts of dried corn, is a far more versatile ingredient than most of us give it credit for, so there's little excuse for a single box of it to stand on the shelf year in and year out (each 1-pound box contains about 3 cups). Have a look at the recipes in the pages that follow, and you'll discover some new and offbeat ways to use cornstarch.

Best Way to Store   In a glass jar (with a screw top) on a cool, dry shelf. Our reason for recommending the glass jar is that it keeps ants, weevils, and roaches at bay. Cornstarch boxes are often frayed or dented about the corners, so the cornstarch may trickle out into the cabinet—an open invitation to insects. Moreover, opened cornstarch boxes cannot be closed air-, moisture-, or bug-tight.

Maximum Storage Time   Although cornstarch appears to keep indefinitely, it may, after a year or so, take on a slightly stale or rancid flavor, so it's wise to use up and replenish your supply within 12 to 14 months.

   Tip   Date the jar of cornstarch so that you'll know exactly how old it is.

Roles in Cooking   Cornstarch (or *corn flour,* as the British call it) is used in place of flour as a thickener of many puddings and dessert sauces because it gives them a sparkling, transparent quality that flour never can (particularly important for thickening cherry or berry sauces, pies, or cobblers, and for making fruit glazes). Cornstarch, by the way, has twice the thickening power of flour—that is, 1 tablespoon of cornstarch will do the work of 2 tablespoons of flour.

   When used to thicken soups, sauces, or puddings, the cornstarch, after being mixed with the liquid and other ingredients, should be boiled 1 to 2 minutes until thickened and clear—but you must stir the mixture constantly lest it scorch, lump, or curdle. Once the cornstarch mixture has thickened, it should be removed from the heat at once; otherwise it will begin to thin out, and no amount of reheating will thicken it up again. It's also important to note that unusually acid and/or sweet mixtures will weaken the thickening power of cornstarch (a lemon pie filling, for example), so you may need to increase the amount of cornstarch as much as 50 percent to compensate.

The British and Europeans use cornstarch in place of part or all of the flour called for in cakes, cookies, pastries, and shortbreads because it produces an exceptionally fine and tender crumb. And the Japanese use it for tempura batters, into which shrimp, raw vegetable chunks, even sprigs of parsley are dipped before they are deep-fat fried, which is why tempura crusts are so light and shattery-crisp.

Recipe Uses   The recipes that follow give a good idea as to the varied functions of cornstarch. To determine other ways to use up more than a tablespoon or two at a time, you might leaf through the pudding and pie sections of your own favorite cookbooks, and through the cake, cookie, and pastry sections of cookbooks featuring English, Scottish, Oriental, or Scandinavian recipes.

N O T E   *For additional recipes, included elsewhere in this book, that call for varying amounts of cornstarch, see the Appendix.*

CREAMY CORNSTARCH FROSTING

Enough to frost a 13 × 9 × 2-inch sheet cake or frost and fill an 8- or 9-inch two-layer cake

This is an excellent frosting because it stands up well and looks like whipped cream. You can use it on any kind of cake, and it's delicious made with brown sugar instead of white (see the variation below).

¼ **cup cornstarch**
1 **cup granulated sugar**
Pinch of salt
1 **cup milk (use part evaporated milk if you have some left over, or part light cream)**
1 **cup (2 sticks) butter or margarine, at room temperature**
1½ **teaspoons vanilla extract**

Blend the cornstarch with ¼ cup of the sugar and the salt in a small, heavy saucepan. Mix in the milk, set over moderate heat, and cook and stir until thickened and smooth—about 3 minutes. Cool to room temperature, whisking now and then to prevent a "skin" from forming on the sauce.

Beat the remaining ¾ cup of sugar with the butter and vanilla at high mixer speed for about 10 minutes, until very fluffy. Add the cooled cornstarch mixture and continue beating at high speed for another 10 minutes, until no sugar grains are discernible and the frosting fluffs up like whipped cream.

N O T E   *In hot weather, it's advisable to refrigerate cakes iced with this frosting.*

V A R I A T I O N

Cornstarch Seafoam Frosting   Prepare as the recipe above directs, but substitute 1 cup firmly packed light or dark brown sugar for the granulated sugar and use 1 teaspoon vanilla and ½ teaspoon walnut or almond extract to flavor. Also use, if possible, part evaporated milk for the milk, which will heighten the "caramel" flavor.

H I G H L A N D S   S H O R T B R E A D

About 2 dozen 1½-inch squares

One reason that this shattery-crisp Scottish shortbread melts in your mouth is that it is made with cornstarch as well as with flour—one part (½ cup) sifted cornstarch to three parts (1½ cups) sifted all-purpose flour, which are the classic proportions. So this recipe is an excellent one for using up the last of a box of cornstarch before replenishing the supply. For a truly tender crumb, however, you must also cream the butter and sugar until light and silvery and until no sugar grains are discernible. For best results, use a food processor or an electric mixer set at high speed.

N O T E   *Do not substitute margarine for butter in this recipe because it has slightly greater shortening power than butter, meaning that your shortbread is likely to thin out and run all over the baking sheet in the oven.*

1 cup (2 sticks) unsalted butter, at room temperature
²/₃ cup granulated sugar

½ teaspoon vanilla extract
Pinch of salt
1½ cups sifted all-purpose flour
½ cup sifted cornstarch

Preheat the oven to moderately hot (375°F.).

Cut the butter into 1-inch pats and cream hard with the sugar, vanilla, and salt for about 5 minutes with an electric mixer set at high speed or by letting a food processor, equipped with the metal chopping blade, run nonstop for about 1½ minutes (you may have to stop the mixer or processor from time to time and scrape the sides of the bowl or work bowl down). Continue to cream until the mixture is silvery-light and fluffy. Combine the flour and cornstarch and add to the butter-sugar mixture, about one-fourth of the total amount at a time, and beating after each addition only enough to blend. (Do not over-beat at this point or your shortbread may be tough.)

Spread the dough out on an ungreased baking sheet into an 8-inch square that is about ½-inch thick. Smooth the surface with a rubber spatula, then prick at regular intervals with a fork (this is to allow steam to escape and to keep the shortbread from buckling or blistering as it bakes). Bake, uncovered, in the preheated oven for 5 minutes, then reduce the heat to very slow (300°F.) and bake for 35 to 40 minutes longer, or until the shortbread is a uniform, pale tan and no longer feels soft to the touch.

Remove from the oven, cool for 5 minutes, then score in 1½-inch squares. Cool completely, then cut into squares. Store in an airtight canister.

CHOCOLATE CRISPIES

About 2 dozen cookies

You won't find that you're keeping cornstarch too long once you become used to the idea that a small amount, used in place of flour in certain cookies and cakes, makes for finer texture. Here is another good cookie recipe using half flour and half cornstarch, a solid cookie that keeps.

CONTINUED

½ cup unsifted all-purpose flour
½ teaspoon baking powder
½ cup unsifted cornstarch
¼ cup unsifted cocoa powder (not a mix)
⅓ cup ground walnuts
½ cup granulated sugar
½ cup (1 stick) butter or margarine, at room temperature

Preheat the oven to moderate (350°F.).

Mix the flour, baking powder, cornstarch, cocoa, and ground walnuts together. In a separate bowl, cream the sugar and butter until light, then knead into the dry ingredients with your fingers.

Scoop up small amounts of dough by teaspoonfuls and push onto a greased and floured cookie sheet with your fingers, spacing the cookies about 1 inch apart. Bake in the preheated oven for 15 to 20 minutes.

Transfer the cookies at once to wire racks to cool.

SUPER-CRISPY FRIED CHICKEN

4 servings

One unusually effective way to use cornstarch is by dredging chicken in it before frying. The cornstarch gives the chicken an almost tempura-crisp coating.

1 broiler-fryer (3 to 3½ pounds), disjointed
1 teaspoon salt
¼ teaspoon freshly ground black pepper
2 eggs, beaten lightly with 1 tablespoon cold water
¾ cup cornstarch, mixed with 1 tablespoon paprika
2 cups peanut, corn, or other vegetable oil

Sprinkle the chicken with the salt and pepper; dip each piece in the egg, then in the cornstarch-paprika mixture. Pour the oil into a deep frying pan and heat to 375°F. on a deep-fat thermometer. Fry the chicken for 25 to 30 minutes, turning once in the hot fat, until golden, crisp, and tender.

Drain on paper toweling, then serve hot or cold.

MELTING MOMENTS

About 2½ dozen cookies

6 tablespoons (¾ stick) butter, at room temperature
6 tablespoons granulated sugar
1 teaspoon finely grated lemon rind
½ teaspoon vanilla extract
1 egg
1 cup sifted cornstarch

Preheat the oven to moderately hot (375°F.).

Cream the butter until fluffy; add the sugar gradually, beating hard after each addition. Beat in the lemon rind and vanilla, then add the egg and beat well. Add the cornstarch, a little at a time, again beating well after each addition.

Drop the dough by half-teaspoonfuls onto lightly greased baking sheets, spacing the cookies at least 2½ inches apart—they will spread as they bake. Bake for 8 to 10 minutes in the preheated hot oven until ringed with tan.

Transfer at once to wire racks to cool.

Corn Syrup

(Light or Dark)

The trouble with corn syrups—both the light and the dark—is that we tend to buy them *seasonally.* That is, around Christmas time when we fly into a frenzy of cake, cookie, and candy making, then again in late summer when we're moved to put up a few quarts of fresh peaches, pears, or plums. The rest of the time these syrups (both now available in pint, quart, half-gallon, and full gallon bottles) do little more than appropriate precious cupboard space and, unless we are meticulous about wiping the bottles clean after each use, attract ants and roaches.

The trouble is, we haven't learned how to use corn syrups with any regularity, although both can be substituted in many recipes for sugar —the dark corn syrup for brown sugar, the light corn syrup for granulated sugar. Our purpose, then, is to show here just some of the many ways to cook imaginatively with corn syrups—and to unclutter your kitchen cabinets at the same time.

Best Way to Store Both light and dark corn syrups should be stored in their original bottles (with the lids screwed down tight) on cool, dark, dry shelves. Each time you use a syrup, wipe any drips or dribbles from the bottle with a damp cloth, and wipe carefully around the cap as well. Ants and roaches both love sweets, and if you leave the slightest trail or scent of syrup on a bottle, they will find it.

Maximum Storage Time We tend to think of corn syrups as being nonperishable, and yet they should be used up within 3 to 4 months, sooner in hot and sticky weather. Sometimes a mold will grow on the surface of the syrup inside the bottle. To remove it, gently pour the syrup into a flat bowl and skim off and discard all traces of mold. Taste the syrup, and if the flavor seems unaffected, the syrup may still be used—but make a point of doing so within a few days.

Roles in Cooking To sweeten foods; to heighten the creaminess of candies, sherbets, and ice creams (the syrup helps keep confections from turning to sugar and sherbets and ice creams from becoming unpleasantly icy); to increase the clarity of fruit punches, preserves, and pickles; and, finally, to glaze hams and roasts as they cook. And one further use: because corn syrups take on moisture from the air, they are frequently used in bar cookies to help keep them nice and chewy.

Recipe Uses So *very* many. Trying to list them here is about as easy (and sensible) as trying to list the uses for granulated sugar.

Special Comments In most recipes, light corn syrup should not be substituted for the dark—or vice versa. Because it is more highly refined, light corn syrup has virtually no more flavor than granulated sugar and should be used in recipes where sweetening alone is required. Dark corn syrup, on the other hand, has a distinct flavor that might best be described as a cross between caramel and molasses (the same might also be said for its color). Dark corn syrup can thus be drizzled over pancakes (and often is), it is the preferred syrup for baked beans, brown breads, and spice cookies and cakes, and it makes a dandy glaze for baked ham.

Light corn syrup, on the other hand, makes for splendid jams, marmalades, and preserves (but do not substitute light corn syrup for more than one-third of the sugar called for, or the jams, marmalades, and preserves may not "set up" or stiffen properly). Light corn syrup may, of course, be used in place of sugar to sweeten fruits, but it should not be substituted for sugar in cakes, cookies, breads, or other baked goods. Or, for that matter, in candies or confections.

How to Use Very Small Amounts Both light and dark corn syrups may be used to mellow the tartness of tomato sauces (1 to 2 tablespoons is usually sufficient) or of a tomato or vegetable soup made with too-acid tomatoes. Also, use light corn syrup to sweeten your coffee or tea instead of sugar (1 teaspoon of light corn syrup has about the same sweetening power as 1 teaspoon of sugar but more calories —20 calories per teaspoon of light corn syrup vs. 15 for sugar).

N O T E *For additional recipes, included elsewhere in this book, that call for varying amounts of light or dark corn syrup, see the Appendix.*

PINEAPPLE-APRICOT PIE

One 9-inch pie

Evaporated milk and light corn syrup are two staples you're apt to have remnants of, and this easy recipe accommodatingly uses up some of each. This pie makes a good company dessert, especially if you decorate it with chocolate curls or orange twists and fluffs of whipped cream.

1 can (8½ ounces) crushed pineapple (do not drain)
1 package (3 ounces) apricot or orange gelatin
¼ cup light corn syrup
Grated rind and juice of 1 lemon
1 cup evaporated milk, chilled in the freezer for about 2 hours, or until ice crystals begin to form around the edge
1 homemade or prepared 9-inch graham-cracker crust

C O N T I N U E D

Dump the contents of the can of pineapple into a medium-sized saucepan and stir in the gelatin. Set over moderate heat and stir constantly for about 3 minutes, or until the gelatin is completely dissolved. Remove from the heat and mix in the corn syrup, grated lemon rind, and one-half of the lemon juice. Chill until the mixture begins to thicken.

Add the remaining lemon juice to the well-chilled evaporated milk and beat hard until the mixture whips into soft peaks. Beat the partially thickened gelatin mixture until frothy, then fold in the whipped milk until no streaks of white or orange show.

Spoon the filling into the graham-cracker crust and chill for several hours, or until firm.

FRESH BLACKBERRY-STRAWBERRY ICE CREAM

6 to 8 servings

Here's a glorious fresh berry dessert in which you can use up anywhere from ¼ to ¾ cup of light corn syrup or honey—it depends upon the tartness of the berries. So taste and add syrup or honey accordingly.

1 quart fresh blackberries, washed and sorted
1 pint fresh strawberries, washed, sorted, and hulled
1 cup granulated sugar
1 teaspoon unflavored gelatin
Juice of 2 large lemons
¼ to ¾ cup light corn syrup or delicate honey
2 cups light cream

Place the blackberries and strawberries in a large, heavy saucepan and crush lightly with a potato masher. Combine the sugar and gelatin and stir into the berries along with the lemon juice. Set over moderate heat and cook, stirring often, for 10 to 15 minutes, or until the sugar is completely dissolved.

Empty the berries into a large, fine sieve set over a heatproof bowl and force as much juice and fruit pulp through the sieve as possible by pressing with a wooden spatula (this is a somewhat tedious job, but don't try to rush the process or the ice cream will not be as richly flavored as it should be). Taste the berry purée and add light corn syrup or honey until it is sweet enough to suit you. Pour into a 9 × 5 × 3-inch loaf pan and freeze for several hours, or until mushy.

Spoon the partially frozen berry mixture into your largest electric mixer bowl and beat at high speed until fluffy. Continuing to beat, add the light cream in a steady stream. Return the mixture to the loaf pan and freeze until soft-firm.

For an exceptionally smooth ice cream, beat once again as soon as the ice cream is mushy, then return to the pan and freeze until soft-firm.

LIME-PINEAPPLE-BUTTERMILK SHERBET

4 servings

This fluffy-smooth sherbet tastes somewhat like Key lime pie, although its calories per serving are significantly lower—about 295 calories per serving vs. 700. You can make the recipe successfully with anywhere from 2 to 2½ cups buttermilk. All that will change is the texture, and that ever so slightly—the larger the amount of buttermilk used, the icier (or grainier) the sherbet. An extra-hard beating, however, will help break down the ice crystals and make the sherbet smooth again.

You can also make this sherbet with lemon or orange juice instead of lime.

    2 eggs
    ½ **cup granulated sugar**
    ½ **cup light corn syrup**
    2 to 2½ cups buttermilk
    ¼ **cup lime juice**
    1 cup drained, crushed pineapple
    1 teaspoon finely grated lemon rind (optional)

Beat the eggs hard until creamy-thick, then add the sugar gradually, beating hard all the while. Mix in the remaining ingredients in the order listed, pour into a refrigerator tray, and freeze until mushy.

Empty into a mixer bowl and again beat hard—just until the mixture fluffs up. Return to the freezer and freeze until firm.

N O T E   *If you have used 2 ½ cups buttermilk, again beat the mixture until fluffy before freezing until firm and serving.*

O R A N G E - A L M O N D   L A C E   C O O K I E S

About 2 ½ dozen

It's best not to attempt this recipe in rainy or humid weather because, under the best climatic conditions, these cookies are difficult to remove from the baking sheets—that's why we both grease *and* flour the baking sheets.

N O T E   *The "dough" is very thin and the cookies will flatten and spread as they bake, so give them 2 or 3 inches in each direction, depending upon how big you make them. Let the first batch of cookies be a test (you can limit it to half a dozen cookies or less), then adjust the heat, the amount of "dough" used for each cookie, and the spacing as needed.*

1 cup sifted all-purpose flour
1 cup finely minced blanched almonds
1 tablespoon finely minced or grated orange rind
¼ cup (½ stick) butter or margarine
¼ cup vegetable shortening
½ cup light corn syrup
⅔ cup firmly packed light brown sugar
¼ teaspoon almond extract

G L A Z E

2 squares (1 ounce each) semisweet chocolate
1 teaspoon butter
3 tablespoons water

Preheat the oven to moderately slow (325°F.).

Combine the flour, almonds, and orange rind in a mixing bowl. Melt the butter and shortening together in a small saucepan; add the corn syrup and sugar and bring the mixture just to a simmer. Add the almond extract and stir quickly into the flour mixture.

Drop the dough by level teaspoonfuls onto well-greased and floured baking sheets, spacing the cookies 2 to 3 inches apart, then bake for 8 to 10 minutes in the preheated oven.

Remove the cookies from the oven and cool for 2 minutes on baking sheets, then transfer to wire racks to finish cooling. (Sometimes it's necessary to loosen the cookies with a sharp knife before using the spatula.)

To make the glaze, cut the chocolate into small pieces and melt directly over very low heat in a small, heavy saucepan with the butter and water. With a pastry brush, brush the top of each lace cookie lightly with the chocolate. Let the cookies harden before you serve them.

CRANBERRY GLAZE

About 1 ½ cups

Here's a festive way to finish a holiday ham or bird—and, at the same time, to use up tag ends of light or dark corn syrup—even maple syrup or honey.

 1 cup cranberry jelly
 ½ cup light or dark corn syrup, maple syrup, or honey
 1 tablespoon cider vinegar
 Pinch of ground cinnamon
 Pinch of ground cloves

Combine all the ingredients in a small, heavy saucepan, set over lowest heat, and warm slowly, whisking briskly, until the jelly melts and the mixture is smooth; keep the glaze warm but do not allow it to boil. With a pastry brush, brush the glaze over roast turkey, chicken, duck, goose, game hens, pork, or ham during the last 30 minutes of cooking; repeat once or twice or until all the glaze has been used and the bird or roast glistens richly.

CHOCOLATE BROWNIE PIE

One 9-inch pie

The nuts called for in this recipe can be any kind—your particular favorite or whatever you have on hand and want to use up. We personally prefer toasted walnuts—just spread the nuts out on a cookie sheet and set them in a 350° F. oven for 10 to 15 minutes. But watch the walnuts closely—at the critical point, they go from not-quite-toasted to *burned!* Also, be sure to spread the nuts out on a sheet of wax paper, paper toweling, or brown paper to cool as soon as they come from the oven; otherwise they will continue to toast and may take on a burned flavor.

2 squares (1 ounce each) unsweetened chocolate
2 tablespoons butter
½ cup granulated sugar
3 large eggs
¾ cup dark corn syrup
¾ cup coarsely chopped pecans, walnuts, or other nuts
1 unbaked 9-inch pie shell

Preheat the oven to moderately hot (375° F.).

Melt the chocolate and butter together in the top part of a double boiler set over simmering water. Beat the sugar and eggs thoroughly; blend in the chocolate mixture, then the corn syrup, and beat until completely combined. Fold in the nuts.

Pour the filling into the pie shell and bake in the preheated oven for 40 to 50 minutes, or until a silver knife inserted in the center of the filling comes out clean.

Serve the pie warm (not hot) or cold, topped, if you like, with ice cream or whipped cream.

EASIEST EVER STRAWBERRY ICE CREAM

6 to 8 servings

It helps to have a food processor or electric blender when making this recipe, because you'll need to buzz the partially frozen strawberries to purée. If you have neither appliance, thaw the berries completely, then force through a food mill. The beauty of this recipe, aside from its wonderfully fresh flavor, is that you can use almost any combination of milk, cream, or yogurt to make it—just so long as you also use 1 cup of heavy cream, whipped.

> **3 packages (10 ounces each) quick-thaw frozen strawberries, partially thawed and buzzed to purée in a blender or processor**
> **1 cup light corn syrup**
> **1 cup light cream, half-and-half, sour cream, plain yogurt, buttermilk, evaporated milk, sweet milk, or any combination thereof (whatever it is you want to get rid of)**
> **Juice of ½ lemon**
> **1 cup heavy cream, whipped to soft peaks**

Combine the strawberry purée, corn syrup, light cream, and lemon juice in a large mixing bowl, then fold in the whipped cream. Pour into a 9 × 5 × 3-inch loaf pan and freeze until mushy.

Spoon into your largest mixer bowl and beat hard with the electric mixer set at high speed until fluffy (or buzz, about half of the total amount at a time, in a food processor fitted with the metal chopping blade). Return the mixture to the pan and freeze until soft-firm.

PEANUT-MAPLE PIE

One 9-inch pie

This recipe's so easy to make it's a joy. You can use light corn syrup instead of the dark if that is what you have in the cupboard, and if you like a stronger maple flavor, substitute maple syrup for some of the corn syrup. You may also use any kind of nuts (or a mixture of them) in place of the peanuts.

1 9-inch unbaked pie shell
1 cup coarsely chopped salted peanuts
1 cup dark corn syrup
½ cup maple syrup
4 eggs, beaten lightly
1 teaspoon vanilla extract

Preheat the oven to moderate (350° F.).

Cover the bottom of the pie shell with the peanuts. Mix together the syrups, eggs, and vanilla and pour on top of the nuts. Bake the pie on a cookie sheet in the preheated oven for 45 minutes.

Cool before cutting, and serve topped with whipped cream or ice cream.

CRACKER CRUMBS, CRACKER MEAL:
See **Crumbs.**

Cream

(Light, Heavy, and Half-and-Half)

Although packed in quantities as small as half a pint (1 cup), light and heavy cream and half-and-half rarely seem to be called for in recipes in 1- or 2-cup amounts, meaning there is a partially used carton of cream slowly souring on the refrigerator shelf. Few of us bother to thumb a recipe file or cookbook to determine easy ways of using up such small amounts, so the cream sours completely, only to be poured down the drain. Soured cream, by the way, can also be used to good advantage (see A Word on Soured Cream, below; see also the special section on sour cream on pages 262–68).

Best Way to Store   In each case, store the cream (whether light, heavy, or half-and-half) in the refrigerator in its own container with the opening pinched shut.

Maximum Storage Time   It depends, to a large extent, upon how fresh the cream was when you bought it (always check the date on the carton). Once opened, creams can usually be kept for about a week, sometimes for as long as 10 days, but they *will* begin to take on unwanted refrigerator odors, especially heavy cream, which has a higher percentage of butterfat (it is the fat that absorbs and holds odors). Once cream has soured, use it as soon as possible—simply substitute for commercial sour cream in baked goods, not in soups or stews or skillet dishes, where the cream is likely to curdle.

Roles in Cooking   Creams impart a special richness and smoothness to soups, sauces, puddings, mousses, and ice creams; they help to bind croquettes and forcemeats together; when boiled down (no, *sweet* cream does not curdle when boiled, although sour cream certainly does), they will thicken sauces and gravies; and, finally, creams enrich —ever so subtly—the flavor of almost every recipe to which they are added, both the sweet and the savory.

Recipe Uses   Cream is another ingredient of infinite versatility. It is integral to dozens of cream sauces and soups and chowders, to puddings and pies, to cake frostings and fillings and confections, to mousses and bombes and ice creams. And it goes without saying that cream, both the whipped and the plain, is a favorite American way "to cut the richness" of a cloyingly sweet dessert.

Special Comments   Half-and-half, a fairly new entry in the cream category, is nothing more than a fifty-fifty blend of milk and light cream that hit the market when people became calorie conscious. Substituted for milk in cakes and quick breads, it will produce a richer, slightly more tender crumb (as will light cream). Used in place of light or heavy cream, it will significantly reduce the calories of puddings, cream pies, mousses, and ice creams (1 cup of half-and-half = 325 calories vs. 505 for light cream and 840 for heavy cream).

On no account, however, substitute heavy cream, measure for measure, for either light cream or half-and-half in baked goods because it is far too rich and will result in leaden, "oily" cakes or breads. In a pinch, you can substitute heavy cream for milk provided you water it down first—that is, ½ cup heavy cream plus ½ cup cold water will *approximate* 1 cup rich milk or half-and-half; and ⅔ cup heavy cream plus ⅓ cup cold water will *approximate* 1 cup of light cream.

If, on the other hand, you should find yourself caught mid-recipe without 1 to 2 tablespoons—or even up to ¼ cup—of required light or heavy cream, don't panic. And don't do as a friend of ours did when making cream scones; having no cream on hand and not even a drop of whole milk, she used skim milk, then tossed in an extra couple of tablespoons of butter to make up for the skim milk's lack of richness. No, the recipe wasn't a flat-out failure, but the scones weren't very good either; certainly, they were not as light and flaky as they should have been. You will have more success—particularly with baked goods —if you substitute evaporated milk for the cream, measure for measure, or, failing that, half-and-half or even sour cream (provided you replace ½ teaspoon of the baking powder called for with baking soda).

A WORD ON SOURED CREAM

As for creams that have gone sour, half-and-half may be substituted for sour milk or buttermilk in cakes, breads, and cookies with good results. And soured light or heavy cream may be substituted for commercial sour cream in the same sorts of baked goods.

Tip   Soured creams may have separated, so buzz them in an electric blender or beat hard with a whisk or rotary beater just long enough to smooth and blend them before measuring and using.

If you try to substitute soured cream for commercial sour cream in soups, stews, and skillet dishes, you will not fare so well, because soured cream is very likely to curdle. (Bringing the soured cream to room temperature before stirring it into a hot dish will help keep the cream from curdling, but you are dealing with an unstable mixture that will most definitely curdle if heated too hot or too long.) Soured creams, moreover, are more strongly flavored than commercial sour cream, so their tartness may overpower the flavor of delicate foods (veal scallops, for example, chicken breasts, fillets of sole or flounder).

The best policy, when substituting soured cream for commercial sour cream, is to let your own instinct and experience guide you; to add the soured cream slowly to any soup or stew or skillet dish, tasting after each addition; and, finally, to keep the burner heat as low as it will go, to add the soured cream at the very last minute, then to bring the mixture *just* to serving temperature.

N O T E   *For additional recipes, included elsewhere in this book, that call for varying amounts of cream (light, heavy and half-and-half), see the Appendix.*

O R A N G E   F R I T T E R S

About 3 dozen

Children love these doughnutlike fritters, which have a nippy orange flavor. They are a splendid way to use up ½ cup of leftover heavy or light cream or evaporated milk.

    2 cups sifted all-purpose flour
    2 teaspoons baking powder
    ¼ teaspoon salt
    ⅛ teaspoon grated nutmeg
    ⅛ teaspoon ground cinnamon
    2 eggs
    ½ cup granulated sugar
    ½ cup cream (heavy or light) or evaporated milk
    Finely grated rind of 1 orange
    ½ cup orange juice
    Shortening or cooking oil for deep-fat frying
    Sifted confectioners sugar

Sift the flour with the baking powder, salt, nutmeg, and cinnamon and set aside. Beat the eggs until light; mix in the sugar and cream. Stir in the sifted dry ingredients, then mix in the orange rind and juice. Drop the batter by teaspoonfuls directly into 375° F. deep fat and fry for about 2 minutes, or until evenly browned.

Drain the browned fritters on paper toweling, then sift confectioners sugar over them lightly while they are still warm.

CURRIED APPLE SOUP

6 servings

A perfectly delicious way to use up ½ to ¾ cup light, heavy, or sour cream. Also to utilize 1 to 1½ cups apple cider that seems to be gaining strength or going cloudy.

> 3 tablespoons butter or margarine
> 1 large Spanish onion, peeled and minced
> 1 clove garlic, peeled and minced
> 2 ribs celery, trimmed, washed, and minced
> 4 tart apples, peeled, cored, and sliced thin
> 2 tablespoons curry powder
> ¼ teaspoon ground ginger
> ¼ teaspoon ground cinnamon
> Pinch of ground cloves
> Pinch of ground mace
> Juice of 1 lemon
> ¼ cup unsifted all-purpose flour
> 3 cups chicken and/or beef broth (use part apple cider or juice if you have any you're trying to use up)
> 2 cups milk, at room temperature
> ½ to ¾ cup cream (light, heavy, or sour), at room temperature
> 1 to 2 tablespoons honey or light brown sugar (to mellow the tartness of the soup)
> Salt and freshly ground black pepper to taste

Melt the butter in a large, heavy saucepan over moderate heat. Add the onion, garlic, and celery and stir-fry for about 10 minutes, or until very lightly browned. Add the apples and stir-fry for 1 to 2 minutes, then cover and simmer for 10 minutes, or until the apples are mushy.

Purée the saucepan mixture in an electric blender or food processor fitted with the metal chopping blade, or put through a food mill; return the purée to the saucepan and blend in the curry powder, ginger, cinnamon, cloves, mace, and lemon juice. Allow to mellow over moderate heat, stirring often, for 2 to 3 minutes, or until no raw curry taste remains.

Blend in the flour, then add the broth (or apple cider–broth mixture) and heat, stirring constantly, until thickened and smooth—3 to 5 minutes. Smooth in the milk and warm gently for 2 to 3 minutes, then smooth in the cream and bring just to serving temperature (do not allow to boil or the soup may curdle).

Season to taste with honey, salt, and pepper, and serve hot. (You can also chill well and serve cold.) To garnish, scatter crisp bacon crumbles on top or, if you prefer, small cubes of ripe avocado that have been dipped in lemon juice to prevent darkening.

APPLE-GINGER PARFAIT

4 servings

Such a quick and easy dessert.

½ teaspoon ground ginger
¼ teaspoon ground cinnamon
Pinch of ground mace or grated nutmeg
3 tablespoons confectioners sugar
½ to ¾ cup well-chilled heavy cream
2 cups well-chilled applesauce

Mix the spices with the confectioners sugar, then stir into the cream and whip to stiff peaks. Layer the applesauce and whipped cream alternately in four slim parfait glasses, beginning and ending with applesauce.

Chill well, then serve.

MOCK CLOTTED CREAM

1 to 1½ cups

Use to top a fresh fruit compote or pie.

½ to ¾ cup heavy cream, whipped to soft peaks
2 tablespoons confectioners sugar
½ to ¾ cup sour cream
1 to 2 drops vanilla extract

Combine all the ingredients and serve.

Crumbs

(Bread, Cracker, Cookie, and Cake)

We shall discuss here bread crumbs (both the soft and the dry), soda cracker crumbs and cracker meal, graham-cracker and cookie crumbs, which are used more or less interchangeably for making crumb crusts and dessert toppings, and, finally, cake crumbs.

SOFT BREAD CRUMBS

These are made by buzzing chunks of 1- or 2-day-old bread to crumbs in an electric blender or food processor or by grating the bread on the second coarsest side of a four-sided grater.

Best Way to Store   In the refrigerator, in a screw-top glass jar.

Maximum Storage Time   About 2 weeks.

Roles in Cooking   To help bind meat loaves, burgers, and croquettes; to extend meat in burgers, meat loaves, and croquettes (thanks to crumbs, you can stretch 1 pound of meat over 6 servings); to absorb moisture in stuffings, puddings, casseroles, uncooked candies, even certain soups, so that the finished consistency is smooth and thick; to form the basis of all manner of meat, poultry, seafood, and vegetable stuffings; to serve as a topping for casseroles, crisps, and cobblers; and to crumb chicken, chops, and cutlets that are to be fried or oven-fried (soft crumbs do not stick well on foods to be deep-fried).

Recipe Uses   The recipes that most often call for significant amounts of soft bread crumbs are steamed puddings, stuffings, meat and fish loaves and puddings, croquettes and casseroles, and streusel- (crumb-) topped cobblers, pies, puddings, and some tortes.

Special Comments   Try substituting whole-wheat bread crumbs or protein or corn bread crumbs for the plain white crumbs now and again. They add a marvelous nutty flavor. Or use a combination of crumbs. You may wonder if soft bread crumbs and dry bread crumbs may be used interchangeably in recipes. Yes, they can, except for stuffings where you want a light, fluffy texture (because they are finer, dry crumbs tend to pack down, producing an unpleasantly heavy, pastelike stuffing; this fineness, on the other hand, makes them a better choice for most breading jobs).

N O T E   *For each 1 cup of soft bread crumbs, you will need 2 standard slices of bread.*

DRY BREAD CRUMBS

These are nothing more than hard, dry bread or toast reduced to crumbs. Again, the simplest way to make them is to buzz chunks of dry bread in either the electric blender or food processor, or to roll the dry bread or toast, several slices at a time, with a rolling pin.

Tip   To keep the crumbs from skittering all over the counter and onto the floor, roll between two large sheets of wax paper or inside a sturdy plastic bag.

Best Way to Store   Tightly covered in a screw-top glass jar or airtight canister on a cool, dry shelf.

Maximum Storage Time   About 2 months. The crumbs can be kept longer, of course, and they will not spoil. But they will be about as tasty as sawdust.

Roles in Cooking   Essentially the same as for soft bread crumbs (see, particularly, the Special Comments above).

Recipe Uses   Again, very much the same as for soft bread crumbs. The dry crumbs are particularly good for breading fish to be fried or, mixed with butter, strewn over such cooked vegetables as asparagus, broccoli, and cauliflower.

Special Comments   To make dry bread crumbs from fresh bread, arrange slices of bread one layer deep on an ungreased baking sheet, set in a slow oven (300° F.) and toast, uncovered, for 15 minutes. Turn the slices and toast for 15 minutes longer, or until dry, crisp, and golden—about like Melba toast.

N O T E   *1 slice of dry bread = about ⅓ cup dry bread crumbs.*

SODA-CRACKER (SALTINE) CRUMBS AND CRACKER MEAL

The difference between these two is that cracker crumbs are ones you prepare yourself (thus you can control the degree of coarseness or fineness), whereas cracker meal is commercially packaged—the left-over crumbs, so to speak, of big-business baking. Their texture is uniformly fine, and for that reason they don't make particularly good casserole toppings (no character or crunch—at least in our opinion). This evenness of texture, however, *does* make them ideal for dredging foods to be fried or deep-fat fried.

Tip Always let breaded foods air-dry on a rack at room temperature for 20 to 30 minutes before cooking them so the breading will stick; this applies to foods breaded with both cracker and bread crumbs.

Best Way to Store Both the crumbs and the cracker meal will keep the longest (and most bug-free) in glass jars with screw tops on a cool, dry shelf.

Maximum Storage Time About 2 months. The crumbs will keep longer, but they will develop a flat, rancid flavor.

Roles in Cooking Coarse cracker crumbs can be used interchangeably with soft bread crumbs (which see, above). Finer cracker crumbs and cracker meal should be used just as you would dry bread crumbs, meaning they are not a good choice for stuffings or, as we mentioned above, for casserole toppings, either. They are excellent, however, for extending meat loaves and puddings, burgers and croquettes; for helping to bind casseroles, and for breading foods to be fried or deep-fat fried.

Recipe Uses See soft and dry bread crumbs (above).

Special Comments For 1 cup of cracker crumbs, you will need about 25 soda crackers (the individual square ones).

GRAHAM-CRACKER, COOKIE, AND CAKE CRUMBS

We group these together because they are used more or less the same way. When we say "cookies," we are referring to the crisp, dry wafers

—vanilla, chocolate and lemon wafers, and gingersnaps. Again, the quickest, easiest way to make crumbs is in an electric blender or food processor. You can also roll the cookies or graham crackers to crumbs with a rolling pin (to spare yourself messy clean-up, pop the cookies or crackers into a large, sturdy plastic bag, fold the top over, then place on the counter and roll). Graham-cracker crumbs are also packaged commercially, but we frankly prefer the coarser texture of the crumbs we roll ourselves.

As for cake crumbs, the most useful are also those you're most apt to have on hand, that is, those from crumbly butter or pound cakes. Cake crumbs may be used interchangeably with cookie or graham-cracker crumbs in dessert stuffings and streusel toppings, but they are too soft for crumb crusts.

Best Way to Store   In screw-top glass jars on a cool, dry shelf. The reason that we keep advocating glass is that it is wholly inert (reacts in no way at all to the foods put into it—not true of metal or plastic, both of which can affect the flavor of foods during long periods of storage).

Maximum Storage Time   About 2 months. The crumbs will not spoil if held longer, but they will begin to taste stale and cardboardy. You can double the shelf life of cookie and graham-cracker crumbs by storing them in the refrigerator (again tightly capped in a glass jar), but if your refrigerator space is as precious as ours is, you may not want to waste it for anything as nonperishable as crumbs.

Roles in Cooking   Both cookie and graham-cracker crumbs are the foundations of crumb crusts, dessert toppings, and many uncooked candies. They also serve as a "filler" or stuffing for a number of fruit desserts (stuffed whole fruits, for example, as well as crisps and cobblers), and they are, of course, integral to streusel—the buttery-sweet crumbs scattered over pies and fruit puddings in lieu of top crusts. Streusel is loaded with character and crunch, an appealing counterpoint to the softness of the fruits underneath. Finally, the crumbs heighten flavor—particularly gingersnap and chocolate- and lemon-wafer crumbs. With them, you can mix and match flavors—a chocolate crumb crust for a mint, mocha, or butterscotch pie, for example; a gingersnap crust for a squash or pumpkin pie; a lemon crumb crust for an apple or peach pie.

Recipe Uses   We show several ways to put cookie and graham-cracker crumbs to imaginative use in the pages that follow. For other ideas, thumb through the cookie, pudding, pie, and gelatin dessert sections of your own recipe files.

Special Comments   How many graham crackers does it take to make 1 cup of crumbs? How many vanilla wafers or gingersnaps? Use the following table as a guide:

> **15 (2¾-inch square) graham crackers = approximately 1 cup crumbs**
> **19 (2-inch diameter) chocolate wafers = approximately 1 cup crumbs**
> **22 gingersnaps, vanilla, or lemon wafers = approximately 1 cup**
> **crumbs (these cookies are all about the same size, that is,**
> **1¾ to 2 inches in diameter)**

N O T E   *For additional recipes, included elsewhere in this book, that call for varying amounts of crumbs (soft and dry bread, soda- and graham-cracker, and cookie crumbs), see the Appendix.*

Soft Bread Crumbs

S O F T   C R U M B   T O P P I N G   F O R   C A S S E R O L E S

Enough for 1 average-size casserole

Bread so quickly hardens beyond a suitable sandwich texture (especially if you refrigerate the bread to keep it from molding in humid weather) that it is often needlessly thrown away. The best solution, we've found, is to buzz the bread to crumbs, to store them in the refrigerator in a tightly covered one-quart preserving jar, then to take out what crumbs are needed—*as* needed—for casserole toppings. Each slice of bread, by the way, will yield about ½ cup of soft crumbs (the handiest way to make crumbs is to buzz torn slices of bread in a food processor fitted with the metal chopping blade or in an electric blender at high speed, but you can also hand-grate the slices using the second coarsest side of a four-sided grater).

To top an average-size casserole, use the following proportions:

1 cup soft bread crumbs (either white or whole-wheat)
1 tablespoon melted butter or margarine
⅛ teaspoon salt
Pinch of freshly ground black pepper

Toss all the ingredients together in a small mixing bowl, then sprinkle evenly over the casserole before baking.

VARIATIONS

Cheese-Crumb Topping   To the above proportions, add ¼ to ½ cup freshly grated Parmesan. Especially good on chicken or tuna casseroles.

Parsley-Crumb Topping   To the above proportions, add ¼ to ⅓ cup minced fresh parsley. Good on any casserole.

Herbed Crumb Topping   To the above proportions, add ½ teaspoon crumbled leaf marjoram, oregano, or sage and a pinch of crumbled rosemary or thyme. Especially good with chicken or turkey casseroles.

Nut-Crumb Topping   To the above proportions, add ¼ to ½ cup finely minced pecans, walnuts, blanched almonds, or hazelnuts. Especially good on poultry, tuna, or salmon casseroles.

Spicy Butter-Crumb Topping for Desserts   Use 1 cup soft bread crumbs as called for above, but increase the melted butter or margarine to 2 tablespoons, and mix in ¼ teaspoon ground cinnamon, and a pinch each ground cloves and grated nutmeg. Use to top fruit Bettys or crisps.

SOUFFLÉ-LIGHT SALMON PATTIES

4 servings

The beaten egg whites, folded in at the last minute, leaven these salmon patties and account for their unusually light texture. If you should have leftover fish on hand (flounder, halibut, cod, bass, whiting —whatever), by all means substitute that for the salmon. Failing that, use one small can (7¾ ounces) of salmon.

CONTINUED

These patties may be made with either whole-wheat bread or white (and if you have heels to use, so much the better because they will enrich the flavor). For the liquid ingredient, you may use evaporated milk, milk, or almost any variety of cream.

> 2 slices stale bread, reduced to moderately fine crumbs (use the second coarsest side of a four-sided grater)
> ½ cup milk, evaporated milk, or cream (heavy, light, half-and-half, sour)
> 1 cup cooked, flaked, boned salmon or 1 can (7¾ ounces) salmon, drained and flaked (pick over carefully to remove bits of dark skin)
> 1 teaspoon salt
> ⅛ teaspoon freshly ground black pepper
> 1 teaspoon butter, at room temperature
> 1 tablespoon finely grated onion
> 2 egg yolks, beaten lightly
> 1 teaspoon lemon juice (optional)
> 2 egg whites, beaten to soft peaks

Combine the bread crumbs and milk and let stand at room temperature for 20 minutes. Mix with all but the last ingredient, then fold in the softly beaten egg whites.

Drop the salmon mixture from softly mounded tablespoons into a liberally greased skillet and cook over moderate heat until nicely browned on each side—about 2 to 3 minutes per side. Serve at once.

These are delicious with young asparagus spears, drizzled with brown butter, or with new garden peas.

LEMON-PECAN TORTE

One 10-inch tube cake

This exquisitely moist and tender cake is made the European way, with bread crumbs and finely ground nuts instead of flour.

> 8 large eggs, separated
> 1½ cups granulated sugar
> 1 cup fine, soft bread crumbs
> 2 cups very finely ground pecans (they should be soft and fluffy, not pasty)

Finely ground rind of 1 lemon
½ teaspoon vanilla extract
¼ teaspoon almond extract

Preheat the oven to moderate (350° F.).

Beat the egg yolks with ½ cup of the sugar in an electric mixer set at high speed until very thick and the color of mayonnaise. Continue beating, adding ¾ cup of the remaining sugar gradually. By hand fold in the crumbs, nuts, lemon rind, and vanilla and almond extracts.

Beat the egg whites to soft peaks, then add the remaining ¼ cup of sugar gradually, beating all the while to fairly stiff, *moist* peaks. Fold the beaten whites into the nut mixture, pour the batter into a very well greased and floured 10-inch tube pan, and bake in the preheated oven for 1 hour.

Remove the cake from the oven; invert and cool it in the upside-down pan for 1 hour (see note below). Loosen the cake around the edges and central tube, then turn out on a cake plate. Cool to room temperature, cut into wedges, and serve topped with billows of whipped cream.

N O T E   *If your tube pan has "feet" projecting above the rim and well above the surface of the risen cake, simply let the cake cool on the counter in the upside-down pan. If not, stand a full, quart-size soft-drink bottle on the counter (a glass one, not one of the new plastic ones) and invert the cake pan over the bottle so that the bottle neck fits inside the pan tube.*

M O T H E R ' S   C H O C O L A T E
B R E A D   P U D D I N G

4 to 6 servings

A bread pudding that belies its name. It's more like a mousse and can become addictive, especially if served just at room temperature with flavored whipped cream or a hard sauce. You *may* even begin to let your bread go stale on purpose!

C O N T I N U E D

2 squares (1 ounce each) unsweetened chocolate
2 cups milk
1 cup solidly packed soft bread crumbs
2 eggs
¾ cup granulated sugar
½ teaspoon ground cinnamon

Cut the chocolate into small chunks and place in a heavy saucepan; add the milk and stir constantly over moderately low heat until the chocolate has melted and combined uniformly with the milk. Off the heat, add the bread crumbs and let the mixture stand for 1 hour.

Preheat the oven to moderate (350° F.).

Beat the eggs lightly, add the sugar and cinnamon, then stir into the bread mixture. Pour into a buttered 6-cup baking dish, set in a shallow baking pan, and pour hot water into the pan to a depth of 1½ inches. Bake the pudding, uncovered, in the hot water bath in the preheated oven for about 1 hour, or until set like custard.

Serve warm or cold, with whipped cream.

KOTLETI (RUSSIAN MEATBALLS SMOTHERED IN CREAM GRAVY)

6 servings

You can look long and hard, but you won't find a better way to use up a lot of stale bread than these feather-light meatballs jacketed in bread crumbs. The meatballs are plumped up with crumbs, too—in fact, the recipe calls for 8 slices of stale bread altogether. It is also a good vehicle for using any beef broth, cream, or sour cream that you may have on hand.

N O T E   *The raw, breaded meatballs can be frozen and kept for about 3 months in a freezer set at 0° F.*

½ pound ground beef chuck
½ pound ground veal shoulder
1 small yellow onion, peeled and minced
¼ teaspoon crumbled leaf rosemary
¼ teaspoon crumbled leaf thyme
¼ teaspoon crumbled leaf marjoram

⅛ teaspoon grated nutmeg or ground mace

¾ teaspoon salt

⅛ teaspoon freshly ground black pepper

8 slices stale, firm-textured white bread, reduced to moderately fine crumbs (you should have 4 cups of bread crumbs in all)

½ cup water

1 large egg, beaten lightly with 3 tablespoons milk, evaporated milk, or cream (light or heavy)

2 tablespoons peanut or vegetable oil

2 tablespoons butter or margarine

G R A V Y

1½ cups strong beef broth or 1 can (10½ ounces) condensed beef broth

2 tablespoons all-purpose flour

¼ to ½ cup cream (sour, light, or heavy) or evaporated milk, at room temperature

Mix together thoroughly the beef, veal, onion, herbs, nutmeg or mace, salt and pepper, 1½ cups of the crumbs, and the water. Shape into 2-inch balls. Dip the balls first in the egg mixture, then in the remaining 2½ cups bread crumbs to coat; as you dip the balls in the crumbs, flatten them into ovals about ½ inch thick. Arrange them one layer deep on a baking sheet, cover loosely with wax paper, and chill for several hours to firm the meat up slightly and to make the breading stick.

N O T E *At this point you may wrap the meatballs individually and freeze them. Partially thaw them—for about 30 minutes—before proceeding with the recipe.*

Preheat the oven to moderate (350° F.).

Heat the peanut oil and butter in a very large, heavy skillet over moderately high heat and brown the meat well on each side; transfer to a shallow baking pan, arranging one layer deep, and set, uncovered, in the preheated oven for 25 minutes.

Meanwhile, prepare the gravy. Combine ¼ cup of the beef broth with the flour and whisk to make a smooth paste; set aside for the moment. Pour the remaining broth into the skillet in which you browned the meat and simmer over moderate heat, scraping up browned bits, for 3 to 4 minutes, until slightly reduced. Smooth in the flour paste and heat, whisking constantly, until thickened and smooth

—about 3 minutes. Turn the heat to its lowest point and allow the gravy to mellow, stirring now and then, for another 3 to 5 minutes—until no raw, floury taste remains. Blend in the cream and bring just to serving temperature (do not allow the gravy to boil or it may curdle).

Arrange the meat on a heated platter and top with some of the gravy; pass the remainder separately.

Dry Bread and Soda-Cracker Crumbs

BREADED LAMB CHOPS

4 servings

Lamb chops are not something we think of breading, yet they are very good indeed prepared this way. Next time you have leftover dry bread crumbs or cracker meal, try this recipe.

> 8 loin or rib lamb chops, cut 1 to 1½ inches thick and trimmed of excess fat
> 2 cloves garlic, peeled and halved lengthwise
> ½ teaspoon crumbled leaf rosemary
> 1 teaspoon salt
> ¼ teaspoon freshly ground black pepper
> 2 eggs, beaten lightly
> ¾ cup fine, dry bread crumbs or cracker meal
> 3 tablespoons butter or margarine
> 2 tablespoons vegetable oil

Rub each lamb chop well on both sides with garlic, rosemary, salt, and pepper, then let stand at room temperature for 30 minutes. Dip the chops first in beaten egg, then in crumbs to coat evenly; let the chops air-dry on a cookie rack at room temperature for 20 minutes (this is to make the crumbs stick better).

Heat the butter and oil in a large, heavy skillet over moderately high heat until a cube of bread will sizzle, then fry the lamb chops for 10 to 12 minutes, turning often with tongs, until nicely browned and cooked the way you like them.

VEAL MILANESE

4 servings

You will find few quicker or more delicious ways to use up dry bread crumbs or cracker meal of doubtful age than this easy skillet dish (just make sure that the crumbs neither smell nor taste stale).

1½ pounds veal round, sliced ¼ inch thick and pounded thin as for scaloppine
1 teaspoon salt
Several grindings of black pepper
1 cup fine, dry bread crumbs or cracker meal
1 to 3 tablespoons very finely minced fresh parsley
1 clove garlic, peeled and crushed
⅓ cup unsifted all-purpose flour
2 large eggs, beaten lightly
⅓ cup clarified butter (melted butter from which the milk solids have been skimmed)
1 lemon, sliced thin

Sprinkle the veal with the salt and pepper. Mix the crumbs with the parsley and garlic. Dip the veal first in flour, then in the beaten eggs, then in crumbs, shaking off excess crumbs. Let the breaded veal scallops air-dry on a cookie rack at room temperature for 20 to 30 minutes (this drying period helps the breading to stick).

Heat the butter in a very large, heavy skillet over moderately high heat until a cube of bread will sizzle. Add the veal and brown for 3 to 4 minutes on each side until golden brown.

Drain quickly on paper toweling and serve topped with lemon slices.

NORWEGIAN-STYLE BREADED HAM PATTIES

4 to 6 servings

Unlike most meat patties, which are simply mixed together by hand, these are beaten hard, so they take on the consistency of a light dough. For best results, use an electric mixer set at high speed or, if you are lucky enough to have one, a food processor (two to three 5-second churnings of the motor should be sufficient). If you have neither mixer nor processor, beat the ham mixture hard with a wooden spoon until uniformly thick and smooth. These patties are an excellent way to use up fine, dry bread crumbs, as well as evaporated milk, if you should have some on hand—and any parsley too wilted to serve as a garnish.

1½ pounds finely ground, fully cooked smoked ham
½ teaspoon salt
½ teaspoon ground ginger
¼ teaspoon ground mace or grated nutmeg
2 tablespoons all-purpose flour or potato flour, approximately
⅓ cup milk, evaporated milk, or cream (heavy, light, half-and-half, or sour)
¼ cup finely chopped fresh parsley
1 large egg, beaten until frothy with 2 tablespoons milk, evaporated milk, or cream
¾ to 1 cup fine, dry bread crumbs
3 to 4 tablespoons bacon drippings or butter

Place the ham, salt, ginger, mace, flour, evaporated milk, and parsley in a large mixer bowl and beat at high speed until uniformly smooth and soft. If the mixture seems too soft (and it may if the weather is rainy or humid), add another tablespoon of flour and beat hard again. Shape into oval patties, using two tablespoons that have been dipped in cold water (it's the same technique that is used for shaping *quenelles,* and you will have to redip the spoons in cold water before shaping each new patty).

N O T E *If the ham mixture seems too soft to shape easily, chill for several hours, or until it stiffens somewhat.*

Dip the patties into the egg mixture, then into the bread crumbs to coat liberally. Arrange on a wax paper-lined baking sheet and let air-dry for 20 minutes (this is to help make the breading stick).

Melt the drippings or butter in a large, heavy skillet over moderate heat, then, when good and hot, add the patties. Reduce the heat slightly and brown them slowly on both sides. Adjust the burner heat as needed so the patties do not brown too quickly—they should be evenly and richly topaz brown.

Serve with fried potatoes and a crisp green salad.

Kalvekarbonader (Norwegian Veal Patties) Prepare as in the recipe above, but substitute 1½ pounds finely ground veal round or shoulder for the ham, and increase the amount of salt to 1½ teaspoons and the mace or nutmeg to ½ teaspoon. Fry in butter only (the strong flavor of the bacon drippings will overpower the more delicate one of the veal).

CRUSTY-CRUMBED OVEN-FRIED CHICKEN

6 to 8 servings

A virtually effortless party dish that is a superlative way to use up bread crumbs and, optionally, grated Parmesan and/or minced parsley.

1 egg, beaten with ⅓ cup milk, sour milk, or buttermilk
2 small cloves garlic, peeled and crushed
1½ to 2 cups fine, dry bread crumbs (white or whole-wheat)
1½ teaspoons salt
1 teaspoon paprika
¼ teaspoon freshly ground black pepper
¼ to ½ cup grated Parmesan cheese (optional)
2 to 4 tablespoons minced fresh parsley (optional)
2 broiler-fryers (3 to 3½ pounds each), disjointed
⅓ to ½ cup (5⅓ tablespoons to 1 stick) butter, melted

Preheat the oven to moderate (350° F.).

Combine egg mixture and crushed garlic in a pie plate. In a second pie plate mix the crumbs, salt, paprika, and pepper, along with the Parmesan and/or parsley, if you like. Dip the chicken first in the egg mixture, then in the crumbs to coat well.

Arrange the chicken one layer deep in a very large, shallow roasting pan and drizzle ⅓ cup of the melted butter on top. Bake, uncovered, in the preheated oven for 1¼ to 1½ hours, or until the chicken is very tender and the crumb coating is crisply brown. Baste now and again during baking with the pan drippings or, if the chicken seems to be drying, with a little additional melted butter.

Graham-Cracker, Cookie, and Cake Crumbs

SCOTTISH GINGER TORTE

One 8-inch round pastry

Such an unusual recipe this is, and a surprisingly delicately flavored one. It's the specialty of Edinburgh friends who graciously shared their recipe with us. It will remind you more of Scottish shortbread than of the cakelike tortes we know. The gingersnap crumbs give it especially good flavor, but if you've cake or other cookie crumbs to use up, simply increase the amount of ground ginger called for to 1½ teaspoons. You may want to add ½ teaspoon of ground ginger to the frosting, too.

TORTE

½ cup (1 stick) butter or margarine, at room temperature
1 cup sifted all-purpose flour
¼ cup granulated sugar
⅓ cup finely ground blanched almonds
⅓ cup fine gingersnap, cake, or other cookie crumbs
1 to 1½ teaspoons ground ginger (use the larger amount if you don't use gingersnap crumbs)

FROSTING

¼ cup (½ stick) butter or margarine, at room temperature
1 cup confectioners sugar
½ teaspoon vanilla extract
½ teaspoon ground ginger (optional)

Preheat the oven to moderate (350° F.).

Rub the butter or margarine into the flour thoroughly; add the remaining torte ingredients and stir well to mix—this will be a stiff dough. Press the dough into an ungreased 8-inch pie pan and bake in the preheated oven for 20 minutes, or until firm and pale tan. Remove from the oven and let the torte cool completely in its pan.

Cream all the frosting ingredients together until smooth, then spread evenly on top of the torte.

To serve, cut in slim wedges just as you would a pie.

BOURBON BALLS

About 2 dozen

These are a great Southern favorite for teas and open houses, particularly at Christmas time. They are not baked at all, merely shaped and rolled in confectioners sugar. Their foundation? Vanilla-wafer crumbs —and plenty of them.

These keep well for several weeks.

> 1¼ cups vanilla-wafer crumbs (about 2¼ dozen vanilla wafers)
> ⅔ cup finely minced pecans, black walnuts, or walnuts
> 3 tablespoons cocoa powder (not a mix)
> 1 tablespoon light or dark corn syrup
> 2 to 4 tablespoons bourbon
> ¼ cup unsifted confectioners sugar

In a large mixing bowl, combine the crumbs, nuts, 1 tablespoon of the cocoa, the corn syrup, and just enough bourbon to make a stiff "dough." Combine the remaining 2 tablespoons of cocoa and the confectioners sugar in a pie plate. Now pinch off bits of the "dough" and shape into balls about the size of walnuts. Roll in the sugar mixture to dredge, then store airtight for at least 2 days before serving (this is to allow the bourbon balls to "season").

CLASSIC GRAHAM-CRACKER CRUST

One 9-inch pie shell

The easiest way to rid your shelves of a lot of graham crackers is to make a crumb crust, which can be used for any favorite cheese or chiffon pie. Snugly wrapped in foil, the pie shell freezes well and may be kept for as long as 4 months in the freezer.

> 1²⁄₃ cups graham-cracker crumbs (about 2 dozen 2¼-inch-square crackers)
> ⅓ cup (5⅓ tablespoons) butter or margarine, melted
> 5 tablespoons granulated sugar
> ¼ teaspoon ground cinnamon (optional)
> Pinch of grated nutmeg or ground mace (optional)

Preheat the oven to moderate (350° F.).

Mix all the ingredients together well and press firmly over the bottom and up the sides of a 9-inch pie plate or spring-form pan. Bake in the preheated oven for about 10 minutes, just until firm and lightly browned.

Remove the crust from the oven and cool before filling.

To Freeze If you intend to freeze the crust, wrap it (pan and all) carefully in aluminum foil so as not to break or damage it, then quick-freeze at 0° F.

VANILLA-WAFER CRUMB CRUST

One 9-inch pie shell

Vanilla wafers hardly qualify as a favorite cookie—at least for eating out of hand—so if you're left with half a box or so of them, make this crumb crust, which can be frozen. Also note the variations for crumb crusts made of chocolate or lemon wafers or gingersnaps.

> 1²⁄₃ cups vanilla-wafer crumbs (about 3 dozen vanilla wafers)
> ⅓ cup (5⅓ tablespoons) butter or margarine, melted
> 2 tablespoons granulated or light or dark brown sugar
> ¼ teaspoon grated nutmeg or ground mace (optional)

Preheat the oven to moderate (350° F.).

Mix all the ingredients together thoroughly, then pat firmly across the bottom and up the sides of a 9-inch spring-form or pie pan. Bake in the preheated oven until firm and lightly browned—8 to 10 minutes.

Remove the pie shell from the oven and cool before filling.

To Freeze Wrap gently but snugly (pan and all) in aluminum foil and quick-freeze by setting directly on the freezing surface of your freezer (preferably one that maintains 0° F.). Do not store the frozen pie shell longer than 4 months or it will begin to taste stale.

VARIATIONS

Lemon-Wafer Crust Prepare as directed but substitute lemon wafers for the vanilla wafers, use granulated sugar, and add, if you like, ½ to 1 teaspoon finely grated lemon rind.

Chocolate-Wafer Crust Roll 2 dozen 2-inch round chocolate wafers to crumbs, mix with ¼ cup melted butter and 2 tablespoons granulated or brown sugar, then shape and bake as directed above.

Gingersnap Crumb Crust Prepare exactly like the vanilla wafer crumb crust, but use 1 tablespoon of sugar only.

FRESH FRUIT PUDDING-COBBLER

6 to 8 servings

The reason we call this a "pudding-cobbler" is that stale bread, cake, cookie, or cracker crumbs are used to thicken the fruit instead of the more conventional cornstarch or flour, so the fruit layer has almost a "steamed pudding" consistency. You'll be pleased to know that the fruit mixture is also an ideal place to use up lumpy brown sugar (as much as 1½ cups of it) and that the topping conveniently takes care of ½ cup of sour milk or buttermilk and as many as 2 egg yolks, which will enrich the mixture.

FRUIT MIXTURE

3 pounds ripe peaches, apricots, pears, or apples, peeled, pitted or cored, and sliced thin, *or* 3 quarts fresh berries, washed and hulled (halve or quarter berries if large)

Juice of 1 large lemon

1½ cups light or dark brown sugar (if hard and dry, break into small lumps; if you do not have 1½ cups brown sugar, use up what you do have and round out the measure with granulated sugar)

CONTINUED

¼ teaspoon salt

2½ to 3 cups fairly fine crumbs (dry bread, cake, vanilla or lemon wafers, gingersnaps, or graham crackers or any combination of these)

TOPPING

1½ cups sifted all-purpose flour

1 teaspoon baking powder

1 teaspoon baking soda

⅓ cup granulated sugar

¼ teaspoon salt

Pinch of grated nutmeg

⅓ cup (5⅓ tablespoons) butter, margarine, or vegetable shortening

½ cup sour milk, buttermilk, or milk (if you use sweet milk, use 2 teaspoons baking powder instead of 1 teaspoon baking powder and 1 teaspoon baking soda)

1 to 2 egg yolks, beaten lightly (optional)

Prepare the fruit mixture first. Place the fruit in a buttered 3-quart casserole and drizzle with lemon juice. Add the sugar and salt and toss well to mix. Let stand at room temperature for 30 minutes, or until the sugar has dissolved in the fruit juices.

Sprinkle the crumbs on top of the fruit and let stand while you make the topping; preheat the oven to hot (400° F.).

Combine the flour, baking powder, soda, sugar, salt, and nutmeg in a mixing bowl. Cut in the butter with a pastry blender until the mixture is the texture of coarse meal. Drizzle the sour milk (or if you are also using the egg yolks, the milk and egg yolks, which have been lightly whisked together) over the surface of the dry ingredients. Toss briskly with a fork just until the mixture holds together.

Quickly toss the crumb and fruit mixture, then drop the topping over the surface of this mixture, using a tablespoon. Bake, uncovered, in the preheated oven for 30 to 35 minutes, or until nicely browned and bubbly.

Cool to room temperature before serving, accompanied, if you like, by cream, whipped cream, or vanilla ice cream.

Dates

(Pitted)

One of the earliest fruits known to man, dates were grown in Mesopotamia (now Iraq) and in Egypt more than 5,000 years ago. Called "the
candy that grows on trees," they served as a sort of early K-ration for
camel caravans making arduous treks across the desert. When dried,
dates kept well, they were good to eat, they were an instant energy
source, and although the early nomads didn't know it, they were also
an excellent source of iron, calcium, phosphorous, copper, vitamin A,
and to a lesser extent of several B vitamins. Today, dates seem to have
fallen from favor across much of America, perhaps because of our
increasing obsession with calories. There is no denying that dates are
a high-calorie food (about 35 calories per average-sized date), still they
are a far better choice for munching than the equally caloric junk foods
now crowding too many cupboard shelves.

The dates we buy in supermarkets are fresh (not dried) and prepack-
aged with just enough moisture added to keep them from drying in
storage. They are available pitted in 8-ounce and 1-pound packages
and, as an added convenience, both pitted and chopped in 8-ounce
packages (these are more perishable than whole dates simply because
they are in smaller pieces, meaning that more surface area is exposed
to the air).

Best Way to Store   Opened packages of dates should be overwrapped
in plastic food wrap and stored either on a cool, dry, dark shelf or,
better yet, in the refrigerator.

Maximum Storage Time   About 1 month at room temperature
(slightly less for chopped dates) and 4 to 6 months in the refrigerator,
depending upon how humid your refrigerator is. Dates absorb atmospheric moisture and odors, and in a humid environment they may
mold (if so, they should be discarded). On the other hand, dates give
their moisture up to the air in arid areas (also in super-heated apartments and houses), becoming quite hard and dry. Hardened dates,

however, can be rehabilitated. Simply plump them in a little water, wine, or fruit juice just as you would plump raisins or dried currants, then drain and use as you would use freshly bought dates.

Roles in Cooking   Dates add color, flavor, sweetness, texture, and nutritive value. When chopped and mixed with a little liquid, dates soften into a paste that can be used to fill (bind together) layer cakes, tortes, pastries, and bar and pinwheel cookies.

Recipe Uses   If you're searching for ways to use up a partial package of dates, you would do well to thumb through your favorite recipes for quick breads, cookies, fruit salads, steamed puddings, and confections.

How to Use Very Small Amounts   If you dice dates fine enough, you can stretch as little as ¼ to ½ cup of dates over a recipe for a dozen muffins. Small amounts of diced dates can also be added to almost any fruit-nut bread, as well as oatmeal, spice, or bar cookie. And when combined with an equal amount of pound cake or macaroon crumbs and just enough wine or fruit juice to bind the two together, they can be used to stuff peach or apricot halves or used to fill whole cored apples before they are baked. Small amounts of finely chopped dates can be kneaded into fondant along with an equal quantity of coarsely chopped pecans or walnuts. Finally, if you are one who likes the combination of fruit and chocolate, you might stir in whatever amount of dates you have left over (coarsely chopped but no more than 1 cup of them) into hot fudge along with the nuts.

N O T E   *For additional recipes, included elsewhere in this book, that call for varying amounts of dates, see the Appendix.*

D A T E   S C O N E S

8 servings

Dates should be used up as soon as possible so that they neither dry out nor become buggy. These scones will accommodate half a package of leftover dates, should you have that many on hand. They make a nice change for breakfast and are good served with honey, although a generous amount of butter is all that's needed.

2 cups sifted all-purpose flour
½ teaspoon baking soda
2 teaspoons baking powder
⅓ to ½ cup diced dates (or up to ½ package, if you should have them)
2 eggs
¼ to ⅓ cup milk
1 tablespoon maple or dark corn syrup
¼ cup (½ stick) butter
2 teaspoons granulated sugar

Preheat the oven to hot (400° F.).

Sift the flour, soda, and baking powder into a medium-sized mixing bowl; measure out ¼ cup of this mixture and toss with the dates in a small bowl (dredging the dates prevents them from clumping or sinking to the bottom of the scones as they bake). Break the eggs into a measuring cup, beat lightly with a fork, then spoon 2 tablespoonfuls of the beaten egg into a ramekin and reserve to use as a glaze. Add enough milk to the eggs in the measuring cup to total ¾ cup of liquid, then blend in the syrup.

Cut the butter into the dry ingredients until the texture of coarse meal; quickly add the combined liquids and stir lightly, just enough to moisten the dry ingredients. Stir in the dates and any remaining dredging flour. Knead the dough quickly once or twice on a lightly floured board—just until it holds together.

Divide the dough in half and shape each into a round about ½ inch thick and 6 to 7 inches across on a lightly greased baking sheet. With a sharp knife, quarter each round of dough, then separate the wedges slightly so that the heat can reach the cut edges. Brush each quarter with the egg glaze, then sprinkle with sugar. Bake in the preheated oven for 15 to 20 minutes, or until lightly browned.

Serve piping hot.

DATE-NUT PUDDING

6 servings

This is an old family recipe, and as good a way as we know to use up dates and bread crumbs.

    2 cups soft bread crumbs
    1 cup milk
    1 egg
    1 cup granulated sugar
    ⅛ teaspoon salt
    1 teaspoon baking powder
    1 cup pecans or walnuts, coarsely chopped
    1 cup pitted dates, coarsely chopped
    1 teaspoon vanilla extract

Put the crumbs and milk in a bowl and let stand for 20 minutes; meanwhile, preheat the oven to moderate (350° F.).

Beat the egg into the crumb mixture; combine the sugar, salt, and baking powder and mix in. Fold in the nuts and dates and, finally, the vanilla. Bake, uncovered, in a buttered 6-cup casserole in the preheated oven for about 1 hour.

Serve with whipped cream.

SPICY DATE-OATMEAL CLUSTERS

About 4 dozen cookies

These cookies are excellent keepers; moreover, they are more nutritious than most sweets because they contain dates, nuts, and oatmeal. Make them when you have a partial package of nuts and/or dates on hand (or, if you prefer, substitute raisins for the dates). Note that the recipe also calls for 1 cup of brown sugar (light or dark), so it's also a good way to use up "the rest of the box" before it hardens and dries.

    1 cup vegetable shortening
    **1 cup firmly packed light or dark brown sugar (or a combination of
      both)**
    2 eggs, beaten lightly

2 cups sifted all-purpose flour
1 teaspoon baking powder
½ teaspoon baking soda
½ teaspoon ground cinnamon
¼ teaspoon ground allspice
¼ teaspoon grated nutmeg
¼ teaspoon salt
2 cups rolled oats
1 cup coarsely chopped, pitted dates or 1 cup seedless raisins
1 cup coarsely chopped pecans, walnuts, blanched almonds, or filberts (whatever nuts you have on hand)
¼ cup milk

Preheat the oven to moderate (350° F.).

Cream the shortening and sugar until fluffy; mix in the eggs. Sift the flour with the baking powder, soda, spices, and salt; add the oatmeal, dates, and nuts and toss lightly to dredge. Stir the oatmeal mixture into the creamed mixture along with the milk. Drop from rounded teaspoonfuls onto greased baking sheets, spacing the cookies 1 inch apart, and bake in the preheated oven for 10 to 12 minutes, or until lightly browned.

Transfer the cookies at once to wire racks to cool.

D R I E D   A P R I C O T S :   See **Prunes and Other Dried Fruits.**

D R I E D   C U R R A N T S :   See **Raisins and Dried Currants.**

D R I E D   F R U I T S :   See **Prunes and Other Dried Fruits.**

Eggs

(Whites, Yolks, Hard-Cooked)

This section will be divided into three parts: egg whites, egg yolks, and hard-cooked eggs (which, believe it or not, can be a problem leftover if there is no one at your house who likes to eat eggs out of hand).

EGG WHITES

Best Way to Store In a tightly covered jar in the refrigerator (be sure to note on the jar the number of egg whites contained inside), but they can be frozen, too.

To Freeze The best way, we think, is to freeze each egg white separately, that is, to drop it into one of the little individual plastic ice-cube cups, to quick-freeze by setting directly on the freezer's freezing surface. As soon as the egg whites are frozen hard, remove them from the cups, bundle them into a plastic bag, seal, date, and label. The advantage of this method is obvious—1 cube = 1 egg white. If stored at 0° F., frozen egg whites will keep well for about 6 months. To use, allow the egg whites to come to room temperature, then use straightaway in any recipes calling for egg whites. Thawed, frozen egg whites spoil rapidly and, *no,* they should not be refrozen.

Maximum Storage Time 10 days in the refrigerator, 6 months if frozen.

Roles in Cooking So very many. Egg whites are the leavener of soufflés and angel food cakes; they are the thickeners of custards, soups, and sauces (1 egg white has approximately the same thickening power as 1 tablespoon of flour); they are the binders of croquettes and meat loaves (egg whites are almost pure protein, which coagulates as it heats, holding other ingredients in place); they serve as the clarifying agent for aspics, consommés, and coffees because they attract and hold stray particles like magic.

Egg whites provide a crisp coating for croquettes and other deep-fried foods (the egg white not only helps the breading to stick but also helps to seal out the fat so that the fried foods aren't greasy). Egg whites, lightly beaten, also help seal pie crusts so that liquid fillings don't seep in and make them soggy (particularly important for custard pies).

Egg whites, moreover, can be used to glaze breads, cookies, and pastries (1 egg white lightly beaten with 1 tablespoon cold water is the traditional proportion and enough to glaze a couple dozen cookies or several loaves of bread). And, finally, egg whites are a stabilizer, meaning that they help keep ice creams and sherbets smooth and creamy because they retard the formation of ice crystals—the culprits in "icy" ice creams.

Recipe Uses In addition to the recipes included in the pages that follow, consult these sections of your favorite recipe files or cookbooks for ideas on how to use up egg whites: omelets, soufflés, meringues, cakes, puddings, cookies, candies.

Special Comments Egg whites are a high-protein, low-calorie food (only 15 calories per large egg white). You may also be interested to know how many egg whites there are in 1 cup: 10 to 12, depending upon the size of the egg.

Tips Eggs will separate more easily if you let them stand at room temperature for about 30 minutes before cracking them. Also, egg whites can be beaten to far greater heights if they are brought to room temperature before they are beaten. You can further increase their volume (and the stability of the beaten whites) by adding a pinch of cream of tartar or a drop of lemon juice to the bowl of unbeaten whites.

How to Use Small Amounts You may safely add up to 3 additional egg whites to any omelet or soufflé, and an extra 1 or 2 to meringues (both pie meringues and meringue cookies). And, of course, you can easily slip an extra egg white or so into plain old-fashioned scrambled eggs. To achieve a chiffon effect, fold 1 to 2 egg whites, beaten to stiff peaks with about 2 teaspoons of sugar, into a stirred custard or not-quite-set gelatin dessert that has been whipped until fluffy.

EGG YOLKS

Best Way to Store Place in a glass jar, add just enough cool water to cover the yolks (it will actually float on top of them, sealing out air and preventing the yolks from drying), cover the jar tight and store in the refrigerator. Drain off the water before using the yolks. Also note on the jar the number of egg yolks inside the jar—this will be hard to determine if any of them should break.

To Freeze   Although some food experts insist that egg yolks cannot be frozen successfully, Cornell food researchers have proved that they can, provided they are prepared this way:

Measure the egg yolks, and for every ½ cup of them, lightly mix in 1½ teaspoons light corn syrup or sugar *or* ½ teaspoon salt (which you choose will determine to some extent how the yolks will ultimately be used—i.e., sweetened yolks should be reserved for sweets, salted yolks for savories). Pour the yolk mixture into a small freezer container, leaving ¼ inch of head space at the top; snap on the lid, date and label, noting how many egg yolks are inside, then quick-freeze by setting the container directly on the freezing surface of a freezer set at 0° F.

Of course, if you freeze as much as ½ cup of egg yolks at a time, you will be committed to a recipe that will use them up at one fell swoop (½ cup will equal 6 to 7 egg yolks), because once thawed the yolks should never be refrozen. Or, if you prefer, mix the egg yolks as directed above with sugar or salt, then apportion them, 1 to 2 yolks at a time, in individual plastic ice-cube cups, noting on each how many egg yolks are contained within. Once the egg yolks are frozen hard, remove from the cups and bundle snugly in a sturdy pliofilm freezer bag. Also note on the bag how many egg yolks each "cube" contains rather than trust to your memory.

Frozen egg yolks will keep well for about 3 months. To use, set the unopened container of yolks on the counter, bring to room temperature, then open and use the thawed yolks promptly in any recipes calling for egg yolks (no need to reduce the amount of sugar in recipes when using the sweetened yolks—they do not contain enough sugar to affect even the most critical recipe).

Maximum Storage Time   3 to 4 days refrigerated, about 3 months if frozen.

Roles in Cooking   Egg yolks aren't quite so versatile as egg whites, yet they are nonetheless one of a cook's best friends. They will, for example, thicken soups, sauces, and custards (2 egg yolks = the thickening power of 1 egg white or 1 tablespoon of flour); they will bind croquettes and meat loaves, they will help keep ice creams creamy-smooth. Egg yolks, moreover, can be used to glaze cookies, breads, and pastries (1 egg yolk beaten with 1 tablespoon cool water is the standard proportion; egg-yolk glaze, unlike egg-white glaze, adds a rich, amber color and a soft patina instead of a hard shine). Egg yolks also help to emulsify mayonnaises, hollandaises, and béarnaises (it gets them together and *keeps* them together). Finally, egg yolks add flavor, color, and creaminess to a wide range of soups, sauces, custards, and cream fillings.

Recipe Uses   Dozens and dozens. See the recipes that follow, also the soup, sauce, cake, cookie, frosting, and dessert sections of your favorite cookbooks and card files.

Special Comments   One of the most glorious custards imaginable is simply the classic recipe made entirely of egg yolks instead of with whole eggs (all you have to do is substitute 2 egg yolks for each whole egg and proceed as the recipe directs). A handy statistic: 12 to 14 egg yolks = 1 cup. As for calories, 1 large egg yolk = about 60 calories.

How to Use Small Amounts   An extra egg yolk or two can be added to any egg-thickened sauce, pudding, or filling (it will merely enrich the color and flavor and, of course, up the calorie count). You can also beat an extra yolk or two into an omelet or scrambled eggs.

HARD-COOKED EGGS

Best Way to Store   In a covered container in the refrigerator.

Maximum Storage Time   About 1 week if the eggs were fresh to begin with, 3 to 4 days if not.

Roles in Cooking   Hard-cooked eggs provide color and flavor, primarily (not to mention nutritive value). But when they are finely chopped, they also serve to thicken sauces, salad dressings, stuffings, meat or fish pies, puddings, and casseroles. Sliced or cut in fancy shapes, they make effective garnishes for meat and fish platters, for vegetables and molded salads.

Recipe Uses   See the recipe ideas that follow, then for more suggestions check the following categories in your recipe files and books: casseroles, molded salads, eggs and cheese, sandwich spreads, hors d'oeuvre, and party dips.

Special Comments   Two problems continually plague people when they deal with hard-cooked eggs: the eggs fail to peel neatly (or at all) and they often have an ugly, dark green layer between the yolk and the white. Fortunately, both difficulties are easily remedied.

The best way to make sure that hard-cooked eggs peel easily is to use eggs that are *not* spanking fresh—you'll have better luck peeling those that are a week to 10 days old. Second, as soon as the eggs are hard cooked, drain them, lightly crack the pointed ends, then immerse the eggs in a big bowl of ice water and keep them there until they are completely cold.

This ice bath, by the way, also helps prevent the formation of the dark green ring (nothing more than the combining of the iron in the yolk with the sulfur in the white into a harmless if unsightly compound called "ferrous sulfide"). Plunging the hot eggs into ice water stops the cooking and stabilizes the iron in the yolk and the sulfur in the white so that the two do not meet and merge. You'll also reduce the risk of the dark green ring forming if you cook the eggs at a slow simmer for 15 to 20 minutes instead of boiling them hard. Or if you start the eggs in just enough cold water to cover, bring them to a boil, then turn the heat off, cover the pan, and let the eggs stand in the hot water for 20 minutes.

N O T E   *For additional recipes, included elsewhere in this book, that call for varying amounts of egg whites, egg yolks, or hard-cooked eggs, see the Appendix.*

Egg Whites

C O C O A - C I N N A M O N R I P P L E   C O F F E E   C A K E

One 9-inch bundt cake

This makes a pretty company coffee cake, and it uses up three egg whites.

1½ cups granulated sugar
½ cup vegetable shortening
½ cup (1 stick) butter, cut in pats and brought to room temperature
3 cups sifted all-purpose flour
1 tablespoon (3 teaspoons) baking powder
½ teaspoon salt

1 cup milk
1 teaspoon vanilla extract
3 egg whites, beaten to soft peaks

RIPPLE MIXTURE

¼ cup granulated sugar or granulated brown sugar
1 tablespoon cocoa powder (not a mix)
1 tablespoon ground cinnamon
¼ cup very finely minced walnuts, pecans, or blanched almonds
(optional)

Preheat the oven to moderate (350° F.).

Cream the sugar with the shortening and butter until fluffy-light. Sift the flour with the baking powder and salt and add to the creamed mixture alternately with the milk (begin and end with sifted dry ingredients). Stir in the vanilla, then fold in the beaten egg whites. Combine all the ripple mixture ingredients and keep separate.

Pour one-third of the batter into a well-greased and floured 9-inch (12-cup) bundt pan, add one-third of the ripple mixture, and swirl lightly into the batter with a spoon. Add another third each of the batter and ripple mixture and swirl as before; repeat once more. Bake in the preheated oven for 1¼ to 1½ hours, or until the cake pulls from sides of pan and is springy to the touch.

Cool the cake upright in its pan for 15 minutes, then loosen around the edges and turn out.

TUTTI-FRUTTI MERINGUES

About 2 dozen

Because these cookies are essentially "dried out" rather than baked, you can—and, indeed *should*—cook the whole 2 dozen of them at once. If the meringue batter stands more than a few minutes at room temperature, it will begin to thin, thanks to the oil in the grated orange rind, which breaks down the beaten egg whites. You can accommodate all of the meringues on two baking sheets, so simply switch their position halfway through baking; that is, put the sheet on the lower shelf above —and vice versa.

Don't attempt this recipe on a rainy or humid day, as the meringues will quickly take on moisture from the air and become soft and sticky.

    4 egg whites
    1 cup granulated sugar, sifted
    ½ teaspoon vinegar or lemon juice
    1 teaspoon vanilla extract
    ½ cup chopped walnuts or pecans
    ½ cup chopped seedless or sultana raisins
    1 tablespoon finely grated orange rind

Preheat the oven to very slow (275° F.).

Beat the egg whites to soft peaks, then add the sifted sugar gradually, beating all the while, until the whites are very stiff. Add the vinegar and vanilla, a few drops at a time, and beat in also. Very gently fold in the nuts, raisins, and orange rind.

Drop the meringue mixture from a teaspoon onto baking sheets that have been lined with aluminum foil (shiny side down), spacing the cookies about 2 inches apart. Bake in the preheated oven for 25 to 30 minutes, or until the meringues are crisp and dry and faintly tinged with color.

Cool and store airtight.

ALMOND TUILES (TILES)

About 3 dozen cookies

So many recipes call for either egg yolks or whites that the "other half of the egg" becomes a frequent and tiresome leftover. What to do with them? Well, these fragile French cookies will take care of 4 egg whites. Do not attempt to make these cookies in humid weather because they will absorb moisture and be difficult to handle.

    4 egg whites
    1 cup granulated sugar
    ½ teaspoon almond extract
    ½ cup sifted all-purpose flour

¼ cup (½ stick) butter, melted and cooled to room temperature (do not substitute margarine)
1 cup finely ground blanched almonds

Preheat the oven to moderate (350° F.). Cover two to three baking sheets with foil, shiny side up, and brush well with cooking oil.

Beat the egg whites to soft peaks, then add the sugar, 1 tablespoon at a time, beating hard after each addition. Add the almond extract and beat the whites to stiff peaks. Fold the flour in alternately with the butter, beginning and ending with the flour, then gently fold in the ground almonds.

Drop the mixture by well-rounded teaspoonfuls onto the foil-covered baking sheets, then, with the back of a spoon, spread into circles about 3 inches in diameter. (These cookies spread considerably as they cook, so allow 5 inches between each.) Bake on the center rack of the preheated oven for 10 to 12 minutes, or until the cookies are golden.

Remove the cookies from the oven and cool on the foil for a few *seconds,* then, using a pancake turner, lift from the foil and curl over a rolling pin or, for a tighter curl, around the handle of a wooden spoon. When firm, carefully transfer to wire racks to cool.

Store the *tuiles* airtight.

N O T E   *If the cookies harden too quickly to shape, return to the oven for a minute to soften.*

UPSIDE-DOWN NUT CAKE

One 9-inch, 2-layer cake

Because the egg whites are added to this cake *unbeaten,* it is a good way to use whites that have had a bit of yolk dropped into them by mistake. The 2½ tablespoons of baking powder called for are more than we're accustomed to using in a cake, but they're necessary for high, light layers.

1 cup finely chopped walnuts, pecans, blanched almonds, or filberts
2½ cups sifted all-purpose flour
2½ tablespoons baking powder

C O N T I N U E D

1 teaspoon salt
1½ cups granulated sugar
⅓ cup vegetable shortening
⅓ cup (5⅓ tablespoons) butter, at room temperature
1¼ cups milk
1 teaspoon vanilla extract
⅔ cup egg whites (unbeaten)
Juice and finely grated rind of 1 lemon

Preheat the oven to moderate (350° F.). Grease and flour two 9-inch layer cake pans well, then divide the nuts between them, covering the bottoms well.

Sift the flour, baking powder, salt, and sugar into a mixing bowl; add the shortening, butter, milk, and vanilla and beat for 1 minute at medium mixer speed, or until well blended. Add the egg whites and lemon juice and rind and beat for 1½ minutes longer.

Spoon the batter into the prepared pans, taking care not to disturb the nuts. Bake in the preheated oven for 35 to 40 minutes, or until the layers have pulled from the sides of the pans and are springy to the touch. Cool the layers for 15 to 20 minutes in their pans before inverting and turning out.

Put the layers together (each nut-side up) with your favorite frosting and/or filling. Seafoam is particularly good, or you might use a rum-spiked vanilla pudding as the filling and a simple lemon glaze on top.

Egg Yolks

NUT-CREAM SOUP

4 to 6 servings

Having a little sour cream or a single egg yolk left over is a fine excuse for making this delicate, old-fashioned soup.

3½ to 4 cups chicken and/or beef bouillon or stock (or 2 cans, 13¼ ounces each)
2 tablespoons butter or margarine
2 tablespoons all-purpose flour

1½ cups finely ground blanched almonds or a combination of almonds and walnuts
1 egg yolk, beaten lightly
3 to 4 tablespoons sour cream (or even as much as ½ cup if that is
the amount you have)
2 to 3 tablespoons dry sherry
Salt and freshly ground black pepper to taste

Heat the bouillon slowly over moderately low heat in a small saucepan. In another, medium-sized saucepan set over low heat, melt the
butter and blend in the flour to form a smooth paste. Add the hot
bouillon slowly, stirring vigorously, and continue heating and stirring
for 3 to 5 minutes, until slightly thickened and no raw, floury taste
remains. Add the nuts and simmer slowly, uncovered, for 20 minutes.

Remove from the heat and cool for 30 minutes, then purée in an
electric blender or a food processor fitted with a metal chopping blade,
or press the mixture through a fine sieve. Whisk in the egg yolk, sour
cream, and sherry; season to taste.

Return to low heat and bring just to serving temperature. Or chill
well and serve cold.

FLAKY EGG PIE CRUST

*Enough for two 9- or 10-inch single-crust pies
or 8 turnovers (5 to 6 inches in diameter)*

This more-or-less foolproof, rich and tender pastry is made with 2 egg
yolks and can be used in place of the more traditional pastry for all
manner of pies and turnovers. The egg yolks add color and flavor to
the pastry, and because of their fat and protein content, they make it
short yet easy to shape.

2¾ cups sifted all-purpose flour
¾ teaspoon salt
²/₃ cup lard or vegetable shortening or a half-and-half mixture of each
2 egg yolks, beaten lightly with ½ cup cold water
1 tablespoon cider vinegar or lemon juice

Combine the flour and salt in a large mixing bowl; cut in the lard
until crumbly, about the texture of oatmeal. Combine the yolk mixture

and cider vinegar and drizzle over the fat-flour mixture, tossing lightly with a fork just until the ingredients hold together. Divide in half and roll as you would any favorite pastry for top and/or bottom crusts or for turnovers.

S A B L É S

About 1½ dozen cookies

Two egg yolks go into this cookie dough and another one into the glaze brushed over them before they are baked. These cookies are an old Norman specialty, traditionally fan-shaped, glossy and tan but not very sweet.

½ cup unsalted butter, at room temperature (do not substitute margarine)
⅓ cup granulated sugar
1½ cups sifted all-purpose flour
¼ teaspoon salt
2 egg yolks, beaten lightly
1 teaspoon finely grated lemon rind or 1 teaspoon vanilla extract

T O P P I N G

1 egg yolk, beaten lightly with 1 teaspoon cold water
Confectioners sugar

Cream the butter until light and blend in the sugar. Combine the flour and salt and add to the creamed mixture alternately with the egg yolks; stir in the rind or vanilla. Knead and squeeze the dough in the bowl until very smooth and no grains of sugar are discernible between your fingers (the dough will be quite soft). Wrap the dough and chill for 3 hours, or until firm enough to roll.

Preheat the oven to moderately hot (375° F.).

Roll out a small portion of the dough at a time on a lightly floured board to a thickness of ¼ inch. Using a round 5- to 6-inch cookie cutter, cut the dough into circles, then quarter each circle, forming four wedges. Transfer gently to lightly greased and floured baking sheets, spacing the cookies 1 inch apart. Prick each cookie well with a fork, brush with egg glaze, and sift a little confectioners sugar on top. Bake in the preheated oven for 10 minutes, or until the cookies are light tan, not brown.

Transfer at once to wire racks to cool, then store the cooled cookies airtight.

VARIATION

Almond Sablés Reduce the amount of flour in the cookie dough to 1⅓ cups and add ¼ cup finely ground blanched almonds, mixing in along with the flour. To flavor, use 1 teaspoon vanilla and ¼ teaspoon almond extract. Otherwise, mix, roll, and bake the cookies as directed.

BOILED DRESSING

1½ cups

If you find this dressing a bit tart (because of your brand of vinegar, perhaps), add a little honey to mellow it. If you would like to use the dressing on fruit, add, in addition to the honey, about ½ cup of heavy cream that has been whipped to soft peaks. This dressing will keep well in the refrigerator in a tightly covered jar for a week to 10 days (without the additional whipped cream). Once the whipped cream has been added, use within 3 to 4 days.

> 2 tablespoons all-purpose flour
> 2 tablespoons granulated sugar
> 1 teaspoon salt
> 1 teaspoon dry mustard
> ⅛ teaspoon cayenne pepper
> 2 to 3 egg yolks, beaten lightly (if you have 2 yolks on hand, use 2; if 3 yolks, use 3)
> ¾ cup milk, evaporated milk, light cream, or half-and-half
> 2 tablespoons butter or margarine, at room temperature

CONTINUED

¾ cup cider vinegar
2 to 3 teaspoons celery seeds, to taste
1 to 3 tablespoons honey, or to taste (optional)
½ cup heavy cream, whipped (optional)

In the top of a double boiler, combine the flour, sugar, salt, mustard, and cayenne. Mix in the egg yolks, milk, and butter and set over barely simmering water, then add the vinegar slowly, stirring constantly. Continue to heat and stir until thick. Remove from the heat and mix in the celery seeds and, if you like, the honey and whipped cream.

WALNUT SHORTCAKES

3 dozen

This recipe is a fine example of taking something that won't keep (egg yolks) and turning it into something that will. Put these cookies in a good tight tin and they'll keep for a month.

1 cup (2 sticks) butter, cut in chunks and brought to room temperature
⅔ cup granulated sugar
3 egg yolks
3 cups sifted all-purpose flour
½ cup finely ground walnuts
1 to 2 tablespoons lemon juice (optional)

TOPPING

½ cup confectioners sugar
1 teaspoon ground cinnamon
¼ teaspoon ground mace

Preheat the oven to moderately slow (325° F.).

Cream the butter and sugar well, then beat in the egg yolks. Gradually add the flour, mixing well after each addition. Add the ground nuts and, if needed, the lemon juice to make a pliable dough.

Pinch off pieces of dough big enough to make balls the size of walnuts. Space the balls about 2 inches apart on ungreased baking sheets, flatten slightly with the back of a spoon, then bake in the preheated oven for 10 to 15 minutes, or just until firm.

Quickly combine all the topping ingredients, then roll the short-cakes in the topping while they are still warm.

MOCHA ICE CREAM SAUCE

About 2½ cups

There is no better way to thicken a sauce, pudding, or pie filling than by using egg yolks, which add a smoothness and richness never achieved with flour. This egg-yolk sauce would be a sensible (and delicious) complement to an egg-white cake—and, of course, it's also delicious with ice cream.

> ½ cup granulated sugar
> 1 tablespoon cocoa powder (not a mix)
> 3 egg yolks, beaten well
> 2 tablespoons strong coffee
> ¼ cup bourbon or light rum
> 1 cup heavy cream, whipped to stiff peaks

Combine the sugar and cocoa in the top of a double boiler, pressing out all lumps, then blend in the beaten yolks, coffee, and bourbon. Set over simmering water and heat, stirring constantly, until the mixture thickens—this will take about 10 minutes. Remove the sauce from the heat and cool to room temperature, stirring occasionally, then fold in the whipped cream.

Store the sauce in the refrigerator.

PYTT I PANNA (SWEDISH HASH)

6 servings

We first tasted this wonderful dish toward the end of a Copenhagen–New York flight aboard Scandinavian Airlines and were delighted when the hostess passed out printed copies of the recipe so we could try it back home. It is a perfectly splendid way to use up 6 egg yolks, not to mention a good bit of leftover roast beef or lamb and smoked ham.

    4 tablespoons (½ stick) butter or margarine
    3 tablespoons vegetable oil
    6 medium potatoes, peeled and cut in ¼-inch cubes
    2 medium yellow onions, peeled and coarsely chopped
    2 cups diced cold roast beef or lamb (or a combination of the two)
    1 cup diced cold smoked or boiled ham
    Salt and freshly ground black pepper to taste
    2 tablespoons finely minced fresh parsley
    6 egg yolks

Warm 2 tablespoons each of the butter and oil in a large, heavy skillet set over moderately high heat. Add the potatoes, turn the heat to moderately low, and stir-fry for about 20 minutes, or until the potatoes are tender and richly browned; transfer them to a large bowl and set aside for the moment.

Add the remaining 2 tablespoons of butter and 1 tablespoon of oil to the skillet; add the onion and stir-fry over moderate heat for 8 to 10 minutes, until limp and golden. Raise the heat slightly, add the beef and ham, and stir-fry with the onions for about 10 minutes, shaking the skillet often so the meat browns evenly. Return the potatoes to the skillet and stir-fry a few minutes with the meats and onions, just until good and hot. Season to taste with salt and pepper.

Dish the hash up on six plates. Make a depression in the center of each portion, sprinkle lightly with parsley, then ease a raw egg yolk into each depression and serve straightaway.

ZABAGLIONE ALLA MARSALA

6 servings

If you have made an angel food cake or meringues and are left with as many as 8 egg yolks, this fluffy Italian dessert will use every last one of them.

    1 cup granulated sugar
    2 whole eggs plus 8 egg yolks

¼ cup Marsala wine
Pinch of salt

Combine all the ingredients in a double boiler top about four times the volume of the combined ingredients (2½ to 3 quarts is a good size because the *zabaglione* will mount to stratospheric heights as it cooks). Set the double boiler top over simmering—*not boiling*—water, then beat constantly with a hand electric mixer set at low speed until the mixture fluffs up, turns pale yellow, and has the consistency of sponge cake batter—this will take about 15 minutes, so have patience.

Spoon the hot *zabaglione* into stemmed goblets or serve as a sauce over angel, pound, chiffon, or sponge cake. Or, better yet, ladle over fresh strawberries, raspberries, or sliced peaches.

Hard-Cooked Eggs

TUNA, ALMOND, AND EGG CASSEROLE

6 servings

Casseroles, perhaps better than any other single recipe category, are the perfect way to use up all sorts of leftovers. This particular casserole proves the point: it takes care of from 2 to 4 hard-cooked eggs, ¼ to ¾ cup of blanched almonds (either raw or toasted), ¼ to ½ cup of capers, and 2 cups of egg noodles. You might also add up to 2 tablespoons of anchovy paste (but *if* you do, eliminate all salt from the recipe), up to 2 tablespoons of minced pimiento, up to ⅓ cup of minced ripe or pimiento-stuffed olives, up to 1 cup of grated Cheddar or Gruyère, and up to 1½ cups of such leftover cooked vegetables as green peas or limas or coarsely chopped broccoli, cauliflower, asparagus, or green beans. Simply improvise with whatever leftovers you have at hand.

CONTINUED

2 medium yellow onions, peeled and coarsely chopped

3 medium ribs celery, trimmed, washed, and chopped

6 tablespoons (¾ stick) butter or margarine

¼ teaspoon crumbled leaf thyme

¼ teaspoon crumbled leaf marjoram

6 tablespoons all-purpose flour

2¾ cups milk or a combination of milk, evaporated milk, or cream (light, heavy, or half-and-half)

¾ teaspoon salt

⅛ teaspoon freshly ground black pepper

2 to 4 hard-cooked eggs, peeled and coarsely chopped

¼ to ¾ cup moderately finely chopped blanched raw or toasted almonds (or pecans, peanuts, or walnuts)

1 can (13 ounces) white tuna, drained and flaked

Juice of 1 lemon

¼ cup minced fresh parsley

¼ to ½ cup drained small capers (if you use ½ cup, eliminate the lemon juice from the recipe)

2 cups egg noodles, cooked according to package directions and drained well

TOPPING

2 slices whole-wheat or white bread, buzzed in a blender or processor or broken into fairly fine crumbs

2 tablespoons melted butter

Preheat the oven to moderate (350° F.).

Stir-fry the onions and celery in 2 tablespoons of the butter in a large, heavy skillet over moderate heat for 8 to 10 minutes, until golden but still crisp. Blend in the thyme and marjoram and remove from the heat.

Melt the remaining 4 tablespoons of butter in a medium-sized heavy saucepan over moderate heat; blend in the flour to make a smooth paste, then add the milk and heat, stirring constantly, for about 5 minutes, or until thickened and smooth. Stir in the salt and pepper.

Empty the reserved onion mixture into a large mixing bowl. Add the hot sauce and all the remaining ingredients except the topping and toss well to mix. Transfer to a lightly buttered 3-quart casserole. Prepare the topping by tossing the bread crumbs well with the butter, then scatter on top of the tuna mixture. Bake, uncovered, in the preheated oven for 45 minutes to 1 hour, or until bubbling and lightly browned.

Serve at once.

CURRIED EGGS

2 to 4 servings

It happens, sometimes, that you've a couple of hard-cooked eggs on hand—perhaps more—that you don't know what to do with. With us, it's when we've resolved to diet, boiled up a batch of eggs to eat, one at a time, for breakfast or lunch, then grown so weary of them that we splurge by stirring the balance of hard-cooked eggs into this easy, relatively low-calorie curry (about 250 calories per serving made with 4 eggs, but served *without* rice or toast).

2 tablespoons butter or margarine
1 large yellow onion, peeled and minced
1 small clove garlic, peeled and minced
1 tablespoon minced fresh gingerroot (optional)
1 to 2 tablespoons curry powder (depending upon how strong you like your curry)
5 tablespoons all-purpose flour
2 cups milk
2 to 4 hard-cooked eggs, peeled and minced
2 tablespoons cider vinegar

Melt the butter in a heavy saucepan over moderate heat; add the onion, garlic, and, if you like, the ginger and stir-fry for 8 to 10 minutes, until limp and golden. Blend in the curry powder and mellow over moderate heat for 2 to 3 minutes, or until no raw curry taste remains.

Blend in the flour and work over the heat for 2 to 3 minutes to form a thick roux. Add the milk and heat, stirring constantly, until thickened and smooth. Reduce the heat to its lowest point, add the minced hard-cooked eggs, and heat for 3 to 5 minutes, stirring now and then.

Mix in the vinegar and serve as is, or over boiled rice or crisp, dry toast.

BIFES ENROLADOS (BRAZILIAN BEEF ROLLS STUFFED WITH HARD-COOKED EGGS AND OLIVES)

4 servings

An absolutely sensational way to utilize leftover hard-cooked eggs, beef broth, ripe olives, nuts, and, if you have it on hand, a dab of tomato paste. The egg filling alone makes an excellent cocktail or sandwich spread.

> 4 very thin slices round steak, pounded thin as for scaloppine (after pounding, the slices should measure 8 to 9 inches long, 4 to 5 wide, and ⅛ inch thick)
> 1 clove garlic, peeled and quartered lengthwise
> ½ cup Madeira or Port
> 4 tissue-thin slices prosciutto ham, cut to fit the beef slices
> 2 tablespoons butter
> ¾ to 1 cup beef broth
> 1 to 2 tablespoons tomato paste (optional)
> ⅛ teaspoon freshly ground black pepper
> Salt to taste
> 2 tablespoons all-purpose flour, blended with ¼ cup cold water

FILLING

> 3 hard-cooked eggs, peeled (sieve the yolks and mince the whites very fine)
> 2 tablespoons butter or margarine, at room temperature
> 1½ teaspoons Dijon or spicy brown mustard
> 3 to 5 tablespoons minced pitted ripe olives or pimiento-stuffed green olives
> ¼ cup finely minced blanched almonds, peanuts, or pignoli (pine nuts) (optional)
> 1 tablespoon minced fresh or frozen chives
> 1 tablespoon minced fresh parsley
> Several grindings of black pepper

Rub each piece of beef with garlic, then place both beef and garlic in a shallow baking dish; add the wine and marinate for 2 hours at room temperature, turning the beef occasionally.

Meanwhile, prepare the filling by blending all the ingredients with a fork until pastelike.

To shape the beef rolls, remove the slices from the marinade (reserve it) and top each with a prosciutto slice. Spread with a thin layer of egg mixture, leaving narrow margins at the sides and about 1½ to 2 inches at one end. Roll up, jelly-roll style, toward the unspread end; fasten with wooden picks.

Brown the beef rolls in the butter in a large, heavy, deep skillet over moderately high heat. Add the reserved marinade and garlic, then lower the heat until the mixture simmers very slowly. Cover and cook for 2 to 2½ hours, until the beef rolls are tender. Turn the rolls in the skillet several times as they cook.

Remove the beef rolls from the skillet and keep warm; discard the garlic. Add the beef broth, tomato paste (if you like), pepper, and salt to taste and boil, uncovered, for about 10 minutes, to reduce slightly. Blend a little of the skillet liquid into the flour paste; stir back into the skillet, then heat, stirring constantly, until thickened and smooth—about 3 minutes. Remove the wooden picks from the beef rolls and discard; return the beef rolls to the skillet, cover, and simmer in the gravy for 10 minutes.

Serve on a bed of cooked rice topped with some of the gravy (pass the remaining gravy separately).

EVAPORATED MILK : See **Milk.**

FIGS : See **Prunes and Other Dried Fruits.**

Flours

(Whole-Grain)

The trouble with whole-wheat flour (also called graham flour), buckwheat, rye, bran, and other whole-grain flours is—from the storage standpoint, at least—precisely that they *are* whole, meaning they contain the oil-rich germ, which absorbs and holds atmospheric odors and, if improperly stored, becomes rancid rather quickly. About the smallest quantity in which you can buy whole-grain flours is the 2-pound bag (approximately 8 cups). So, unless you're into baking in a heavy way, you're bound to have leftovers.

Best Way to Store   Weevils, ants, roaches, and mice all dote upon whole-grain flours, so we recommend storing them in half- or full-gallon preserving jars with lids that can be sealed airtight. Store the jars of flour on a cool, dark, dry shelf and be sure to wipe the outside of the jar each time you remove flour (be sure, too, to wipe up any light spills or dustings of flour on your cupboard shelves).

Maximum Storage Time   About 2 to 3 months, or until a flour begins to taste "off" or stale.

Roles in Cooking   To form the framework of breads, crackers, steamed puddings, and so on; to impart a delicate nutlike flavor; to add texture to food (and roughage to the diet); and, finally, to supply valuable nutrients (principally B vitamins and vegetable protein).

Recipe Uses   It is with breads that you can put whole grains to the best use, particularly the rough country breads of Scandinavia, Germany, Austria, Hungary, Czechoslovakia, Poland, and Russia. A number of drop cookies also call for whole-grain flours, as do certain pancakes, and steamed puddings and breads.

How to Use Very Small Amounts   You can safely substitute up to ½ cup of whole-grain flour for all-purpose flour in streusel toppings, in bar cookies, in oatmeal and peanut butter cookies, even in muffins, biscuits, and pancakes, provided the total amount of flour is at least 2 cups.

N O T E *For additional recipes, included elsewhere in this book, that call for varying amounts of whole-grain flours, see the Appendix.*

HONEY-WHOLE-WHEAT ROLLS

About 1½ dozen

If you like to bake bread and have experimented with recipes calling for different kinds of flours, you know that those flours are packaged in quantities too large to use up at once unless you bake in a big way. You also know that whole-wheat flours quickly stale (because of the oils in the germ) and that they attract ants and weevils. An excellent way to use up some of the leftover flour is to make these easy, healthful rolls. They require no kneading and they freeze well.

  ¾ cup scalded milk
  3 tablespoons vegetable shortening
  ¼ cup honey or sugar (granulated or light or dark brown)
  1 teaspoon salt
  ¼ cup cool water
  1 package active dry yeast
  1 egg
  2 cups sifted all-purpose flour
  1 cup *unsifted* whole-wheat or graham flour
  ¾ cup chopped pecans, walnuts, peanuts, or almonds

In a large mixing bowl combine the milk, shortening, honey, and salt and stir until the shortening melts; add the water, then the yeast, and stir until the yeast dissolves. Mix in the egg. Combine the flours and nuts and mix into the yeast mixture, a cup at a time. Mix hard until the dough is springy.

Pinch off bits of dough with floured hands and roll into balls about the size of large marbles; place three balls in each cup of greased muffin pans to form cloverleaf rolls. Cover the rolls with a clean, dry cloth and let rise in a warm, dry, draft-free spot until doubled in bulk—about 1 hour.

Toward the end of the rising time, preheat the oven to hot (400° F.); bake the rolls in the preheated oven for 20 minutes, or until they are nicely browned and sound hollow when thumped.

Serve warm, with plenty of fresh butter.

RYE MUFFINS

About 1 dozen

1 cup sifted all-purpose flour
1 cup *unsifted* rye flour
2½ teaspoons baking powder
¼ cup granulated sugar
½ teaspoon salt
¼ cup melted shortening or vegetable oil
1 egg, beaten lightly
1 cup milk

Preheat the oven to hot (400° F.).

Combine the flours, baking powder, sugar, and salt in a mixing bowl and make a well in the center. In a separate bowl, combine the melted shortening, egg, and milk, then pour all at once into the well in the dry ingredients. Stir briskly but lightly, just enough to combine the liquid and dry ingredients—no longer or your muffins may be tough and filled with tunnels.

Spoon the batter into well-greased muffin-pan cups, filling each no more than two-thirds full. Bake in the preheated oven for about 25 minutes, or until the muffins are lightly browned and feel springy to the touch.

Serve oven-hot, with plenty of butter and jam or marmalade.

STEAMED APPLESAUCE BREAD

Four 1-pound loaves

So few of us make steamed breads these days, and yet they are so very easy. This one is a superlative way to use up 1½ cups of whole-wheat or graham flour that you may have left over from a bread-baking session, as well as ½ cup of corn meal and ⅔ to ¾ cup of leftover applesauce. The best containers we've found for steaming the bread are simply 1-pound cans—the size many fruits and vegetables are packed in.

These loaves freeze beautifully, by the way (directions for freezing are included at the end of the recipe).

1 cup sifted all-purpose flour
1½ cups *unsifted* graham or whole-wheat flour
½ cup yellow or white corn meal
1 teaspoon salt
1 teaspoon baking powder
1 teaspoon baking soda
¼ cup honey
¾ cup molasses
1²/₃ cups milk
²/₃ to ¾ cup applesauce
1 cup seedless raisins or dried currants

Combine the flours, corn meal, salt, baking powder, and soda in a large mixing bowl; make a well in the center. In a separate bowl, combine the honey, molasses, milk, and applesauce, then add all at once to the dry ingredients and stir briskly to mix. Stir in the raisins.

Grease four 1-pound cans well, then fill each two-thirds full of batter. Cover snugly with several thicknesses of aluminum foil and tie around the tops with string to seal. Place a rack in the bottom of a deep kettle (one with a snug-fitting lid), pour in 1 to 1½ inches of boiling water (it should not come above the level of the rack), then stand the four sealed cans on the rack (not touching); cover the kettle and steam for 3 hours. (If at any time the kettle should threaten to boil dry, add more boiling water.)

When the breads have steamed for 3 hours, remove from the kettle and cool upright in their cans for 20 minutes. Uncover, ease the breads out of the cans, and cool to room temperature before slicing.

Delicious spread with cream cheese.

To Freeze   Wrap the cooled loaves individually in aluminum foil, pressing out all the air pockets; label, date, and store in a freezer set at 0° F. Keeping time: about 6 months.

Whenever you want a slice or slices of the steamed applesauce bread, simply cut off the amount you need, using a serrated knife. Rewrap the balance and return to the freezer.

Ginger

(Fresh, Candied, and Preserved)

Not until recently, with our mounting curiosity about the cuisines of China, has fresh ginger become a supermarket item. These gnarled, fawn-skinned roots of the ginger plant may not yet have reached your community, but in big-city groceries across the country they are almost as routine an item as the tomato. They are rarely lavishly displayed, it's true—they are, after all, a specialty and, quite frankly, not particularly pretty. But for cooking they are magnificent—crisp, lemony, slightly sweet but with plenty of bite, too. Ground ginger pales in comparison.

Better substitutes, should you be unable to buy fresh ginger, are preserved ginger (packed in syrup in small bottles) and candied (crystallized or Canton ginger, stocked by most good candy stores). These, to be sure, are sweet. But it's a simple enough matter to rinse off all syrup or sugar.

Best Way to Store Fresh ginger should be tightly wrapped in plastic food wrap and stored in the refrigerator. It should not be washed or peeled—both will shorten its shelf life. As for preserved ginger, any opened bottles should be refrigerated. Candied ginger should simply be stored airtight at room temperature.

To Freeze We have had great success freezing fresh ginger, and here's the way we do it. Do not wash or peel the gingerroot, but do trim off all small or wizened nubs so that you have a more-or-less uniform piece. This is simply to make wrapping easier. Now wrap the trimmed ginger snugly in either aluminum foil or plastic food wrap and seal airtight with freezer tape. Date and label and set directly on the freezing surface of your freezer. When frozen, transfer to some spot in the freezer where the ginger (a small packet) won't get lost. To use, unwrap, then, using a sharp knife, cut off whatever amount of ginger you need; rewrap the balance airtight and return to the freezer. Frozen ginger keeps well for about 4 months at 0° F.

Maximum Storage Times   About 3 to 4 weeks in the refrigerator for fresh ginger (4 months in the freezer), 3 months for preserved ginger, and, depending upon humidity, 3 to 4 months for candied ginger. In overly dry seasons or in superheated apartments, candied ginger will dry brick-hard; in humid weather, it will become gummy and susceptible to mold. If candied ginger hardens, it can be slivered and teamed with fresh fruit compotes or added to skillet dishes (it will absorb moisture and plump right up). Gummy ginger is more difficult to deal with, but it, too, can be mixed into fruit salads and Oriental stir-fried recipes.

N O T E   *Once fresh, candied, or preserved ginger molds, discard it.*

Roles in Cooking   To add flavor, texture, and bite (piquancy). Preserved and candied ginger are used primarily to decorate pastries, cakes, cookies, and candies, but these trimmings are as much for flavor as for show.

Recipe Uses   Fresh ginger is integral to East Indian curries and chutneys, to dozens of Chinese recipes (particularly the spicier dishes of Hunan and Szechuan). The English brew fresh ginger into beer and add bits of candied or preserved ginger to steamed puddings, fruit cakes, and compotes.

How to Use Very Small Amounts   A 1-inch cube of fresh ginger, finely minced, is a tantalizing addition to a pound of ground beef, lamb, or ham that is to be made into a meat loaf. The same quantity will spark the flavor of almost any beef or lamb stew or casserole, and it will add dash to a pound of glazed carrots or a casserole of candied sweet potatoes or winter squash.

And what about leftover candied or preserved ginger? Try folding 1 to 2 tablespoons of finely minced candied or preserved ginger into 1 cup of heavy cream that has been stiffly whipped into a dessert topping. Or scatter 2 to 3 tablespoons of candied or preserved ginger into an apple, peach, or pear pie, crisp, or cobbler. And for a marvelous, almost instant dessert, fold 2 to 4 tablespoons of finely minced or slivered preserved or candied ginger into a pint of mushy vanilla ice cream (or orange, lemon, or lime sherbet) and refreeze. What could be easier?

N O T E   *For additional recipes, included elsewhere in this book, that call for varying amounts of fresh, candied, and preserved ginger, see the Appendix.*

GINGER-GLAZED CARROTS

4 servings

1 pound carrots, peeled and coarsely shredded
¼ cup water
3 tablespoons butter or margarine
1 cube (1 inch) fresh gingerroot, peeled and minced very fine
Juice of ½ lemon
3 tablespoons orange marmalade or tart fruit jelly
Salt and freshly ground black pepper to taste

Place the carrots, water, butter, and ginger in a medium-sized heavy saucepan and bring to a gentle simmer over moderately low heat. Cover and cook for about 15 minutes, or until the carrots are quite tender. Add the lemon juice and marmalade and heat and stir for 3 to 5 minutes over moderately high heat, just until most of the pan liquid has evaporated and the carrots are nicely glazed.

Season to taste with salt and pepper and serve.

SZECHUAN DRY-SAUTÉED BROCCOLI

4 servings

Szechuan is to Chinese cooking what Tex-Mex is to American, that is to say, plenty hot and spicy. Now that Szechuan restaurants are proliferating over much of the United States, most of us have tasted the Szechuan specialties and found the Cantonese to be bland by comparison. What makes Szechuan food so hot is a liberal use, not only of red peppers, but also of fresh ginger.

The most popular—and successful—Szechuan way to prepare vegetables, particularly green beans and broccoli, is to dry-sauté them, that is, to stir-fry them in the barest minimum of oil. And what about leftover broccoli stems, since this recipe uses only the tender florets? Save them to add to soup or to boil, purée, and serve another time; if wrapped in plastic food wrap and stored in the refrigerator, the stems will keep well for about a week.

1 medium clove garlic, peeled and minced

1 cube (1 to 1½ inches) fresh gingerroot, peeled and minced

⅛ teaspoon crushed dried red chili peppers (¼ teaspoon if you like things really hot)

2 tablespoons peanut or vegetable oil

1 large bunch of broccoli, washed, trimmed, and divided into small florets

1 teaspoon granulated sugar

3 tablespoons water

1 tablespoon dry sherry or Port

2 tablespoons soy sauce

Stir-fry the garlic, ginger, and chili peppers in the oil in a very large, heavy skillet or wok over moderately high heat for about 3 minutes, or until the garlic and ginger are golden but not brown. Add the broccoli and sugar and stir-fry for 1 to 2 minutes, or until the broccoli turns bright green. Mix in the water, sherry, and soy sauce, then cover and steam the broccoli for about 5 minutes—just until crisp-tender.

Toss well and serve.

N O T E   *Broccoli prepared this way is particularly good with broiled chicken, chops, or steak.*

VARIATION

Dry-Sautéed Green Beans   First of all, buy 1 pound of the youngest, tenderest green beans you can find. Wash them well, then tip them but leave them whole. From here on out, the cooking procedure is precisely the same as for the broccoli (above), except that you may need to stir-fry the beans slightly longer (say for 3 to 5 minutes). Taste a bean after 3 minutes of sautéing—it should still have plenty of crunch but should not taste dead raw. If it does taste raw, stir-fry 1 to 2 minutes longer.

You may also need to steam the beans slightly longer in the water, sherry, and soy sauce. The wisest plan is to taste them after 5 minutes, and if they still seem raw to your taste, to re-cover them and steam a couple of minutes longer. Do *not,* however, cook the beans so long that they soften; properly dry-sautéed, they should retain plenty of crunch.

ORANGE AND GINGER SAUCE

About 2 cups

This nippy sauce is marvelous spooned over gingerbread, pound cake, or vanilla or rum-raisin ice cream. It's quick and easy to make and a superlative way to use up oddments of candied or preserved ginger (even if the candied ginger is hard and dry, it will plump right up in the hot sauce). This sauce keeps well in the refrigerator for about a week. Warm briefly and gently before serving.

1 cup granulated sugar
2 tablespoons cornstarch
1½ cups water
Juice of 1 orange
Juice of 1 lemon
2 teaspoons finely grated orange rind
1 egg yolk
2 tablespoons butter or margarine
¼ to ⅓ cup chopped candied or preserved ginger

Combine the sugar and cornstarch in a small, heavy saucepan, then blend in the water and orange and lemon juices. Set over moderate heat and cook, stirring constantly, until the mixture boils. Reduce the heat and continue to cook and stir for 3 minutes—just until sauce is thickened and clear and no longer tastes of raw starch. Mix the orange rind with the egg yolk, then spoon a little of the hot sauce into the yolk, forking vigorously; stir the yolk mixture into the pan and heat and stir for 1 to 2 minutes.

Remove the sauce from the heat, stir in the butter and ginger, and let stand at room temperature for about 5 minutes before serving (this is to give the flavors a chance to mellow).

GINGER ICE CREAM

1 quart

An "instant" that's uncommonly good—and that uses up from ½ to 1 cup of chopped preserved or candied ginger.

1 quart vanilla ice cream, softened until mushy
½ to 1 cup chopped preserved or candied ginger
2 tablespoons rum or brandy

Beat all the ingredients hard in an electric mixer set at high speed for about 1 minute or until fluffy. Spoon back into the original ice cream cartons or spoon into 2 freezer trays and freeze until firm.

QUAKER "CRACKERS"

About 4 dozen

We always called these "crackers," although they are actually shattery-crisp cookies studded with small chips of candied or preserved ginger. The recipe comes from the late Dr. Helen Price, a classics professor from Swarthmore, Pennsylvania. When she shared the recipe with us, Dr. Price (or "Aunt Helen," as we called her) said that it had been a favorite in her mother's family for several generations, which would make it more than two hundred years old.

¼ cup granulated sugar
1 tablespoon firmly packed light brown sugar
½ cup (1 stick) unsalted butter, at room temperature (do not substitute margarine; the cookies will spread too much during baking)
1 egg, beaten well
1 teaspoon vanilla extract
⅞ cup sifted all-purpose flour (to simplify the measuring, measure out ¾ cup of flour and add 2 level tablespoons to it)
48 thin slivers of candied or drained, preserved ginger (measuring about ½ inch square)

Preheat the oven to moderate (350° F.).

Cream the granulated sugar, brown sugar, and butter hard until light and silvery, then beat in the egg and the vanilla. Stir (don't beat) the flour in, then drop the mixture by half-teaspoonfuls onto lightly greased baking sheets, spacing the cookies about 2 inches apart. Center a piece of ginger on each cookie, pressing in lightly, then bake for 8 to 10 minutes, or until the cookies are nicely edged with tan.

Remove the cookies from the oven and transfer at once to wire racks to cool; store airtight (they will keep for about a month).

GRAHAM-CRACKER CRUMBS: See
Crumbs.

Green (Bell) Peppers

(Also Sweet Red and Yellow)

Including peppers as a troublesome leftover among for-the-most-part
boxed and packaged foods may seem as if we're forcing it. Not at all.
Peppers must be bought by the piece. Recipes so often require ½ small
green pepper, minced (or ½ medium or ½ large—and to some extent
you can solve the leftover problem by using 1 whole small pepper
instead of ½ medium, or 1 whole medium instead of ½ large). Unfortunately, there are also recipes that call for minced pepper by the cup
—¼ cup or ⅓ or ½—again *less* than 1 whole pepper. So there you are
—with half a pepper or less, which will quickly soften and spoil, even
in the refrigerator. What to do? Here are a few suggestions.
Best Way to Store   Tightly wrapped in plastic food wrap in the
refrigerator. But first, wash the leftover pepper in cool water, trim of
any blemishes, discard seeds, inner membranes, and pith. Pat dry on
paper toweling, then wrap and refrigerate.
   To Freeze   You can freeze diced sweet pepper (the green, the red,
and the yellow), but it will lose its crispness and, in the case of green
pepper, its dazzling color—immaterial if the pepper is to be used in
stews, soups, casseroles, and the like where crispness and color are
unimportant. Here, then, is the way to prepare sweet pepper for freezing: wash and trim as directed for storing (above), then mince, measure, bundle in foil or plastic food wrap, seal with freezer tape, and
label, noting both the quantity and the date. Set the packet of pepper
directly on the freezer's freezing surface and quick-freeze. Do not
blanch the minced pepper prior to freezing it—blanching will merely
make it mushier after it is thawed. To use, simply dip into the packet

of pepper with a tablespoon, removing whatever amount you need and stirring directly into the dish (no need to thaw the pepper—it will thaw fast enough on its own). Be sure to reseal the package of frozen pepper meticulously, and to mark on the label the amount you have removed so you have some record of what's left.

Maximum Storage Time   5 to 7 days in the refrigerator, 6 months in a freezer set at 0° F.

Roles in Cooking   To serve as a container for a variety of savory fillings; to add flavor, color, texture, and nutritive value. Red, yellow, and green peppers are unusually rich sources of vitamins A and C. Cooking will destroy a percentage of the vitamin C, it's true, but it will not affect the vitamin A content.

Recipe Uses   Can you imagine cooking without green peppers? So many recipes depend upon them: Chinese skillet dishes, Hungarian specialties, most recipes prepared the Creole way (the two other integral ingredients are tomatoes and gumbo filé or filé powder, made of ground dried sassafras leaves), the vast repertoire of stuffed pepper recipes—not to mention all manner of salads, dips, spreads, sandwich fillings, dressings and stuffings, soups, stews, gumbos, meat loaves, burgers, casseroles, vegetables, sauces, pickle relishes. The list goes on and on—particularly among the Cajuns of the Louisiana bayou country, who claim to use sweet peppers—the red and the yellow as well as the green—"in everything except ice cream."

Tip   If raw peppers disagree with you, blanch 30 seconds before using, then drain well. You'll find them more digestible.

How to Use Very Small Amounts   You can heighten the flavor of hamburgers and meat and ham loaves by adding up to ½ cup finely minced sweet pepper (red, green, or yellow) per pound of meat. Finely slivered, butter-sautéed sweet pepper teams well with scalloped potatoes or cooked, shredded carrots. And try scattering minced pepper, again sautéed a few minutes in butter, over your favorite pizza. Or stirring it into an omelet or scrambled eggs. Small amounts (up to ¼ cup minced) can be added to almost any casserole, stuffing, vegetable or tomato soup, or meat gravy with good results. Small amounts of sliced, diced, or finely minced raw sweet pepper can be slipped into cole slaws, tossed salads, or into tuna, turkey, or chicken salads.

N O T E   *For additional recipes, included elsewhere in this book, that call for varying amounts of sweet peppers, see the Appendix.*

CHEROKEE CHOWDER

About 6 servings

This recipe, and the three that follow, all offer easy, economical, and imaginative ways to utilize bits and pieces of green or other sweet peppers that you may have in the refrigerator.

> 4 slices bacon, cut crosswise into julienne strips
> 4 scallions, washed, trimmed, and sliced thin (include some green tops), or 1 medium yellow onion, peeled and chopped
> ¼ to ⅓ cup chopped sweet green, yellow, or red pepper (and you won't harm the chowder if you add even more)
> 1 medium potato, peeled and coarsely chopped
> 1 cup water
> 2 cups fresh or frozen whole-kernel corn
> 1½ cups milk or light cream or half-and-half (or any combination thereof)
> 2 tablespoons minced fresh parsley
> Salt and freshly ground black pepper to taste

Stir-fry the bacon in a large, heavy skillet (not unenameled iron, because the chowder may taste rusty) over moderately high heat for 2 to 3 minutes, until crisp and brown; remove the bacon with a slotted spoon, spread out on several thicknesses of paper toweling to drain, and reserve.

Drain the bacon drippings from the skillet, then measure out and return 2 tablespoons of them to the skillet. Add the scallions, green pepper, and potato and stir-fry over very low heat about 15 minutes —just until the potato begins to become tender. Add the water, then cover and simmer for 5 minutes. Now add the corn, re-cover, and simmer for 10 minutes, or just until the corn no longer tastes raw. Add the milk and heat, uncovered, for 10 minutes, stirring now and then.

Stir in the parsley and the reserved bacon, season to taste with salt and pepper, and serve.

N O T E   *Do not allow the finished chowder to boil or it may curdle.*

CREAMED DICED CARROTS WITH GREEN PEPPER

4 servings

1 pound carrots, peeled and diced fairly fine
1 cup water or chicken broth or consommé
3 tablespoons butter or margarine
1 small yellow onion, peeled and minced
¼ to ⅓ cup chopped sweet green pepper (or yellow pepper, if you
   have that on hand)
Pinch of crumbled leaf rosemary
Pinch of ground mace or grated nutmeg
3 tablespoons all-purpose flour
Carrot cooking liquid plus enough milk, light cream, or half-and-half
   to total 1½ cups
Salt and freshly ground black pepper to taste

Boil the carrots in the water or broth in a snugly covered, medium-sized saucepan over moderate heat for about 10 to 12 minutes, or until crisp-tender (watch the pot closely, and if it threatens to boil dry, add a bit more water). Meanwhile, melt the butter in a second medium-sized saucepan over moderate heat; add the onion, green pepper, rosemary, and mace and stir-fry for about 5 minutes, or just until the onion is golden. Blend in the flour and stir over moderate heat for about 1 minute—just enough to mellow the roux; set off the heat until the carrots are done.

Quickly drain the carrot cooking liquid into a measuring cup, then add enough milk or cream to total 1½ cups liquid. Set the carrots off the heat for the time being but keep them warm. Mix the liquid into the roux, set over moderate heat, and cook and stir for 3 to 5 minutes, or until the sauce is thickened and smooth and no longer tastes of raw starch.

Mix the sauce into the carrots, season to taste with salt and pepper, then heat and stir for about 2 minutes—just long enough to bring the carrots to serving temperature.

N O T E   *Carrots prepared this way are particularly good with turkey, chicken, pork, and ham.*

CAJUN RICE DRESSING

4 to 6 servings

Rice dressing resembles jambalaya except that it contains no ham (the name "jambalaya" comes from *jambon,* the French word for ham). Cajuns, by the way, do not use rice dressing as a stuffing but as a side dish, a potato substitute to accompany roast turkey, chicken, pork, or baked ham.

2 tablespoons bacon or ham drippings or butter
1 tablespoon butter or margarine
1 medium yellow onion, peeled and chopped
1 large rib celery, peeled and chopped
⅓ to ½ cup chopped sweet green or yellow pepper
1 small clove garlic, peeled and minced
1½ cups converted rice
3 cups water or chicken or beef broth or consommé
2 tablespoons minced fresh parsley (optional)
Salt and freshly ground black pepper to taste

Melt the bacon drippings and butter (or just butter) in a large, heavy pan over moderately low heat; add the onion, celery, green pepper, and garlic and stir-fry for 8 to 10 minutes, until the onion is translucent and golden but not brown. Mix in the rice, raise the heat to moderate, and stir-fry for about 2 minutes—just until the rice is richly golden. Pour in the water or both, bring to a gentle boil, and cook, uncovered, for about 20 to 25 minutes, or until all the liquid is absorbed and the rice is tender but not mushy (it should be, as the Italians say, *al dente* —offering a bit of resistance to the teeth).

Fork in the parsley, if you like, then add salt and pepper to taste and serve.

PEPPER BREAD

One 8 × 8 × 2-inch loaf

4 slices bacon, cut crosswise into julienne strips
½ to ¾ cup chopped sweet green, yellow, or red pepper
1 cup sifted all-purpose flour

1 cup yellow or white corn meal
1 tablespoon (3 teaspoons) baking powder
1 tablespoon granulated sugar
1 teaspoon chili powder
½ teaspoon salt
1 egg, beaten lightly
1 cup milk
2 tablespoons corn, peanut, or vegetable oil

Preheat the oven to hot (400° F.).

In a small, heavy skillet, stir-fry the bacon over moderately high heat for 2 to 3 minutes, until brown and crisp; using a slotted spoon, transfer the bacon crumbles to paper toweling to drain. Pour all the bacon drippings from the skillet; return 1 tablespoon of them to the skillet and reserve the remainder. Stir-fry the green pepper in the 1 tablespoon of drippings over moderate heat for 3 to 5 minutes—just until the pepper no longer tastes raw (it should still be somewhat crisp). With the slotted spoon, transfer the pepper to paper toweling and spread it out so that most of the excess bacon fat is absorbed.

Combine the flour, corn meal, baking powder, sugar, chili powder, and salt in a mixing bowl and make a hollow in the center. In a small bowl or large measuring cup, combine the egg, milk, 2 tablespoons of bacon drippings, and peanut oil. Pour all at once into the dry ingredients and fork briskly—just enough to incorporate the combined liquids. Lightly fold in the reserved bacon and green pepper and spoon into a well-greased 8 × 8 × 2-inch baking pan. Bake, uncovered, in the preheated oven for 20 to 25 minutes, or until the bread is lightly browned and feels springy to the touch.

Cut into large squares while hot and serve with plenty of butter.

G R I T S :   See **Corn Meal and Grits.**

Herbs

(Fresh)

Unless you grow your own herbs or have a greengrocer from whom you can buy them, you will rarely be caught with more than leftover fresh parsley (which is discussed elsewhere in this book; see page 237). Still, more and more supermarkets are selling pots of fresh basil in season (May to September), chives year round, and sometimes even bouquets of fresh dill, mint, or tarragon. Fresh herbs, not surprisingly, are expensive, a luxury we buy only when we have a specific need for a specific herb. Unfortunately, we must invariably buy more of that herb than we need. What to do with the balance? The suggestions below may help.

Best Way to Store   It differs somewhat from herb to herb, but these are the methods we've found most reliable:

Dill, tarragon, and chives: Remove coarsest leaves and stem ends, as well as wilting or fading leaves. Do not wash; wrap loosely in plastic food wrap and store in the refrigerator.

Basil or mint: Remove coarse stem or root ends by slicing diagonally through each with a sharp knife (the same technique you would use when trimming cut flowers); also remove coarse or discolored leaves. Wash each sprig gently in cool water, then stand the sprigs in a jar or glass of cool water and slip a plastic bag loosely on top. Store in the refrigerator—but not in the coldest section, because the leaves may shrivel or freeze.

To Freeze   There are two highly successful ways to freeze fresh herbs—in ice cubes or as herbal butters.

• *In ice cubes:* Place 1 tablespoon of freshly minced herb into each compartment of an ice cube tray, add 2 to 3 tablespoons of cold water to each, then freeze until hard. Pop the frozen herb cubes into a plastic bag, label, and date, then store in the freezer. Use in any recipe calling for herbs, remembering that 1 frozen cube = 1 tablespoon freshly minced herb (or about ½ teaspoon of dried herb).

• *As herbal butters:* Dill, tarragon, and chives make particularly fragrant butters, delicious when spread on grilled steaks and chops, broiled fish or chicken. To make, soften 1 cup (2 sticks) unsalted butter to room temperature, then mix in 3 to 4 tablespoons finely minced dill, tarragon, or chives. Chill the butter until firm enough to shape, then mold into 2 sticks or rolls, wrap individually and freeze until firm. To use, simply slice off pats of the herb butter and plop on top of sizzling hot steaks, chops, fish, or chicken. These herbal butters will keep well in the freezer for about 4 months.

• Gardening friends of ours have told us of a third way to freeze fresh herbs, and it's one with which we've had some success. In our experience, however, only certain varieties of herbs—the smaller and hardier leafed ones such as thyme, chervil, oregano, and marjoram—freeze well by this method. Parsley freezes beautifully this way, too, but tarragon, dill, and fennel are too fragile; basil and mint both too big-leafed and too perishable (because of the greater surface area of their leaves, basil and mint seem especially prone to freezer-burning and blackening when frozen whole). But by all means experiment as you like with the technique, which, quite simply, is this: Divide the herb you intend to freeze into small sprigs and select for freezing only those that are young, springy, and unblemished. Wash the sprigs gently in cool water, pat dry on several thicknesses of paper toweling, then pop the herb sprigs into a double plastic bag (we simply slip one bag inside another). Smooth the double bag up around the herb, pressing out as much air as possible, twist the top into a gooseneck, and secure with a twist-band. Quick-freeze by setting the herb packet directly on the freezing surface of your freezer. Keeping time: about 3 months at 0° F. To use, simply reach into the bag and remove whatever amount of herb you need (no need to thaw it before chopping or mincing), then reseal carefully, again pressing out all air, twisting the top, and securing.

Maximum Storage Time About 5 to 7 days in the refrigerator for all of the herbs, depending, of course, upon how fresh they were when you bought them; see the section on freezing (above) for freezer storage time.

Roles in Cooking Fresh herbs add flavor—and, to some extent, color —to a wide range of savory recipes.

Recipe Uses Fresh herbs are used primarily in soups, stews, sauces, salads and dressings, dips, spreads, and seasoned butters.

Special Comments If you grow your own herbs, gather them just before they bloom (this is when herbs are at their peak of flavor), and in the cool of the morning before the dew dries (herbs are more succulent and fragrant then).

Many herbs, by the way—dill, thyme, sage, and coriander—have a lemony, almost salty flavor, so they're ideal seasonings for those on low- or no-salt diets.

N O T E *For additional recipes, included elsewhere in this book, that call for varying amounts of different kinds of fresh herbs, see the Appendix.*

CHUNKS OF VEAL BRAISED WITH WINE AND FRESH BASIL

6 servings

Make this fragrant fricassee when you have fresh basil on hand— either in your own garden or in the refrigerator. The recipe also enables you to use tag ends of dry white wine and tomato sauce, and, best of all, it freezes beautifully. Cool the finished stew to room temperature, ladle into half-pint containers (ideal if you live alone), pints (two servings) or quarts (four servings), filling each container to within ½ inch of the top. Snap on the lids, label, date, and quick-freeze at 0° F. Keeping time: about 6 months.

> 3 pounds boned veal shoulder, cut in 1½-inch cubes
> 2 tablespoons olive oil
> 1½ tablespoons butter
> 1 medium yellow onion, peeled and coarsely chopped
> 1 medium clove garlic, peeled and minced
> ²/₃ cup dry white wine
> ¹/₃ to ½ cup chopped fresh basil
> 1 teaspoon minced fresh marjoram or ½ teaspoon crumbled leaf marjoram
> ½ teaspoon minced fresh rosemary or ¼ teaspoon crumbled leaf rosemary
> 1 large, ripe tomato, peeled, cored, and chopped, or ¹/₃ to ½ cup tomato sauce or purée

1 teaspoon salt, or to taste
⅛ teaspoon freshly ground black pepper, or to taste

Brown the veal, a few cubes at a time, in the oil and butter in a large, heavy kettle set over high heat. (The veal, being very lean, will not brown as nicely as beef; it will, rather, be a rich golden color.) As the veal browns, transfer to paper toweling to drain, using a slotted spoon.

Turn the heat under the kettle to low; add the onion and garlic and sauté, stirring, for 12 to 15 minutes, until very limp—do not brown. Add the wine and simmer, uncovered, for about 10 minutes, until reduced slightly. Add all the remaining ingredients and simmer, stirring occasionally, for about 5 minutes. Return the veal to the kettle; spoon some of the wine-tomato mixture on top, cover, and simmer slowly for 2 to 2½ hours, or until the veal is very tender.

Taste for salt and pepper; add more, if needed, just before serving.

HERBAL VINEGARS

1 pint

If you grow your own herbs or if you've bought a bigger bunch than you need, you can turn the excess into an herbal vinegar that will keep well on the cupboard shelf for several months. The best fresh herbs to use for making herbal vinegars are the aromatic, tender-leafed ones: tarragon, chervil, thyme, dill, marjoram, and oregano. The formula remains the same for all.

N O T E   *Use only the very freshest, most sparkling vinegar; otherwise the herbal vinegar may not keep.*

1½ cups tightly packed, carefully washed and dried tender young
   herb sprigs (for the most fragrance, pick the herbs before they are
   ready to bloom)
1 pint boiling white wine vinegar or cider vinegar

Place the herbs in a 1-quart preserving jar, pour in the boiling vinegar, cover, and allow to steep for about 1 week at room temperature.

C O N T I N U E D

Line a funnel with several thicknesses of cheesecloth, stand the funnel in the neck of a sterilized 1-pint bottle, and then slowly pour in the flavored vinegar. Discard the strained-out herbs.

Cap the bottle tight and use the herbal vinegar as a dressing for green salads.

VARIATION

Fines Herbes Vinegar Place ½ cup *each* carefully washed and dried tender young sprigs of chervil, tarragon, and parsley, along with 1 peeled and quartered shallot, in a 1-quart preserving jar. Pour in 2 cups boiling white wine vinegar, then steep and filter as directed for herbal vinegars (above).

FRESH MINT JELLY

4 half-pints

If you have mint that is on the point of wilting, here's a delicious way to put it to good use—and to convert a highly perishable food into a nonperishable that you can keep on the pantry shelf for about a year.

> 2 cups fresh mint sprigs, washed
> 1 cup boiling water
> ⅓ cup lemon juice, strained through a very fine sieve
> 3 cups granulated sugar
> ½ cup bottled liquid pectin
> Green and yellow food coloring (to tint the jelly a pretty spring green) (optional)

Steep the mint in the boiling water for 15 minutes, then strain the infusion through several thicknesses of cheesecloth. Discard the mint. Place the mint liquid, lemon juice, and sugar in a large enameled or stainless-steel saucepan; set, uncovered, over high heat and bring to a boil without stirring. Mix in the pectin and the food coloring, if you like, and boil for exactly 30 seconds. Remove from the heat, skim off froth, then fill four sterilized jelly glasses (8 ounces each) to within ¼ inch of the tops. Seal with a thin layer of melted paraffin; cool, cap, and label.

Store on a cool, dark, dry shelf.

N O T E   *The jelly will keep well for about a year, although after 6 to 8 months it may begin to lose color.*

V A R I A T I O N S

Fresh Rosemary, Thyme, or Sage Jelly   Prepare as you would the mint jelly, but substitute 2 cups of rosemary, thyme, or sage sprigs for the mint.

Fresh Parsley or Basil Jelly   Prepare exactly as directed above, but substitute 2 cups parsley or basil sprigs for the mint; omit the lemon juice and increase the quantity of water to 1⅓ cups.

P E S T O   S A U C E

Enough to dress 4 servings of spaghetti

Pre-blender or food processor, this was one of the most tedious recipes on earth to make because it involved grinding fresh basil leaves, garlic, and pignoli (pine nuts) to a paste with a mortar and pestle (Italian women still prepare *pesto* this way). The quantity of sauce this particular recipe makes will dress 1 pound of thin spaghetti and use up 2 cups of basil leaves and ½ cup of leftover parsley sprigs, which may sound like a lot for leftovers. Not so if you grow your own and are cleaning up the garden at the end of summer.

    ¼ cup (½ stick) unsalted butter, at room temperature
    ¼ cup best-quality olive oil
    2 medium cloves garlic, peeled
    2 cups tightly packed tender young basil leaves, washed and patted
       very dry on paper toweling
    ½ cup loosely packed parsley sprigs, washed and patted very dry on
       paper toweling

C O N T I N U E D

    3 to 4 tablespoons pignoli (pine nuts)
    ½ teaspoon salt
    Several grindings of black pepper

Place all the ingredients in an electric blender or a food processor equipped with the metal chopping blade and buzz to a smooth purée —two to three 1-minute churnings of the blender, about 1 minute nonstop with the processor.

Use to dress well-drained, hot spaghetti that has been tossed with a good chunk of butter, and serve with plenty of freshly grated Parmesan cheese.

N O T E   *If you should have a quantity of fresh basil on hand, make up several batches of* pesto *and freeze in half-pint containers, filling each to within ½ inch of the top. Label and date each container, then quick-freeze by setting the containers directly on the freezing surface of a freezer set at 0° F. Frozen* pesto *sauce will keep well about 6 months.*

Herbs and Spices

(Dried)

What's the difference between an herb and a spice? Botanically, herbs are considered to be the leaves of such fragrant plants as marjoram, oregano, rosemary, tarragon, thyme, mint, basil, etc. They may be annuals, biennials, or perennials, but they almost invariably grow in temperate climes. Spices, on the other hand, thrive in the tropics or subtropics; they are the tougher, woodier portions of aromatic plants —gingerroot, for example, cinnamon (which is the bark of the cassia tree), and nutmeg (the hard oval kernel of the nutmeg tree—mace, by the way, is the webbing that encloses nutmeg, which is why these two spices taste very much the same). There is, in addition, a third category —aromatic seeds, which include anise, cardamom, caraway, coriander, fennel, mustard, and poppy seeds. Do these all qualify as leftovers? We think so because they *should* be used up within a reasonable period (1 year).

Best Way to Store All herbs, spices, and aromatic seeds should be stored more or less the same way, that is, tightly capped on a cool, dry shelf and away from the fading effects of direct sunlight (delicate leafy herbs, in particular, will lose almost all color in a matter of weeks if stored on a sunny windowsill).

Maximum Storage Time 1 year. You can, of course, keep herbs and spices much longer. And most people certainly do—year in and year out. But herbs, spices, and aromatic seeds will all lose their fragrance if kept too long. So the point is to use them frequently and to replenish them after about a year—especially the more delicate herbs like tarragon, chervil, dill weed, basil, and marjoram.

Roles in Cooking To add fragrance, flavor, piquancy, and sometimes color as well (paprika, turmeric, and saffron).

Recipe Uses It's a rare recipe, indeed, that does not call for an herb or spice of some kind—the simplest cakes and cookies, perhaps, although they are usually flavored with vanilla, the aromatic bean of a wild Latin American orchid.

Special Comments You'll find that herbs last longer if you buy the "leaf" variety instead of the ground or powdered. To heighten the flavor of herbs, crumble them gently between your fingers as you add them to a recipe—the warmth of your hands will activate the aromatic oils in the herbs.

If you have an electric blender, food processor, or small coffee grinder in which you can grind aromatic seeds, by all means buy whole such seeds as dill, cumin, coriander, cardamom, and caraway. You'll be astonished at how much more flavorful freshly ground seeds are than their commercially pulverized counterparts.

N O T E *For additional recipes, included elsewhere in this book, that call for varying amounts of dried herbs or spices, see the Appendix.*

VITELLO ALL'UCCELLETTO (VEAL SCALOPPINE WITH BAY LEAVES)

4 to 6 servings

If your dried bay leaves are beginning to brown and lose their fragrance, you can use them up in this recipe with superb results. If you do not have a partial bottle of white wine on hand with which to make this recipe and do not want to open a fresh one, substitute dry vermouth.

> ¼ cup olive oil
> 2 cloves garlic, peeled and quartered
> 6 to 8 bay leaves
> 2 pounds veal round, sliced ¼ inch thick and pounded thin as for scaloppine
> 1 tablespoon lemon juice
> ²/₃ cup dry white wine
> ¼ teaspoon salt
> Several grindings of black pepper

Heat the oil, garlic, and bay leaves in a very large, heavy skillet over low heat, stirring and mashing the garlic, for 8 to 10 minutes, or until the garlic is tender (do not brown the garlic, as it will give off an unpleasant, bitter flavor). Remove the garlic from skillet and discard.

Raise heat to high and brown the veal quickly on both sides (keep the bay leaves on top of the veal so they don't scorch). Reduce the heat to low; add all the remaining ingredients, cover, and simmer for 12 to 15 minutes, or until the veal is tender enough to cut with a fork. Discard the bay leaves.

Serve the veal topped with the skillet juices. A bowl of tender young green peas makes a perfect accompaniment.

POPPY SEED SAUERKRAUT

6 servings

To finish a boiled tongue or baked ham, steamed knackwurst, or frank-furters, bed on a platter of this poppy seed sauerkraut. It's one of the easiest recipes imaginable to prepare, and a cinch for using up 2 table-spoons of poppy seeds of doubtful age.

> 1 can (1 pound, 14 ounces) sauerkraut, drained and rinsed
> 2 tablespoons butter, margarine, or bacon drippings
> 2 tablespoons poppy seeds
> Freshly ground black pepper to taste

Place all the ingredients in a medium-sized saucepan, set over mod-erately low heat, and bring just to the serving temperature—about 5 minutes. Stir the mixture from time to time lest it threaten to stick in spots.

SESAME CRISPS

About 2½ dozen cookies

Quick and easy drop cookies that will utilize from ¼ to ½ cup of leftover sesame seeds.

> ½ cup (1 stick) butter (do not substitute margarine)
> 1 cup firmly packed light brown sugar
> 1 egg
> 1¼ cups *unsifted* all-purpose flour
> ¼ teaspoon baking soda
> Pinch of salt
> Pinch of ground cinnamon
> ¾ teaspoon vanilla extract
> ¼ to ½ cup sesame seeds, plus enough finely chopped walnuts or
>   pecans to total ¾ cup

Preheat the oven to moderately hot (375°F.).

Cream the butter and sugar until fluffy-light; beat in the egg. Com-bine the flour with the soda, salt, and cinnamon and stir in. Mix in the vanilla, then the sesame-nut mixture. Drop from a teaspoon onto lightly greased baking sheets and bake in the preheated oven for about 10 minutes, or until lightly browned.

Transfer at once to wire racks to cool.

CHICKEN SESAME

6 to 8 servings

If you've ever bought a jar of sesame seeds, chances are you did so for a particular recipe and still have the balance tucked away on the spice shelf—going stale. For sesame seeds *do* stale (because of their high oil content). Actually, they're more versatile than most of us think, as this recipe demonstrates.

> ¾ cup (1½ sticks) butter or margarine, melted
> Juice of 1 lemon
> ½ teaspoon crumbled leaf rosemary
> 3 cups moderately fine, soft bread crumbs (for this amount you will need about 6 slices of firm-textured white bread)
> ¼ cup minced fresh parsley (optional)
> ⅓ cup sesame seeds
> ¼ teaspoon crumbled leaf thyme
> 2 teaspoons salt
> ¼ teaspoon freshly ground black pepper
> 2 small broiler-fryers (about 2½ to 3 pounds each), disjointed

Preheat the oven to moderate (350°F.).

In a small mixing bowl, combine the melted butter, lemon juice, and rosemary. In a pie plate, combine the crumbs, parsley (if you like), sesame seeds, thyme, salt, and pepper. Dip the pieces of chicken first in the melted butter, then in the crumb mixture to coat evenly. Arrange one layer deep in a large, shallow baking pan and drizzle any remaining butter evenly over the chicken. (At this point you may refrigerate the chicken, loosely covered with wax paper, until about 1 hour before serving; if you do, preheat the oven just before you bake the chicken.)

Bake the chicken, uncovered, in the preheated oven for about 1 hour, or until golden-crisp and tender, basting now and then with pan drippings.

Serve hot or cold.

Honey

What accounts for the difference in flavor, aroma, and color in honey? The flowers from which the bees have gathered nectar. Sweet clover and alfalfa honeys, for example, are light and mild (more than half of the honey produced in the United States is clover honey). Other popular domestic honeys are sourwood (an amber-hued, rich Appalachian honey that's highly prized in the South), citrus honey (delicate, almost fruitlike), and buckwheat honey (dark and heavy). As a rule, the darker the honey, the stronger and heavier it will be. There are also dozens of exotic, often expensive imported honeys, including the heather honeys of Scotland, the jasmine honeys of the Mediterranean, and the precious Hymettus honey of Greece ("nectar of the Gods" made by bees feeding upon the acacia blossoms on the slopes of Mount Hymettus, near Athens).

Best Way to Store   In a screw-top glass bottle or jar (which is the way most honeys are sold, although, sadly, an increasing number are now being packed in plastic) on a dry shelf at room temperature. It's important that honey be kept tightly covered, because on exposure to the air it loses aroma and flavor and absorbs household odors and moisture. *Do not refrigerate honey*—it will crystallize (turn sugary). In fact, as it ages, honey will begin to crystallize and to darken somewhat. You can't do anything about the change of color, but you can reliquefy sugary honey by setting the jar in a pan of warm water—the crystals should dissolve quickly. If not, warm the honey on a rack in a pan of barely simmering water for 3 to 5 minutes. Do not let the water in the pan boil and do not let the honey stand for more than a few minutes in the hot water because its flavor will be altered.

N O T E   *Be sure to wipe the honey bottle well with a damp cloth after each use to avoid attracting ants and roaches, and pay special attention to the cap and screw-top ridges so the cap does not stick fast in future.*

Maximum Storage Time   About 1 year, but if you notice the honey darkening or crystallizing, these are your cues to use it up more quickly.

Roles in Cooking   First and foremost, honey is a sweetener, but it also makes a splendid glaze for ham, poultry, and such vegetables as carrots, beets, and winter squash. Because one of the sugars contained in honey is levulose (or "invert sugar"), it has the power to absorb moisture from the air, meaning that breads, cakes, cookies, and confections made with honey will remain moister far longer than will those made with sugar.

What about substituting honey for sugar in your favorite cakes and cookies? In all but the most fragile cakes, it is usually safe to substitute honey for half of the sugar called for. You may also substitute honey for half of the sugar in such chewy bar cookies as brownies, but for crisper types—gingersnaps, for example—replace no more than one-third of the sugar with honey. When making jams, marmalades, conserves, and preserves, it's safe to substitute honey for half—but no more—of the sugar called for. As for candies, better not monkey around with the proportions—candies are too critical (apt to fail). Instead, choose recipes that were developed specifically for honey. Needless to add, in less crucial recipes you can substitute honey measure for measure for sugar—in custards, for example, in puddings, pie fillings, sweet-and-sour meats and vegetables.

Recipe Uses   See, first of all, the recipes that follow. For additional ideas, you'll find the most recipes containing honey among your collections of breads, pastries, puddings, pies, cakes, cookies, and candies, as well as in Middle Eastern cookbooks.

Special Comments   Natural food advocates prefer honey to sugar—and with some justification. Honey *is* more easily digested by some people than refined sugars; in fact, it is believed to help babies metabolize calcium. Honey also contains *small amounts* of protein, B complex vitamins, iron, copper, sodium, potassium, manganese, calcium, magnesium, and phosphorous. But it also contains more *calories* than sugar: 1 tablespoon of honey, for example, contains about 65 calories, as compared with 45 per tablespoon for granulated sugar and 50 for brown sugar.

N O T E   *For additional recipes, included elsewhere in this book, that call for varying amounts of honey, see the Appendix.*

STRAWBERRY BUTTER

1 cup

If you're down to a dab of honey (and if it's the strawberry season), you might want to make one of the most delicious spreads we've ever tasted. In fact, you might want to make up multiple batches, pack them in attractive crocks, and present them to friends as gifts. The recipe comes from the old Mayflower Hotel on New York's Central Park West. Traditionally served every breakfast, the strawberry butter has now become so popular that it is also served at dinner. It is delicious on waffles and pancakes, as well as on warm bread. And it's a "company" touch that's impressive but easy. Don't, of course, buy strawberries merely to make the strawberry butter (unless you're going to do several batches), just save back 4 big ripe ones—that's all you need for the recipe

> **1 cup (2 sticks) unsalted butter, at room temperature**
> **2 tablespoons honey**
> **4 large ripe strawberries, washed, hulled, and halved**

Cream all the ingredients together in an electric mixer set at high speed (or in an electric blender or food processor equipped with the metal chopping blade) until fluffy-smooth and the honey and strawberries have been completely "homogenized" with the butter. Pack into a decorative 1-cup crock (or into two jelly or jam jars), cover, and store in the refrigerator (the butter keeps well for about 10 days).

Bring to room temperature before serving (simply scoop out however much strawberry butter you need instead of warming the entire crock of it).

HONEY-SOY GLAZE

About ¾ cup

This recipe is both an easy and an excellent way to utilize honey that has perhaps stood on the shelf longer than necessary occupying valuable cupboard space. If the honey has by chance molded on top, simply scrape the mold off and use the clear honey underneath. It is perfectly safe. This glaze is equally delicious on chicken, turkey, duck, goose, game, hen, roast pork, or baked ham.

> ½ cup soy sauce
> ¼ cup honey
> ¼ cup dry sherry, Madeira, or Port
> 1 clove garlic, peeled and crushed
> 1 tablespoon minced fresh gingerroot, candied or preserved ginger,
>   or, as a last resort, ¼ teaspoon ground ginger

Combine all the ingredients in a small, heavy saucepan; cover and simmer slowly for 5 minutes. Using a pastry brush, "paint" the glaze on chicken, turkey, goose, duck, game hen, pork, or ham during the final 20 minutes of roasting, baking, or broiling; repeat, if necessary, until the meat is nicely glazed.

HONEY FRENCH DRESSING

About 2 cups

If your family are big salad eaters, and if you have a small amount of honey on hand, you may want to make up a batch of this French dressing to keep on hand. It's equally delicious on mixed green or fruit salads and will keep well for about 10 days in the refrigerator.

> 1 cup corn or vegetable oil
> ⅓ cup best-quality olive oil
> ⅔ cup vinegar (cider, wine, or tarragon)
> ¼ to ⅓ cup honey
> 1 teaspoon salt
> 1 tablespoon paprika
> 1 teaspoon dry mustard

Place all the ingredients in a 1-quart shaker jar and shake well to combine. Store, tightly covered, in the refrigerator and shake well before using.

HONEY-GLAZED BEETS AND SWEETS

6 servings

With its reds and oranges, this vegetable dish is decidedly Latin in color, but then it was in Acapulco that we first tasted it. Frankly, it was far better than we'd expected, and we have since served it at home to high compliments. Try the recipe when you have the last of a jar of honey to use up. It's particularly good with roast pork or fowl.

> 1 pound medium beets, scrubbed well and trimmed of all but 1 inch of the tops (do not peel the beets or cut off the root ends so the beets will retain as much of their dazzling scarlet color as possible)
> 1 pound small sweet potatoes or yams, scrubbed but not peeled
> ¼ to ⅓ cup honey
> 2 tablespoons melted butter or margarine
> ¼ teaspoon salt
> 1 teaspoon finely grated orange rind (optional—use if you have an orange from which some of the rind has already been grated)
> Several grindings of the pepper mill

Parboil the beets in just enough lightly salted water to cover for about 30 minutes, or until firm-tender. Drain and cool until easy to handle, then peel and cut in 1-inch cubes. Meanwhile, boil the potatoes for 20 minutes, or until firm-tender; drain, cool, peel, and cut in 1-inch cubes.

Preheat the oven to hot (400° F.).

Arrange the beets and potatoes in a 9-inch baking pan or pie plate. Combine the honey, melted butter, salt, orange rind (if you like), and pepper. Drizzle over the vegetables and bake, uncovered, in the preheated oven, basting occasionally with the mixture, for 20 to 25 minutes, or until richly glazed.

Serve at once.

HONEY–CHOCOLATE CHIP COOKIES

About 4 dozen

⅓ cup vegetable shortening
½ cup honey
1 egg, beaten well
1¼ cups sifted all-purpose flour
½ teaspoon salt
½ teaspoon baking soda
1 package (6 ounces) chocolate bits
⅔ cup coarsely chopped pecans or walnuts
1 teaspoon vanilla extract

Preheat the oven to moderately hot (375° F.).

Cream the shortening until fluffy, then add the honey gradually, beating all the while until creamy. Mix in the egg. Combine the flour, salt, and soda, then mix into the creamed mixture, one-half of the total amount at a time. Stir in the chocolate bits, nuts, and vanilla.

Drop the mixture from a teaspoon onto greased baking sheets, spacing the cookies about 2 inches apart. Bake in the preheated oven for 10 to 12 minutes, or until lightly browned around the edges.

Transfer at once to wire racks to cool.

ATHENIAN HONEY-CINNAMON CHEESECAKE

8 to 10 servings

For this cheesecake, Greeks would use the highly prized, flowery Hymettus honey, but any liquid honey with a pronounced flavor will do nicely.

CRUMB CRUST

20 square graham crackers, rolled to fine crumbs
3 tablespoons granulated sugar
¼ teaspoon ground cinnamon
Pinch of ground mace
⅓ cup (5⅓ tablespoons) butter or margarine, melted

FILLING

3 cups cottage cheese
¾ cup honey
1 teaspoon ground cinnamon
¼ teaspoon salt
4 eggs

Preheat the oven to moderately hot (375° F.).

Combine all the crust ingredients, then pat firmly over the bottom and up the sides of a 9-inch spring-form pan. Bake for 5 minutes in the preheated oven, then remove the crust from the oven and let cool.

Reduce the oven heat to moderately slow (325° F.).

In a food processor fitted with the metal chopping blade or an electric mixer set at high speed, cream the cottage cheese until smooth. Beat in the honey, cinnamon, and salt, then the eggs, mixing only enough to blend. Pour the filling into the crumb crust, then bake in the moderately slow oven for about 1 hour, or until the filling is set.

Remove the cheesecake from the oven, cool to room temperature, then chill for several hours—or, better yet, overnight—before serving.

HERBED HONEY GLAZE
FOR POULTRY, PORK, OR HAM

1 to 1¼ cups

¼ cup boiling water
½ teaspoon crumbled leaf sage
½ teaspoon crumbled leaf thyme
¾ to 1 cup honey
1 to 2 tablespoons vinegar (cider, tarragon, or white wine)

Pour the boiling water over the herbs and let them steep for 10 minutes. Strain out the herbs and mix the herb infusion with the honey and vinegar. Warm gently over lowest burner heat in a small, heavy saucepan; do not allow the mixture to boil. Brush the mixture over poultry or pork several times during the last half hour of cooking.

HONEYED APPLE CHUTNEY

4 to 6 half-pints

You may be interested to know that, in pickling and preserving, you may substitute honey for one-half of the total amount of sugar called for. Some recipes—like this one—are made altogether with honey, in this case 1 cup. This is also a handy way to use 1 to 1½ cups dried currants or raisins that may be hardening.

> About 10 to 12 medium greenings or other tart apples, washed, cored, and very coarsely chopped but not peeled (enough to make 2 quarts)
>
> 2 medium sweet green and/or red peppers, washed, cored, seeded, and coarsely chopped
>
> 3 medium yellow onions, peeled and coarsely chopped
>
> 1 to 1½ cups dried currants or raisins
>
> 1 cup honey
>
> Juice of 2 lemons
>
> Grated rind of 1 lemon
>
> 1½ cups cider vinegar
>
> ¾ cup cranberry, orange, or grapefruit juice
>
> 1½ teaspoons salt
>
> 1 teaspoon ground ginger
>
> ¼ teaspoon cayenne pepper
>
> 1 cinnamon stick, broken in several pieces
>
> 1 teaspoon whole cloves
>
> 1 clove garlic, peeled and halved

Place all but last three ingredients in a large, heavy enameled or stainless-steel kettle. Tie the cinnamon, cloves, and garlic in cheese-cloth and drop into the kettle. Simmer the mixture slowly, uncovered, for about 2½ hours, or until the volume is reduced by about one-half; stir often toward the end of cooking to prevent scorching. When the mixture is thick and glossy, remove the cheesecloth bag and discard.

Using a wide-mouthed canning funnel, ladle the boiling hot chutney into clean, hot half-pint preserving jars, filling to within ¼ inch of the tops. Wipe the jar rims and seal the jars; process for 10 minutes in a boiling water bath.

Remove the jars from the water bath; cool and check the seals, then store in a cool, dark, dry place for several weeks before serving.

Jams, Jellies, Marmalades, and Preserves

Can these truly be problem leftovers? Yes, if you're counting calories and foregoing breakfast toast with all the trimmings or if you're not very keen on jams, jellies, and the like in the first place. Unfortunately, certain recipes do call for them in less than full-jar amounts (jelly rolls, thumbprint cookies, cake fillings, trifles, and other desserts). So you're stuck with a half or third or fourth of a jar, which clutters up the cupboard and, in time, gathers mold and/or insects.

Best Way to Store Tightly capped on a cool, dry cupboard shelf. And, most important, do sponge off both the jar and the cap (paying special attention to the screw-top ridges) each time you dip into a jar of jam, jelly, marmalade, or preserves. Any spills or dribbles are an open invitation to ants and roaches. Moreover, if you don't clean around the screw top, the lid will stick fast and you won't be able to open the jar without considerable rapping, tapping, or soaking in hot water.

Maximum Storage Time About 6 months, but it's better to use up leftovers sooner because jams, jellies, marmalades, and preserves will begin to liquefy or crystallize, to lose color and flavor.

Roles in Cooking To add color and flavor; also to glaze meats and vegetables.

Recipe Uses In fillings for cakes, cookies, candies, and sandwiches; in puddings, sauces, gravies, and glazes.

Special Comments If a jam, jelly, or preserve should mold, no harm done. Simply scrape off and discard all moldy portions, then use the balance as fast as possible because it will quickly re-mold (such molds, by the way, aren't dangerous or poisonous—merely unsightly; penicillin, remember, is a mold). If the jams, jellies, or preserves are either sugary or runny, it's wisest to use them in glazes, sauces, or gravies (the cooking heat will dissolve any sugar crystals and render lumpy, weepy jellies uniformly smooth).

How to Use Very Small Amounts Try adding a tablespoon or two of jelly, jam, marmalade, or preserves to any favorite meat gravy (particularly good with gravies made from lamb, turkey, chicken, or game drippings). And to mellow a too-tart tomato sauce or soup, smooth in a tablespoon or so of jam, jelly, or preserves; this works every bit as well as brown sugar or honey. Or substitute for all or part of the sugar in an apple, pear, or peach pie.

And, finally, use odds and ends to glaze beets, carrots, turnips, rutabagas, winter squash, or parsnips. It's as easy as adding a table-spoon or two to the drained, cooked vegetable along with an equal amount of butter and shaking briskly over low heat until the vegetable pieces glisten. Glazing acorn squash is even easier—simply plop a spoonful or two of jam, jelly, marmalade, or preserves into the hollow of each unbaked half of acorn squash, add 1 to 2 tablespoons of butter, and bake, uncovered, for 45 minutes to 1 hour in a moderately hot oven (375° F.), or until the squash is fork-tender. That's all there is to it.

N O T E *For additional recipes, included elsewhere in this book, that call for varying amounts of jams, jellies, marmalades, and preserves, see the Appendix.*

Ä B B L E K A G E
(N O R W E G I A N   A P P L E   C A K E)

6 to 8 servings

Most people do not find jams or jellies problem leftovers. But others of us use them so occasionally that we do indeed have partial jars of jams and jellies sitting around, and this recipe offers one solution. You may wonder why this flourless dessert is called a "cake" (as indeed we do). All we can say is, don't let a Norwegian hear you call it a pudding. To Norwegians this is *the* traditional Christmas "cake."

> 4 to 5 medium cooking apples (McIntoshes, Baldwins, or greenings), peeled, cored, and sliced into very thin rings
> ½ jar (10-ounce size) raspberry or other berry jam (²/₃ cup)
> ¼ to ⅓ cup fine, dry bread crumbs
> 1 tablespoon granulated sugar

4 eggs
1 cup heavy cream
⅛ teaspoon salt
1 tablespoon butter

Preheat the oven to moderate (350° F.).

Arrange a layer of apple rings in the bottom of a buttered 6-cup casserole; dab a little jam in the hole of each ring, then sprinkle lightly with crumbs and sugar. Continue building up apple layers until the dish is filled to the brim, spooning dabs of jam in the center of each apple ring and sprinkling each layer *lightly* with crumbs and sugar (hold back a tablespoon of crumbs to scatter over the top layer of apples).

Beat the eggs with ¼ cup of the cream and the salt and pour evenly over the apples. Sprinkle the reserved crumbs on top and dot with butter, then bake, uncovered, in the preheated oven for 45 minutes; cover and bake for 15 minutes longer, or until the apples are tender.

Serve warm or cold—simply cut into wedges and top with the balance of the cream, which has been whipped to soft peaks.

N O T E   *This dessert is even more delicious if made one day and served the next.*

O V E R - T H E - T O P   C O O K I E S

3 dozen 1½-inch squares

This old family recipe is sinfully sweet, and although it's a delicious way to use leftover marmalade or jam, don't feel compelled to add the marmalade or jam. In fact, do so only if you have some to use up (or if your family has an insatiable sweet tooth). The second egg white is optional, too, but do include it, if you can, because it makes for a meringuelike topping.

½ cup (1 stick) butter or margarine, at room temperature
1 cup granulated sugar
1 egg plus 1 egg yolk
½ teaspoon vanilla extract

C O N T I N U E D

½ teaspoon almond extract
1½ cups sifted all-purpose flour
1 teaspoon baking powder
⅛ teaspoon salt

TOPPING

½ jar (10-ounce size) orange marmalade or raspberry jam (⅔ cup)
   (optional)
1 or 2 egg whites
1 cup firmly packed light or dark brown sugar (for best results, use
   soft brown sugar that's totally devoid of lumps)
¼ cup chopped walnuts

Preheat the oven to moderately slow (325° F.).

Cream the butter and sugar until light; add the egg, egg yolk, and vanilla and almond extracts, beating after each addition. Sift together the flour, baking powder, and salt, then add to the egg mixture and stir just enough to incorporate.

Spread the dough in a greased 9 × 9 × 2-inch baking pan and, if you like, spread the marmalade on top. Beat the egg white or whites to fairly stiff peaks, then fold in the brown sugar and nuts and spread on top of the marmalade. Bake in the preheated oven for 45 minutes (if the meringue topping is browning too quickly, cover the pan with foil during the last 10 minutes of baking).

Cool for 20 to 25 minutes, then cut into 1½-inch squares; cool completely before removing from the pan.

CURRANT-GLAZED CHUNKS OF VEAL

4 to 6 servings

A particularly accommodating recipe that will use up not only ½ to ¾ cup of currant or other tart fruit jelly that is going sugary, runny (or begging), but also odds and ends of chicken and/or beef broth and wine.

2 pounds boned veal shoulder, cut in 1-inch cubes
½ cup unsifted all-purpose flour
1 teaspoon salt

¼ teaspoon freshly ground black pepper
¼ cup vegetable oil
2 medium yellow onions, peeled and minced
Juice of 2 lemons
½ cup dry white or red wine
1 cup chicken or beef broth or water or a combination of them
½ to ¾ cup currant or other tart jelly (cherry, plum, apple)
1 tablespoon Dijon mustard

Dredge the veal by shaking, a few cubes at a time, in a paper bag with the flour, salt, and pepper. Brown, again a few cubes at a time, in the oil in a large, heavy kettle set over moderately high heat; remove the veal to paper toweling to drain.

Reduce the heat under the kettle to moderate; add the onions and stir-fry for 8 to 10 minutes, or until lightly browned. Return the veal to the kettle and add the lemon juice, wine, and broth; cover and simmer slowly for about 1½ hours, or until the veal is very tender.

Remove the veal to a bowl with a slotted spoon and boil the cooking liquid, uncovered, for 5 to 10 minutes, or until slightly thickened. Whisk in the jelly and mustard and heat and stir for about 5 minutes, or until smooth and glazelike. Return the veal cubes to the kettle and heat, uncovered, for 10 minutes, turning them in the glaze.

Serve with boiled rice or new potatoes.

Maple Syrup

If you've wondered why pure maple syrup is so precious, consider this:

A maple tree is usually 30 years old before it is tapped. Small trees (those about 10 inches in diameter) can safely receive only a single tap, which will yield about 10 gallons of sap during the annual, 8- to 10-week, winter's-end mapling season. This may sound like a lot of sap, but, boiled down, these 10 gallons produce only 1 quart of maple syrup.

Best Way to Store   Believe it or not, opened cans or bottles of maple syrup should be stored in the freezer or, failing that, in the refrigerator. The syrup contains too much sugar to freeze hard, although it will thicken to the point that it cannot be poured easily. So let the can or bottle of syrup stand at room temperature just until liquid enough to pour; pour off the amount you need, then reseal and return the balance to the freezer.

If you should buy maple syrup by the gallon, you may, for convenience's sake, want to repackage it in smaller containers. Here is the method recommended by the New York State Maple Producers:

Pour the maple syrup into sterilized pint or half-pint preserving jars, filling each right to the top. Seal the jars, then process for 10 minutes in a simmering water bath (180°F.). Cool to room temperature, label, and date the jars, then store in freezer or refrigerator. (Transferring maple syrup to glass jars is a good idea, because left in the can it may turn unpleasantly dark and take on a metallic taste.)

As for unopened cans or bottles of maple syrup, they may be stored on a cool, dark, dry shelf.

N O T E   *If maple syrup should mold, skim the mold off, then bring the syrup to a simmer. Stir in skim milk (¾ cup skim milk for each 1 gallon of syrup is the recommended proportion), then continue heating until the mixture boils. Strain the syrup at once through a filter (several thicknesses of cheesecloth or a paper coffee filter will work), then bottle, seal, cool, and store in freezer or refrigerator. This is to kill the mold and keep the syrup smooth.*

Maximum Storage Time   About 1 year.
Roles in Cooking   To sweeten and flavor food.
Recipe Uses   The best recipes in which to use maple syrup are milk drinks (shakes, sodas, and flavored milk), fruit desserts and puddings, custards and mousses, pies and frozen desserts, yeast breads and quick breads, confections, and, finally, glazes for meats and vegetables.
Special Comments   Can maple syrup be substituted for sugar? Yes, it can, in most puddings, cobblers, fruit pies, ice creams, and frozen mousses. Do not try, however, to use maple syrup in place of sugar in cakes, cookies, or confections, where the success of a recipe depends upon precise ingredient proportions. Because maple syrup is not quite

so sweet as granulated or brown sugar, use 1¼ cups syrup for each 1 cup of sugar called for when making substitutions.

Tip   When buying maple syrup, read package labels carefully to determine whether or not you are indeed buying maple syrup. Pure maple syrup will be so marked on the label (and it will be expensive). Many of the so-called "maple syrups" (the ones we buy for waffles and pancakes) are nothing more than corn syrups to which artificial maple flavoring has been added. Such syrups are usually designated "maple flavor" instead of "pure maple."

N O T E   *For additional recipes, included elsewhere in this book, that call for varying amounts of maple syrup, see the Appendix.*

MAPLE-ORANGE GLAZE FOR POULTRY AND PORK

About 1½ cups

There are few easier or more elegant ways to use aging maple syrup than to stir it into this sweet-sour glaze. It is equally good with turkey, chicken, goose, duck, game hen, roast pork, baked ham, or ham loaf.

½ cup maple syrup
½ cup orange juice
Juice of 1 lemon
½ cup orange or ginger marmalade or any tart fruit jelly

Combine all the ingredients in a small, heavy saucepan and warm slowly over low heat, whisking constantly until smooth. Keep warm but do not allow the mixture to boil. Using a pastry brush, brush the glaze on poultry, pork, or ham two to three times during the last half hour of cooking, or until the meat glistens richly.

MAPLE-NUT SAUCE

2 to 2½ cups

You can vary the quantity of maple syrup in this recipe according to how fond you are of maple or how much syrup you have to use up. But you must reduce the amount of milk used proportionately so that the combined volume of milk and syrup totals 2 cups. This sauce is particularly good with a light spice cake or vanilla ice cream.

> ¼ cup firmly packed light or dark brown sugar
> 6 tablespoons unsifted all-purpose flour
> ½ to 1 cup maple syrup, plus enough milk (or evaporated milk or light or heavy cream) to total 2 cups
> ⅓ cup (5⅓ tablespoons) butter or margarine
> ¼ to ½ cup coarsely chopped walnuts (or pecans, if you prefer)

Stir the sugar, flour, and maple-milk mixture together in the top of a double boiler. Set over barely simmering water and cook and stir until thickened. Remove from the heat, add the butter, and beat well, then stir in the nuts.

Serve warm or cold.

MAPLE SPONGE CAKE

One 9 × 9 × 2-inch cake

Published in a 1917 county farmers' bulletin, this cake is such an easy and inexpensive one that we consider it a real find.

> 2 eggs, separated
> ¾ cup hot maple syrup
> 1 cup *unsifted* all-purpose flour
> 2 teaspoons baking powder
> ⅛ teaspoon salt
> 1 teaspoon lemon juice

Preheat the oven to moderate (350° F.). Grease and flour a 9 x 9 x 2-inch pan.

Beat the egg yolks until thick, then drizzle in the hot syrup, beating constantly until cool. Sift together the flour, baking powder, and salt and stir into the syrup mixture. Beat the egg whites to stiff peaks, then fold in along with the lemon juice.

Turn into the prepared pan and bake in the preheated oven for 25 minutes, or until springy to the touch. Let the cake cool in the pan for 10 minutes before turning out on a wire rack. Frost with your favorite brown sugar frosting or with Cornstarch Seafoam Frosting (see page 94).

MAPLE-APPLE-YAM CASSEROLE

8 servings

This is an especially good accompaniment for baked ham.

4 medium apples, peeled, cored, and sliced about ¼ inch thick
1 cup maple syrup
5 tablespoons butter or margarine
¼ teaspoon salt
4 medium yams, boiled until tender, peeled, and sliced about ¼ inch
  thick
½ cup soft bread crumbs

Preheat the oven to hot (400° F.).

Cook the apple slices in the syrup in a heavy saucepan over low heat for 8 to 10 minutes, or until soft. Add 4 tablespoons of the butter and the salt and stir gently to mix. Layer the yams and the apple mixture in a buttered 2-quart casserole; top with the crumbs and dot with the remaining 1 tablespoon of butter. Bake, uncovered, in the preheated oven for about 30 minutes, or until heated through.

N O T E   *It will not harm this dish if it is left in the oven for another 15 to 20 minutes—good to know, should dinner be delayed.*

MARMALADES: See **Jams, Jellies, Marmalades, and Preserves.**

Milk

(Evaporated and Sweetened Condensed)

Our discussion here will be limited to the two milks that are bought by the can and apt to be problem leftovers because they are not drunk like fresh whole milk: evaporated milk and sweetened condensed milk. For information on buttermilk and sour milk, see pages 37–38.

EVAPORATED MILK

Three major steps go into the conversion of fresh whole milk into evaporated milk: (1) evaporation, during which about 60 percent of the water is removed; (2) homogenization, by which the particles of butter fat are broken up and distributed uniformly throughout the milk (this accounts for the creaminess of evaporated milk); and (3) fortification with vitamin D. The evaporated milk is then vacuum-packed in small (5⅓-ounce) and large or tall (13-ounce) cans containing about ⅔ and 1⅔ cups respectively.

Best Way to Store   Once a can of evaporated milk is opened, it should be put into the refrigerator immediately. We transfer leftovers to a glass jar, screw the lid down tight, then set the jar in the refrigerator. It's perfectly safe to store leftover evaporated milk in its own can, but it does tend to absorb refrigerator odors no matter how carefully you've tried to seal the can with aluminum foil or plastic food wrap.

Maximum Storage Time   5 to 7 days.

Roles in Cooking   To provide a creamy-smooth foundation for a variety of soups, sauces, milk drinks, scalloped and creamed foods, custards, ice creams, candies, and confections. Because of its high protein content, evaporated milk also helps to bind meat loaves, burgers, croquettes, and stuffings together. Finally, it adds to recipes a mellow, almost nutlike flavor that whole milk lacks.

Recipe Uses   Evaporated milk can be used in any recipes that call for milk—which, of course, includes virtually every recipe category. Undiluted evaporated milk is about twice as rich as whole milk (and slightly less rich than light cream). It is perfect for most desserts, particularly those flavored with chocolate or butterscotch. For our money, evaporated milk makes the finest chocolate sauces, frostings, puddings, and hot cocoas imaginable (simply substitute it measure for measure for the whole milk called for). For the majority of soups, savory sauces, and milk drinks, evaporated milk should be mixed about half and half with cold water so that it is the equivalent of whole milk.

Special Comments   Evaporated milk can be whipped and substituted for whipped cream—both as a dessert topping and as an ingredient in almost any mousse, pudding, chiffon pie, or gelatin salad calling for whipped cream. Best of all, this substitution enables you to cut calories significantly—1 cup of evaporated milk contains only 348 calories per cup vs. 840 per cup for heavy cream.

To Whip Evaporated Milk   Measure the milk and make a note of the quantity. Pour the milk into a shallow pan or ice-cube tray, set in the freezer, and let stand until ice crystals begin to form (about 30 minutes). Set in the freezer as well the bowl in which you'll whip the milk and the beater. When the evaporated milk has partially frozen, empty into the chilled bowl, then add 1 tablespoon of lemon juice for each ½ cup of milk. Beat hard until the mixture peaks stiffly. If you're going to use the whipped evaporated milk as a topping, sweeten to taste with confectioners sugar.

SWEETENED CONDENSED MILK

This canned milk is altogether different from evaporated milk, and the two cannot be used interchangeably. The milk is sweetened, yes (it is mixed with sugar), but it is also cooked to a satiny thickness, then condensed (60 percent of the water is removed), then canned under pressure. The result is a very thick milk product about the consistency of a good hot fudge sauce and very nearly as rich (1 cup of sweetened condensed milk = 1,000 calories; 1 tablespoon of it = 62 calories—scarcely diet fare). It should also be noted, however, that sweetened condensed milk is surprisingly nutritious; each 14-ounce can (which is the most common size) contains as much protein, calcium, vitamins B_1 and B_2 as an entire quart of fresh milk.

Best Way to Store   Tightly covered in the refrigerator, in either its own can or in a screw-top jar (again, we prefer the screw-top jar because it seals out refrigerator odors).

Maximum Storage Time   About 1 week.

Roles in Cooking: Sweetened condensed milk possesses a number of unique properties: (1) when combined with an acid ingredient (lemon or lime juice, for example), it firms up magically (Key lime pie, you may remember, is nothing more than sweetened condensed milk "congealed" with plenty of tart Key lime juice); (2) when heated with chocolate, it becomes so smooth and thick that it can be cooled into a practically foolproof fudge that will not turn sugary; (3) when used in ice creams, it minimizes the formation of ice crystals so that there is no unpleasant grittiness; and (4) when mixed with fruits and nuts in cakes, cookies, puddings, and pies, it helps bond all the other ingredients together—both physically and flavorfully.

Recipe Uses   Sweetened condensed milk provides the basis for a wide variety of recipes: appetizer dips, sandwich spreads, beverages, salad dressings, sweet-sour sauces and soups, and, of course, all manner of puddings and pies, frozen desserts and candies.

Special Comments   Do not try to use sweetened condensed milk in your favorite recipes in place of whole milk and sugar. Use only in recipes that were developed especially for it. Sweetened condensed milk is a tricky substance, highly unpredictable.

Tip   When unopened cans of sweetened condensed milk are stored too long (keep them on a cool, dry shelf), they may begin to caramelize—that is to thicken and darken. They are perfectly safe to use, but may have become so thick that they cannot be easily mixed with other ingredients (in such cases, it's best to eat the stuff like candy). The wisest policy is to pay attention to the label date and to use the sweetened condensed milk well in advance of it.

N O T E   *For additional recipes, included elsewhere in this book, that call for varying amounts of evaporated or sweetened condensed milk, see the Appendix.*

Evaporated Milk

LEMON-CARDAMOM PILLOWS

About 3½ dozen cookies

The recipe to make when you have a small amount of evaporated milk or light or heavy cream cluttering up the refrigerator shelf. This cookie dough is frozen, so you can consider it a "frozen asset," to be brought out, a little bit at a time, and baked as needed.

> 2 cups sifted all-purpose flour
> 2 teaspoons baking powder
> 2 teaspoons ground cardamom
> ¼ teaspoon grated nutmeg
> ¼ teaspoon salt
> ½ cup (1 stick) butter, at room temperature
> ⅔ cup granulated sugar
> 1 egg
> ¼ cup evaporated milk or cream (light or heavy)
> Finely grated rind of 1 lemon

Sift the flour with the baking powder, spices, and salt onto a piece of wax paper and set aside. Cream the butter until light, then beat in the sugar until smooth. Mix in the egg, then the evaporated milk and lemon rind, beating well after each addition. Stir in the dry ingredients, a small amount at a time, and mix thoroughly. Spoon the dough onto a piece of foil, wrap, and freeze until firm.

When ready to bake, preheat the oven to moderately hot (375°F.).

To shape the cookies, pinch off small bits of dough and roll into 1-inch balls.

N O T E   *Work fast because the dough softens quickly. If it becomes too sticky to handle, firm up by chilling briefly in the freezer.*

Space the balls of dough about 1½ inches apart on lightly greased baking sheets and bake in the preheated hot oven for 12 to 15 minutes, or until pale tan.

Transfer at once to wire racks to cool.

PORK CHOPS
WITH PEANUT STUFFING

6 servings

Although we used this stuffing as a topping for pork chops, it is also a nice change of pace for stuffing a chicken. The amount of evaporated milk used in the recipe is adaptable to the amount you have on hand —less will make for a crispier topping (or stuffing), more for a moister one. It's good either way.

> 1 small yellow onion, peeled and minced
> 1 tablespoon butter or margarine
> 1 cup fine, soft bread crumbs
> ½ cup finely minced, roasted peanuts
> ½ teaspoon salt
> ¼ teaspoon cayenne pepper
> ⅓ to ⅔ cup evaporated milk (or any amount in between)
> 6 center-cut loin pork chops, about ¾ inch thick

Preheat the oven to moderate (350°F.).

Stir-fry the onion in the butter in a medium-sized heavy skillet for 5 to 8 minutes, until limp; stir in the crumbs, nuts, salt, cayenne, and evaporated milk. Spread on top of the pork chops, dividing the total amount of stuffing as evenly as possible.

Place the chops, stuffing side up, in a shallow roasting pan and bake, uncovered, in the preheated oven for 1 hour, or until the stuffing is lightly browned and the pork chops are well done (test by making a small slit near the bone). Serve at once.

N O T E   *If you intend to use this stuffing to stuff a 4- to 5-pound roasting chicken, triple the recipe so you don't run short (any leftover stuffing may be baked separately in a small, buttered, foil-covered casserole alongside the bird for the final 30 minutes of roasting).*

PAPRIKA-ROLLED FLOUNDER FILLETS IN DILL-WINE SAUCE

4 servings

Although the main point of this recipe is to use up small amounts of evaporated milk (or cream) and dry white wine, it also enables you to use—as a recipe ingredient rather than a garnish—paprika that may be losing its dazzling red color simply because it's stood on the shelf too long.

> 1 pound flounder fillets (preferably fresh, although frozen thawed fillets may be used)
> 2 tablespoons lemon juice
> 1 tablespoon paprika
> 2 tablespoons butter or margarine
> 1 tablespoon all-purpose flour
> ½ cup evaporated milk, light cream, or half-and-half
> ¼ cup dry white wine or vermouth
> 1 tablespoon minced fresh dill (or ½ teaspoon dill weed)
> ¼ teaspoon salt
> ⅛ teaspoon freshly ground black pepper

Preheat the oven to moderate (350°F.).

Brush the fillets with the lemon juice, then sprinkle liberally with paprika. Roll each fillet up jelly-roll style and fasten with 2 wooden picks—or more, as needed. Halve the flounder rolls crosswise, then arrange in a lightly buttered 8 × 8 × 2-inch baking dish. Cover with foil and bake in the preheated oven for 10 minutes.

Meanwhile, melt the butter in a small, heavy saucepan and blend in the flour. Gradually add the milk and cook, stirring constantly over low heat, until thickened. Cool slightly, then blend in the remaining ingredients.

Pour the sauce over the partially cooked flounder rolls, re-cover, and bake for 15 minutes longer. Remove the wooden picks and serve.

POTATO PUFF

6 servings

For this recipe you may either boil or bake the potatoes, whichever is easier for you or whichever method best suits the potatoes you have on hand. None of the amounts in this recipe must be exact—add more potato, if you like, and adjust the seasonings to your taste.

> 2 to 4 eggs yolks (depending upon how many you have on hand)
> ½ cup evaporated milk, milk, or cream (light or heavy)
> 4 cups mashed potatoes (for this amount you will need 5 to 6 medium potatoes)
> 2 tablespoons melted butter or margarine
> ¼ teaspoon crumbled leaf thyme
> ¼ teaspoon crumbled leaf rosemary
> ⅛ teaspoon freshly ground black pepper
> 1 teaspoon salt
> Pinch of grated nutmeg or ground mace
> ¼ cup grated Parmesan, Gruyère, or Cheddar cheese

Preheat the oven to hot (400°F.).

Beat the egg yolks and milk just enough to combine, then mix in the mashed potatoes and all the remaining ingredients. Spoon into a well-buttered 1½-quart casserole or soufflé dish and bake, uncovered, in the preheated oven for 15 to 20 minutes. Raise the oven temperature to 450°F. and bake for 10 minutes longer, or until lightly browned.

N O T E   *Up to 1½ cups of chopped leftover green beans, carrots, cauliflower, or other cooked vegetable can be added to this dish.*

SCALLOPED EGGPLANT

4 servings

An easy dish that can be prepared several hours ahead, then baked whenever you are ready for it. We prepare it up to the point of stirring in the milk and topping with buttered crumbs, then add those just before popping the casserole into the oven. This may seem like a great deal of eggplant (8 to 10 cups of raw cubes), but these will boil down to half that amount.

> 1 large or 2 small eggplants, washed (but not peeled) and cut in 1-inch
>   cubes
> 1 cup boiling water, mixed with 1 teaspoon salt
> 1 large yellow onion, peeled and chopped
> 2 tablespoons butter or margarine
> ⅛ teaspoon freshly ground black pepper
> 2 cups soft bread crumbs
> ½ cup evaporated milk, milk, or cream (light or heavy)

T O P P I N G

> ½ cup soft bread crumbs tossed with 1 tablespoon melted butter

Preheat the oven to moderate (350°F.).

Boil the eggplant in the salted water in a covered pan over moderate heat for about 5 minutes, or until tender; drain well and reserve. Stir-fry the onion in the butter in a medium-sized heavy skillet over moderate heat for 8 to 10 minutes, until limp and golden but not brown. Combine with the eggplant, pepper, bread crumbs, and evaporated milk in a buttered 1½-quart baking dish. Sprinkle the topping evenly over all and bake, uncovered, in the preheated oven for about 30 minutes, or until browned and piping hot.

EASY BREAKFAST WAFFLES

4 servings

What accounts for these waffles' unusually mellow flavor is the evaporated milk, used as the liquid ingredient in place of regular milk. The recipe calls for only ½ cup of it, so it's a fast and effective way to use up a leftover. If you should have less than ½ cup of evaporated milk and don't want to open a fresh can, round out the ½ cup measure with plain milk, light cream, or half-and-half.

This batter, by the way, may be dropped onto a lightly greased griddle and cooked like pancakes.

C O N T I N U E D

1 cup sifted all-purpose flour
1½ teaspoons baking powder
1 tablespoon granulated sugar
¼ teaspoon salt
2 eggs, beaten lightly
2 tablespoons melted butter or margarine
½ cup evaporated milk or light cream·

Preheat waffle iron according to manufacturer's instructions.

Sift the flour, baking powder, sugar, and salt into a bowl. Combine the eggs, butter, and milk and add to the sifted dry ingredients, one-half of the total amount at a time. Beat well after each addition until the batter is smooth. Pour the batter into a pitcher, then pour directly into the preheated waffle iron, again following the manufacturer's directions. Bake the waffles at medium heat until steaming stops and the waffles are golden brown.

Serve with plenty of butter and maple syrup or other topping.

VARIATION

Nut Waffles Prepare the waffle batter as directed, and at the end mix in ¼ cup very finely minced walnuts, pecans, blanched almonds, or filberts. Bake as directed above.

CURRIED TUNA MOUSSE

6 to 8 servings

What's best about this recipe is that it's so adaptable. The liquid ingredient used, for example, can be evaporated milk, light cream, a half-and-half mixture of tomato sauce or purée and water, chicken or beef broth, juice drained from a can of apricots or peaches. You might even try leftover vegetable or fish stock. The point is to use whatever you have on hand.

1 envelope unflavored gelatin
2 teaspoons curry powder
1 cup liquid (evaporated milk, cream, broth, fruit nectar, etc.)
½ cup mayonnaise or salad dressing

1 tablespoon cider vinegar
2 tablespoons finely grated onion
1 tablespoon Worcestershire sauce
½ cup heavy cream, whipped
2 cans (6½ to 7 ounces each) tuna, drained and flaked
1 to 4 tablespoons minced capers (optional—use if you should have
  an almost empty jar of them)

Combine the gelatin and curry powder; pour ¼ cup of the liquid into a small, heavy saucepan, then sprinkle in the curry-gelatin mixture. Bring the remaining liquid to a boil in a separate small saucepan. Pour into the gelatin mixture and stir until the gelatin is dissolved, then blend in the mayonnaise, vinegar, onion, and Worcestershire. Chill until tacky-firm.

Beat the chilled mixture lightly, then fold in the whipped cream, tuna, and, if you like, the capers. Pour into an oiled 1-quart ring mold and chill until firm.

Unmold and serve on crisp greenery.

BAKED POTATOES
STUFFED THE PORTUGUESE WAY
WITH CREAMED SALT COD

6 servings

Almost everywhere you travel in Portugal, you will see *bacalhão* (salt cod) on the menu—from such fancy Lisbon restaurants as Aviz and Tavares to the most remote and rustic village inn. But of all the Portuguese ways to prepare salt cod, this one remains a favorite. It is also, by the way, an excellent way to use up oddments of evaporated milk and/or cream.

½ pound dried salt cod
1 medium yellow onion, peeled and minced
¼ cup (½ stick) butter or margarine
¼ teaspoon crumbled leaf marjoram
¼ teaspoon crumbled leaf rosemary

CONTINUED

Pinch of ground mace or grated nutmeg

⅛ teaspoon freshly ground black pepper

¼ cup unsifted all-purpose flour

2 cups milk and/or cream mixture (use any combination; you might even use part chicken, beef, fish, or vegetable stock if you have that on hand)

6 large Idaho potatoes, baked for 1 hour in a hot oven (400°F.), then cooled to room temperature

Soak the salt cod in just enough cold water to cover for 8 hours or overnight, changing the water at least twice to leach out most of the salt. Drain and rinse the cod well, place in a saucepan, and add just enough fresh cold water to cover; bring to a simmer over moderate heat. Cover the pan and simmer for 8 to 10 minutes, or until the cod will flake at the touch of a fork. Drain the cod well, cool until easy to handle, then pick over carefully to remove any bits of bone. Flake the cod moderately fine and place in a mixing bowl.

Sauté the onion in the butter in a medium-sized heavy saucepan over moderate heat for 8 to 10 minutes, until limp and golden; add the herbs, mace, and pepper and allow to mellow for 3 to 5 minutes. Blend in the flour and heat, stirring constantly, for 1 to 2 minutes, to form a thick paste. Pour in the milk and/or cream mixture and heat, whisking vigorously, until thickened and smooth. Turn the heat to its lowest point and let the sauce mellow until no floury taste remains—5 to 10 minutes. Pour the sauce over the flaked cod.

Preheat the oven to moderate (350°F.).

Scoop out the baked potatoes, leaving shells about ⅛ inch thick. Cut the scooped-out potato flesh into ½-inch cubes and add to the cod mixture; toss lightly but well to mix. Stuff each potato with cod mixture, then bake, uncovered, in the preheated oven for 30 minutes, or until tipped with brown.

Serve as a lunch or supper main dish accompanied by chunks of crusty garlic bread and a crisp green salad.

WHIPPED TOPPING

1½ to 2 cups

There are few easier or more efficient ways to use up a small amount of leftover evaporated milk than to turn it into a mock whipped cream that can be drifted over almost any dessert.

    ½ to ¾ cup evaporated milk
    Juice of ½ small lemon
    ⅓ cup confectioners sugar
    ½ teaspoon vanilla extract

Pour the evaporated milk into a small metal bowl, and set in the freezer until ice crystals begin to form around the edges of the bowl —this will take about half an hour. Chill as well your beater and the bowl in which you will whip the milk. Pour the chilled milk into the chilled bowl and beat hard until soft and billowing; add the remaining ingredients and continue whipping until the mixture forms stiff peaks.

Sweetened Condensed Milk

PLANTATION PEANUT SOUP

6 servings

This updated version of the old Southern classic is an excellent repository for leftover sweetened condensed milk, beef or chicken broth, evaporated milk and/or cream and chopped peanuts.

This soup freezes well (directions are included at the end of the recipe).

    1 large yellow onion, peeled and chopped
    2 tablespoons butter or margarine

CONTINUED

1 large, very ripe tomato, peeled, cored, and chopped, or ½ cup tomato sauce
½ teaspoon crumbled leaf thyme
⅛ teaspoon freshly ground black pepper
Pinch of ground mace
2 cups beef or chicken broth
3 to 4 tablespoons sweetened condensed milk or 1 tablespoon honey or light or dark corn syrup (or 2 tablespoons light brown sugar)
1 cup firmly packed cream-style peanut butter
1½ cups milk-cream mixture (use any combination of milk, evaporated milk, cream—light, heavy, sour, or half-and-half)
¼ teaspoon cayenne pepper
3 tablespoons tawny Port or sherry
2 tablespoons minced fresh or frozen chives
1 cup chopped roasted peanuts

Stir-fry the onion in the butter in a large, heavy saucepan over moderate heat for 8 to 10 minutes, until limp and golden. Stir in the tomato, thyme, black pepper, and mace and simmer, stirring now and then, for about 5 minutes until quite thick. Add the broth, sweetened condensed milk, and peanut butter and heat, stirring often, for 10 minutes.

Purée the mixture in an electric blender or food processor or by putting through a food mill. Return to the pan, add the milk-cream mixture and cayenne and bring just to serving temperature. Stir in the Port and chives and heat for 1 to 2 minutes longer; do not allow to boil or the soup may curdle.

Ladle into soup bowls and serve, topped with a scattering of chopped peanuts.

To Freeze   Cool the soup to room temperature (do not add the chopped peanuts), then ladle into freezer containers of a size appropriate to your needs, filling each to within ½ inch of the top. Snap on the lids, label, and date, then place in a freezer set at 0°F. Keeping time: about 4 months.

MACARONI AND TURKEY SALAD WITH SWEET MUSTARD DRESSING

6 servings

Both the salad and the dressing recipes are flexible, enabling you to use up a variety of leftovers: a partial can of sweetened condensed milk, a cup of diced leftover turkey (or chicken, ham, or pork). You might also add a cup of leftover cooked peas or carrots or green beans if you should have them on hand.

DRESSING

⅓ to ½ cup sweetened condensed milk
¾ cup mayonnaise or salad dressing
½ cup lemon or lime juice
½ cup cream (sour, light, or heavy), evaporated milk, or milk
2 tablespoons Dijon or spicy brown mustard
¼ teaspoon crumbled leaf marjoram
¼ teaspoon dill weed
⅛ teaspoon freshly ground black pepper

SALAD

2 cups elbow macaroni, cooked according to package directions and drained
1 cup diced, cooked turkey (or chicken, ham, or pork)
1 small yellow onion, peeled and chopped fine
1 rib celery, trimmed and diced fine
½ cup minced sweet green, red, or yellow pepper
Salt to taste

Whisk all the dressing ingredients together to combine. Place the salad ingredients in a large bowl, pour the dressing over all and toss well to mix. Taste for salt and add as needed. Cover and chill for several hours before serving.

If, after standing in the refrigerator, the salad seems dry—and it may, even though it seemed soupy in the beginning, because the pasta absorbs liquid like a sponge—moisten with a little additional cream or milk, toss well again, and serve.

Molasses

The finest, mellowest, and clearest of the many types and grades of molasses available is the unsulfured (meaning that sulfur was not used in the sugar-refining process as it sometimes is when the sugar cane is less than fully ripe). The lowest grade of molasses, as well as the darkest and strongest, is blackstrap, to which food faddists have attributed magical powers. The truth is, blackstrap amounts to little more than the dregs, and most of the iron and other minerals it contains are not present in a form that the body can use.

Best Way to Store   Tightly capped in its own bottle on a cool, dry shelf. Each time you use molasses, wipe both the bottle and the cap well with a damp cloth so you do not attract insects—and so you will be able to open the bottle easily the next time around.

Maximum Storage Time   Although it seems that molasses keeps almost indefinitely, it's best to use up and replenish your supply within a year to 15 months.

Roles in Cooking   To add color and flavor, to glaze meats.

Recipe Uses   Cakes, cookies, gingerbreads, candies, steamed puddings and breads, rye and whole-wheat breads, barbecue sauces, pies, and confections—they often call for molasses and sometimes for plenty of it.

How to Use Small Amounts   For a refreshing drink, stir 1 to 2 tablespoons of molasses into a glass of milk; also try spreading a tablespoon or so into a peanut butter sandwich or drizzling a couple of tablespoons over vanilla, chocolate, or coffee ice creams.

N O T E   *For additional recipes, included elsewhere in this book, that call for varying amounts of molasses, see the Appendix.*

GINGERY SWEET-SOUR
BEEF STEW WITH MOLASSES

6 to 8 servings

This easy, all-in-one-kettle party stew is a good one to prepare if you have an almost-empty bottle of molasses on hand (the recipe calls for ¼ to ⅓ cup). Via optional additions, the stew also enables you to use up any small amounts of raisins, wine, and tomato paste you may have on hand. So make the stew when you have leftovers to get rid of, then freeze, if you like, to enjoy later (directions for freezing are given at the end of the recipe).

  3 pounds boned beef chuck, trimmed of excess fat and cut in 1½-inch
    cubes
  ⅔ cup unsifted all-purpose flour
  ⅓ cup peanut or vegetable oil
  3 medium yellow onions, peeled and coarsely chopped
  2 cloves garlic, peeled and minced
  2 tablespoons finely minced fresh gingerroot or preserved or candied
    ginger (rinsed of syrup or sugar) or 1 teaspoon ground ginger
  ½ teaspoon crumbled leaf thyme
  ½ teaspoon crumbled leaf marjoram
  2 cups peeled, coarsely chopped fresh tomatoes or 2 cups canned
    tomatoes (do not drain)
  1 to 3 tablespoons tomato paste (optional)
  ¼ to ⅔ cup dry red or white wine (optional)
  ⅓ cup cider vinegar
  ¼ to ⅓ cup molasses
  ⅓ to 1 cup seedless raisins (optional)
  1 pound carrots, peeled and cut in ½-inch chunks (halve lengthwise
    any unusually chunky carrots)
  Salt and freshly ground black pepper to taste

Shake the beef, a few cubes at a time, in the flour in a heavy paper bag. Brown in the oil in a large, heavy kettle set over moderately high heat, again a few cubes of beef at a time; drain on paper toweling.

Add the onions, garlic, and ginger to the kettle and stir-fry in the drippings over moderate heat for 8 to 10 minutes, or until golden. Add the thyme, marjoram, tomatoes, tomato paste and wine (if you like), vinegar, and molasses and bring to a simmer. Return the beef to the kettle, adjust the heat so the liquid stays at a gentle simmer, then cover and cook for 1 hour 15 minutes. Add the raisins, if you like, and carrots, then re-cover and simmer for about 1 hour 15 minutes longer, or until the beef and carrots are fork-tender. Season to taste with salt and pepper.

If the stew seems too liquid, boil, uncovered, for 10 to 15 minutes, or until the gravy thickens slightly. If, on the other hand, the stew seems too thick, thin with a little water.

Serve over fluffy boiled rice or boiled noodles.

To Freeze Cool the stew to room temperature, then ladle into freezer containers (half-pints if you live alone, pints if there are two of you, quarts for families or for entertaining). Fill each container to within ½ inch of the top, snap on the lid, label, and date, then put in a freezer set at 0° F. Keeping time: about 6 months.

When ready to serve, bring the stew gently to serving temperature over low heat, stirring often to prevent sticking. Thin, if necessary, with a little water.

'LASSES BREAD

One 9 × 9 × 2-inch loaf

This old Southern gingerbread makes a good breakfast cake if left unfrosted and served with unsalted butter. Topped with whipped cream or an orange sauce, it makes a fine dessert. Note that the recipe not only enables you to use up "the last" of a bottle of molasses, but also small amounts of brown sugar and buttermilk, sour milk, or sour cream.

> ¾ cup (1½ sticks) butter, at room temperature
> ½ cup firmly packed light or dark brown sugar
> ½ cup molasses
> 3 eggs, separated
> 2 cups sifted all-purpose flour
> ½ teaspoon ground cinnamon
> ½ teaspoon ground mace
> 1 tablespoon ground ginger
> 1 teaspoon baking powder
> ½ teaspoon baking soda

½ cup buttermilk, sour milk, or sour cream
Finely grated rind of ½ orange

Preheat the oven to moderately slow (325° F.).

Cream the butter well, then add the sugar and cream well again. Add the molasses, then the egg yolks, mixing well after each addition. Sift the flour with the spices, baking powder, and soda and add to the creamed mixture alternately with the buttermilk, beginning and ending with the dry ingredients. Stir in the orange rind.

Beat the egg whites to soft peaks, then fold into the batter. Pour into a well-greased 9 × 9 × 2-inch baking pan and bake in the preheated oven for about 40 minutes, or until the bread pulls away from the sides of the pan and the top springs back when pressed lightly with a finger.

STEAMED BROWN BREAD

Four 1-pound loaves

This is the classic "Boston brown bread," traditionally served with baked beans. This recipe calls for 1½ cups whole-wheat or graham flour (a good way to use up leftovers), as well as 2 cups of buttermilk and ¾ cup molasses. Freeze whatever loaves your family cannot eat right away (see the directions at the end of the recipe); the bread seems even better after a stint in the freezer.

The ideal containers for steaming the bread are #303 cans (the 1-pound size) in which fruits and vegetables are commonly packed.

1½ cups *unsifted* graham or whole-wheat flour
1 cup sifted all-purpose flour
½ cup yellow corn meal
½ teaspoon salt
1 teaspoon baking powder
1 teaspoon baking soda
¾ cup molasses
2 tablespoons honey
2 cups buttermilk or sour milk
1 cup seedless raisins

In a large mixing bowl combine the flours, corn meal, salt, baking powder, and soda; make a well in the center. Mix together the molasses, honey, and buttermilk and pour all at once into the dry ingredients; mix briskly—just enough to dampen the dry ingredients. Stir in the raisins.

Spoon the batter into four well-greased 1-pound cans, filling each no more than two-thirds full. Cover each can with several thicknesses of aluminum foil, then tie string around the tops of the cans to seal. Stand the cans on a rack in a large, deep kettle containing 1 to 1½ inches of boiling water (the water should not touch the bottoms of the cans); cover and steam for 3 hours, adding more boiling water to the kettle if necessary to keep it from boiling dry.

Remove the breads from the kettle after they have steamed the allotted time and cool for 20 minutes. Uncover the breads, ease them from their cans, and cool to room temperature before slicing.

To Freeze   Wrap the cooled loaves individually in aluminum foil, pressing out all air pockets; label, date, and store in a freezer set at 0° F. Keeping time: about 6 months. No need to thaw the bread before slicing—simply cut off the amount you need, using a serrated knife, then rewrap the remainder and return to the freezer.

ALL-PURPOSE BARBECUE SAUCE

3 to 3½ cups

Here's a way to turn odds and ends of molasses, ketchup or chili sauce, and honey and/or soy sauce into a useful, versatile seasoning that will keep well in the refrigerator for about 1 month.

> 1 cup molasses
> ½ cup prepared mustard
> ½ cup ketchup or chili sauce
> 1 cup cider vinegar or wine vinegar, or a half-and-half mixture of the two
> 1 to 4 tablespoons honey (optional)
> 1 to 3 tablespoons soy sauce (optional)
> 1 clove garlic, peeled and crushed

Place all the ingredients in a 1-quart jar with a close-fitting lid and shake well to combine. Store, tightly covered, in the refrigerator and use for barbecuing chops, chicken, meat loaf, hamburgers, short ribs, or spareribs. Shake well before each use, then brush liberally over the food to be broiled, roasted, baked, or braised.

Any foods requiring 30 minutes or more to cook should be brushed several times during cooking with additional barbecue sauce.

Mushroom Stems

Mushrooms, it's said, were a great favorite of the pharoahs of Egypt, and later of the Caesars. In fact, only within the twentieth century have they become available (and affordable) to any but the rich and the royal. Mushrooms scarcely qualify as cheap food yet—all the more reason why we should use every scrap of them. Too many recipes blithely call for mushroom caps, and too few of us, unfortunately, save the stems to use another time, although they can be very good indeed.

Best Way to Store   First of all, wipe the mushroom stems as clean as possible with a damp cloth and trim away any blemishes. Wrap the stems *en masse* in several thicknesses of damp paper toweling, pop the bundle into a large plastic bag (do not seal or close the bag), then store in the refrigerator.

Maximum Storage Time   About 5 days.

Roles in Cooking   Principally to add flavor, color, and texture. Finely minced sautéed mushrooms (duxelles) have a pastelike consistency that can be used to fill (and hold together) rolled cutlets, steaks, boned and rolled roasts, even omelets and rolled pancakes.

Recipe Uses   So many French classics call for mushrooms (sauces; forcemeats, stuffings; fish, meat, and poultry recipes; soufflés and omelets), as do dozens of Russian, Scandinavian, German, Austrian, and Italian specialties. The French, by the way, are so fond of mushrooms, so enchanted by their shape, that they fashion "dessert mushrooms" out of delicately tinted meringue.

Special Comments   Whenever a recipe calls for chopped or minced whole mushrooms, you may substitute an equal amount of chopped mushroom stems. They—like whole mushrooms—add almost no calories (about 120 per pound!) but plenty of flavor.

How to Use Very Small Amounts   Scramble ½ cup or less of minced or chopped mushroom stems into eggs, or sauté in butter until soft and pastelike and use as a spread for toast. Mix lightly sautéed minced mushroom stems into meat loaves or hamburgers or pasta sauce. Or scatter over pizza or toss with cooked, drained, and seasoned green beans.

N O T E   *For additional recipes, included elsewhere in this book, that call for mushrooms, see the Appendix.*

M U S H R O O M   C R U S T

One 8-inch pie shell

Here's an unusual way to make the most of mushroom stems—to combine them with butter and crumbs and shape them into a pie shell. This particular pie shell is excellent for quiches, for hamburger, creamed chicken, turkey or tuna fillings, or for the Rice and Onion Pie included in this book (see page 258).

> 1¼ to 1½ cups mushroom stems (this is the quantity you will get
>   from a pound of medium mushrooms)
> 5 tablespoons butter or margarine
> 4 cups fine, soft bread crumbs
> ¼ teaspoon rubbed sage
> ⅛ teaspoon crumbled leaf thyme
> ¼ teaspoon salt
> ⅛ teaspoon freshly ground black pepper
> 2 tablespoons milk (if needed to hold the mixture together)
> 1 egg white, beaten until frothy

Preheat the oven to moderate (350°F.).

Wipe the mushroom stems clean with a damp cloth, then mince very fine; stir-fry in the butter in a large, heavy skillet over moderate heat for about 10 minutes, or until pastelike. Mix in the crumbs, herbs, salt, and pepper and mix well. If the mixture still seems crumbly, scatter the milk over the surface, then mix well again.

Pat the mushroom mixture firmly over the bottom and up the sides of a lightly greased 8-inch pie pan to form a pie shell. Bake in the preheated oven for 25 to 30 minutes, or until the crust is lightly browned around the edges. Remove from the oven and cool, then brush well with beaten egg white to seal any cracks and let air-dry for 10 minutes (this is to help keep the filling from seeping into the crust and making it soggy).

The crust is now ready to fill with your favorite savory filling and to bake as individual filling recipes direct.

SKILLET VEAL IN MUSHROOM AND WINE SAUCE

2 servings

This is a low-calorie recipe that "weighs in" at about 180 calories per serving.

2 tablespoons butter or margarine
Stems from ¾ to 1 pound mushrooms, wiped clean and coarsely chopped
½ pound veal round, sliced and pounded thin as for scaloppine
¼ teaspoon salt
⅛ teaspoon freshly ground black pepper
⅓ cup dry white wine

Melt 1 tablespoon of the butter in a large, heavy skillet over moderate heat; add the mushrooms and stir-fry for 2 to 3 minutes, until beginning to color. Turn the heat to low and let the mushrooms cook for about 10 minutes, uncovered, then remove from the skillet to a large plate and keep warm.

Wipe the skillet dry with paper toweling; add the remaining 1 tablespoon butter and melt over high heat. When bubbly, add the veal and brown quickly on each side—just about a minute for each side is all that's needed. Remove the veal to two heated serving plates and sprinkle with salt and pepper.

Add the wine to the skillet and boil rapidly, scraping up browned bits, for 1 minute. Return the mushrooms to the skillet and cook and stir for 1 minute longer. Pour over the veal and serve.

DUXELLES (MUSHROOM PASTE)

About ½ cup

There is no reason why this concentrated mushroom-onion paste cannot be made with mushroom stems, which would normally be thrown away. And that is precisely what we have done in developing this recipe. It calls for the *stems* of 1 pound of mushrooms (about 1⅓ to 1½ cups when finely minced). If you should have more stems—say from 1½ to 2 pounds of mushrooms—simply prepare 1½ or 2 times this basic recipe.

The beauty of duxelles is that it can be frozen (it will keep well for about 4 months in the freezer) and dipped into as needed to flavor soups, sauces, gravies, stews, stuffings, and so on. Remember that it is highly concentrated, so 2 to 3 tablespoons should be sufficient for most recipes. But by all means taste as you add, and continue adding the duxelles until the flavor of a particular recipe suits you.

> Stems from 1 pound of mushrooms, wiped very clean and minced very fine
> 1 small yellow onion, peeled and minced very fine
> 2 medium shallots or scallions (white part only), peeled or trimmed and minced very fine
> 3 tablespoons unsalted butter
> ¼ teaspoon salt
> Pinch of freshly ground black pepper

Bundle the minced mushrooms into a clean, dry dishtowel and wring out as much liquid as possible; set aside for the time being.

In a small, heavy saucepan, stir-fry the onion and shallots in the butter over moderately low heat for about 10 minutes, until very soft and golden; do not brown the onion mixture, as this will give the duxelles a tinge of bitterness. Add the mushrooms and sauté, stirring now and then, over low heat for about 15 minutes, or until very thick and pastelike. Season with salt and pepper.

Shape the duxelles on a double thickness of foil into a bar about the size of a stick of butter, then wrap snugly and freeze. To use, simply slice off ¾-inch pats (about the equivalent of 1 tablespoon) and use to flavor soups, sauces, gravies, stews, and the like. No need to thaw the duxelles—simply add the solidly frozen pats.

Nuts

The information given here applies to a wide variety of shelled nuts, most of which can be used interchangeably in recipes: pecans, walnuts and black walnuts, filberts and hazelnuts, cashews, Brazil nuts, macadamias, pine nuts (known in Italian as *pignoli* and in Spanish as *piñon*), almonds, and, of course, peanuts, which are not true nuts at all but rather the fruits of a legume related to peas and beans.

Best Way to Store   If the nuts are fresh, unsalted, and unroasted, store in tightly covered glass jars, snugly sealed heavy-duty vapor-proof plastic bags, or in plastic cartons with snap-on lids. Salted, roasted nuts are best stored in glass jars, because glass is a wholly inert material impervious to the corrosive effects of salt.

To Freeze   Fresh, unroasted, unsalted, shelled nuts freeze beautifully and will keep as long as 2 years at 0° F. The best way to package them is exactly as you would for refrigerator storage.

Maximum Storage Time   About 9 months for fresh, raw, unsalted nuts; about 4 to 6 weeks for nuts that were vacuum canned, bottled or bagged—both the raw and the roasted. See the section on freezing (above) for freezer storage time.

Roles in Cooking   Primarily to add crunch and flavor. But when nuts are finely ground, they also provide body (for cookies, breads, and cakes); and in the case of sauces they actually serve as a thickener.

Special Comments You may be interested to learn that the pecan, a variety of wild hickory, is as American as the turkey, the cranberry, and the ear of corn. De Soto, traveling the Gulf Coast and Mississippi River Valley in his search for the Fountain of Youth, tried pecans and liked them. He noted that they were a great favorite among the Indians, who munched them much as we do candy.

Nuts, the Indians seemed instinctively to know, are nutritional powerhouses, rich in high-quality protein, vitamins, and minerals. They are also an instant energy source but *low in saturated fats.*

NOTE *For additional recipes, included elsewhere in this book, that call for varying amounts of different kinds of nuts, see the Appendix.*

CABBAGE AND WALNUTS IN SOUR CREAM

6 servings

Cabbage quickly cooked (and therefore *un*smelly), then tossed with sour cream and leftover walnuts. If you should have half a large cabbage on hand (left over from making cole slaw), use it in place of the medium-sized cabbage.

> 1 medium yellow onion, peeled and minced
> ¼ cup (½ stick) butter or margarine
> 1 medium cabbage, trimmed, quartered, and cored, then sliced ¼ inch thick
> Pinch of ground mace or grated nutmeg
> Pinch of crumbled leaf savory
> Pinch of crumbled leaf thyme
> ¼ cup water or beef or chicken broth
> ¾ to 1 cup sour cream (at room temperature)
> ¾ to 1 cup finely chopped walnuts (or pecans, if that is what you have on hand)
> Salt and freshly ground black pepper to taste

Stir-fry the onion in the butter over moderately high heat in a very large, heavy skillet for about 5 minutes, just until limp and golden. Add the cabbage, mace, savory, and thyme and stir-fry for 8 to 10 minutes longer, just until the cabbage is nicely glazed. Add the water, cover, and simmer for 10 to 15 minutes, or until the cabbage is done the way you like it. Uncover, mix in the sour cream and walnuts and bring just to serving temperature, stirring constantly (do not boil or the cream will curdle).

Season to taste with salt and pepper and serve.

P E A R - P E C A N P U D D I N G - C A K E

One 8 × 8 × 2-inch cake

¼ cup (½ stick) butter or margarine
¾ cup firmly packed light brown sugar
2½ cups peeled, cored, and thinly sliced pears (about 3 to 4 medium-
  to-large pears)
¾ to 1 cup coarsely chopped pecans or walnuts
¾ teaspoon ground mace or grated nutmeg
Juice of 1 lemon
⅓ cup vegetable shortening
⅔ cup granulated sugar
1 egg
1½ cups sifted all-purpose flour
2 teaspoons baking powder
¼ teaspoon salt
⅔ cup milk
1 teaspoon vanilla extract

Preheat the oven to moderately slow (325° F.).

Melt the butter in an 8 × 8 × 2-inch baking pan and sprinkle or crumble in the brown sugar. Layer the pears on top, overlapping the slices, then sprinkle with the nuts, mace, and lemon juice. Set aside.

Cream the shortening and granulated sugar in a mixing bowl until fluffy; beat in the egg. Combine the flour, baking powder, and salt and add to the creamed mixture alternately with the milk, beginning and ending with the dry ingredients. Stir in the vanilla.

Pour the batter evenly over the fruit and bake in the preheated oven for 1 hour, or until the top seems springy to the touch. Remove from the oven, cool for 20 minutes, then cut into squares and serve, topped, if you like, with whipped cream or vanilla ice cream.

H O N E Y - H A Z E L N U T   B R E A D

One 9 × 5 × 3-inch loaf

3 cups sifted all-purpose flour
1 tablespoon (3 teaspoons) baking powder
1 teaspoon salt
½ cup vegetable shortening
½ cup granulated sugar
½ cup honey
1 egg
¾ cup milk
1 cup blanched, chopped, lightly toasted hazelnuts (or chopped pecans or walnuts)

Preheat the oven to moderate (350° F.).

Sift the flour, baking powder, and salt together onto a piece of wax paper and set aside. Cream the shortening and sugar until fluffy; beat in the honey, then the egg. Add the sifted dry ingredients to the creamed mixture alternately with the milk, beginning and ending with the dry ingredients. Stir in the nuts.

Spoon the batter into a well-greased and -floured 9 × 5 × 3-inch loaf pan and bake in the preheated oven for 45 minutes to 1 hour. Remove the pan from the oven and loosen the bread around the edges. Cool upright in the pan on a wire rack for 10 minutes, then invert and turn the bread out.

Cool to room temperature before slicing.

L E M O N - N U T   B U N D T   C A K E

One 9½-inch cake

This is a dense-textured cake not unlike pound cake, and it can be made, if you prefer, with the grated rind of an orange and ¼ cup of orange juice instead of with the lemon rind and juice called for below. You may also use a half-and-half mix of raisins (or dried currants) and nuts instead of chopped nuts alone, so the cake is a good one for ridding your shelves of partial boxes of this and that.

Note, too, that the batter calls for ¾ cup sour cream (you can also use heavy or light cream that has gone sour).

¾ cup (1½ sticks) butter, at room temperature
1 cup granulated sugar
Finely grated rind and juice of 1 lemon
2 eggs
2 cups sifted all-purpose flour
1 teaspoon baking soda
½ teaspoon salt
¾ cup sour cream
¼ cup milk
1½ cups chopped nuts (walnuts or pecans are best)

G L A Z E

1 cup sifted confectioners sugar
Juice of 1 lemon
¼ cup rum (optional)

Preheat the oven to moderately slow (325° F.).

Cream the butter and sugar until fluffy; add the lemon rind and juice. Beat the eggs in, one at a time. Sift the flour with the soda and salt; in a separate bowl, combine the sour cream and the milk. Add the sifted dry ingredients to the batter alternately with the sour cream mixture, beginning and ending with the dry ingredients. Fold in the nuts.

Pour the batter into a well-greased and -floured 9½-inch (12-cup) bundt pan and bake in the preheated oven for 1 hour and 15 to 20 minutes, or until the cake pulls from the sides of the pan and is springy to the touch.

Cool the cake upright in its pan on a wire rack for 15 minutes, then loosen around the edges and turn out on a cake platter. Quickly combine all the glaze ingredients and drizzle evenly over the cake.

N O T E   *You can, if you prefer, sprinkle the rum over the cake as soon as you invert it, then glaze with a mixture of the confectioners sugar and lemon juice (this way the rum penetrates the cake more deeply).*

Oatmeal

(Rolled Oats)

Both the quick-cooking and the old-fashioned types of oatmeal are made of whole grains; they will, therefore, become rancid in time because they contain the rich, perishable oat germ as well as the bran and endosperm.

Best Way to Store Tightly covered in a rustproof canister or jar on a cool, dark, dry shelf.

Maximum Storage Time About 4 months.

Roles in Cooking To provide crunch, flavor, body, and nutritive value (the B-complex vitamins, in particular). Oatmeal is a frugal and filling way to extend ground meats; it can be used as a crisp topping for cobblers and open-faced fruit pies; it will thicken soups and broths (just add it as you would rice or barley); and, as every good Scottish cook knows, it helps to bind croquettes and meat puddings together. Gillies (Scottish hunting guides) often "bread" fresh-caught trout with oatmeal, then pan-fry them in bacon drippings—and very good they are, too. Finally, oatmeal is the foundation of a variety of nourishing porridges.

Recipe Uses Bar cookies, drop cookies, quick breads, meat loaves, and burgers are your best bets for using up what your family won't eat for breakfast.

Special Comments If you should have any *cooked* oatmeal left over, chill until firm, shape it into flat cakes, dip into fine dry bread crumbs so that each side is nicely coated, then brown quickly in butter and serve as you would hot cakes—that is, with plenty of melted butter and maple syrup.

N O T E *For additional recipes, included elsewhere in this book, that call for varying amounts of oatmeal, see the Appendix.*

CROFTER'S OAT, APPLE, AND LAMB LOAF

6 to 8 servings

A nourishing, old Scottish recipe that uses oatmeal as a meat extender and binder in place of bread crumbs.

> 2 pounds lean ground lamb shoulder (or lean ground beef chuck or a half-and-half mixture of the two)
> 1 cup rolled oats
> 1 medium yellow onion, peeled and minced
> ½ cup apple cider, milk, or evaporated milk
> 1 cup finely chopped, peeled tart apple
> 1 cup finely grated carrot
> 2 eggs
> 2 teaspoons salt
> ¼ teaspoon crumbled leaf rosemary
> ¼ teaspoon crumbled leaf thyme
> ¼ teaspoon crumbled leaf sage
> ¼ teaspoon freshly ground black pepper

Preheat the oven to moderate (350° F.).

Mix all the ingredients together well and pack into a well-greased 9 × 5 × 3-inch loaf pan. Bake, uncovered, in the preheated oven for about 1 hour, or until the loaf is richly browned and has pulled from the sides of the pan. Remove from the oven and cool for 10 minutes; drain off accumulated drippings (these may be saved and used to make gravy or added to a soup or stew).

Loosen the meat loaf with a spatula or thin-bladed knife, then turn out on a heated platter. Slice about ½ inch thick and serve.

PARKIN

2½ dozen small bars

The time to make these chewy, gingery Scottish bars is when you are down to a small amount of oatmeal and/or dark brown sugar and/or molasses.

CONTINUED

    1 cup sifted all-purpose flour
    ¼ teaspoon salt
    1½ teaspoons baking soda
    1 teaspoon ground ginger
    ¼ teaspoon ground mace
    ¼ teaspoon ground cinnamon
    ½ cup (1 stick) butter or margarine
    ½ cup firmly packed dark brown sugar
    ¼ cup molasses
    1 cup rolled oats
    1 egg, beaten lightly
    2 tablespoons milk or cream (light, heavy, or sour)

Preheat the oven to moderate (350° F.).

Sift the flour, salt, soda, and spices together onto a piece of wax paper. In a large saucepan set over moderate heat, stir the butter constantly with the sugar and molasses until the butter melts. Off the heat, blend in the remaining ingredients and the reserved sifted ingredients.

Spoon the batter into a well-greased 9 × 9 × 2-inch pan and bake in the preheated oven for 25 to 30 minutes, or until the top springs back when touched. Cool to room temperature in the pan, then cut in small squares.

OATMEAL-BANANA MUFFINS

1½ dozen

So often our resolve to eat a hot cereal during cold weather falls by the way, and we find that, come spring, we have an almost full box of rolled oats on hand. Rather than keep the oatmeal through the summer (when it's likely to attract insects), try to use it up before the hot and sultry days hit. This recipe will help.

    1¼ cups rolled oats
    ¾ cup milk
    1 egg, beaten lightly
    ½ cup vegetable oil
    ⅓ cup firmly packed light or dark brown sugar

1 large, ripe banana, peeled and mashed
1¼ cups sifted all-purpose flour or unsifted whole-wheat or graham
   flour
4 teaspoons baking powder
1 teaspoon salt

Preheat the oven to hot (425° F.).

Soak the oats in the milk in a mixing bowl for 30 minutes, or until all the milk has been absorbed. Combine the egg, oil, brown sugar, and mashed banana, beating until smooth, and stir into the oat mixture.

Combine the dry ingredients in a second mixing bowl and make a well in the center. Pour in the banana-oat mixture and stir lightly—just until the dry ingredients are moistened; do not overbeat at this point or your muffins will be tough and shot through with tunnels.

Line muffin pans with crinkly paper cupcake liners and spoon in the muffin batter, half filling each cup. Bake in the preheated oven for 15 minutes, or until the muffins are lightly browned and feel springy to the touch.

Olives

(Green or Ripe)

Olives may seem an unlikely leftover, and yet they can present problems. What so often happens is that there's half a jar remaining after a party (or after you've prepared a particular recipe) and in your haste to clean up, that half-jar gets shoved to the back of the refrigerator—and forgotten. Olives are not particularly perishable, but they do preempt precious refrigerator space, so the best plan is to put them to good use—in good time. You can, of course, eat them out of hand like peanuts—just remember that one jumbo-sized ripe olive contains about 15 calories and 1 jumbo green olive approximately 10. Hardly diet fare.

Best Way to Store   In the refrigerator, submerged in their own liquid in a tightly covered jar. If the olives were canned (as ripe olives often are), transfer them and their liquid to a screw-top jar, then refrigerate.

Maximum Storage Time   About 1 month for pimiento-stuffed green olives and canned ripe olives (the heavily brined Greek-style black olives will last 3 to 4 months); about 3 to 4 months for unpitted green olives.

N O T E   *If a white scum should form on either the olives or their brine, skim it off, then rinse the olives before using them (the scum is nothing more than crystallized salt).*

Roles in Cooking   In ancient Egypt, Mesopotamia, and Greece, where milk animals were scarce, olives provided man with sorely needed fat. Indeed, the Old Testament is strewn with references to olives and olive oil. Today olives still provide a valuable source of oil ("the butter of the Mediterranean"). But the whole fruits are also used for flavor, color, texture, and decoration.

Recipe Uses   The women of southern Italy and France, of Spain, Portugal, Greece, Turkey, Lebanon, and North Africa, could not cook without olives or olive oil, so look to recipes from these countries for ideas on how to use olives imaginatively. Olives are also popular in Latin America and Mexico, where they were introduced by Jesuit missionaries in the seventeenth century. Here olives are teamed with spicy meat and fish dishes; see Picadinho (page 235) and Bifes Enrolados (page 154), two Brazilian classics that offer splendid ways to use up small amounts of olives as well as a number of other troublesome leftovers.

How to Use Very Small Amounts   The easiest way to use small amounts of ripe or green olives is to mince them and then mix them into deviled-egg fillings, cole slaws or potato salads, hamburger relishes, chicken or tuna salads, or cheese spreads. You might also try scrambling ¼ to ⅓ cup of minced ripe or green olives into eggs, or folding them into a cheese soufflé, or mixing them into a meat loaf, hash, beef or lamb stew, or chili.

Tip   Whenever you add olives to a recipe, reduce the quantity of salt to compensate for that in the olives.

N O T E   *For additional recipes, included elsewhere in this book, that call for varying amounts of black or green olives, see the Appendix.*

TUNA- AND OLIVE-STUFFED POTATOES

4 servings

4 large, hot baked potatoes
⅓ cup evaporated milk or light cream, at room temperature
¼ cup (½ stick) butter or margarine, at room temperature
1 can (7 ounces) tuna, drained and flaked
¼ to ⅓ cup minced pimiento-stuffed green or pitted ripe olives
¼ cup minced yellow onion
2 tablespoons minced fresh parsley
Salt and freshly ground black pepper to taste

Preheat the oven to hot (400° F.).

Cutting lengthwise, slice ½ inch off the top of each baked potato. Scoop out the flesh, taking care not to tear the potato shells; mash the potato well, then add the evaporated milk and butter and beat until light. Stir in the tuna, olives, onion, parsley, and salt and pepper to taste.

Fill the potato shells with the tuna mixture, then bake in the pre-heated oven for 10 to 15 minutes, or until piping hot.

Serve as a main course.

WALES SALAD

6 to 8 servings

This party-pretty gelatin mold is a splendid way to use up leftover pimientos, pimiento-stuffed or pitted green olives, and blanched almonds. Adjust the proportions of chopped pimiento and olives to fit your supplies on hand—the two together should total 1 cup.

> 1 package (3 ounces) lemon-flavored gelatin
> Juice of 1 lemon
> 1 cup boiling water
> 1 cup moderately coarsely grated sharp Cheddar cheese
> ½ cup slivered blanched almonds
> ½ cup finely chopped pimiento
> ½ cup thinly sliced pimiento-stuffed or pitted green olives
> ¼ teaspoon salt
> 1 cup heavy cream, whipped

Heat the gelatin, lemon juice, and water, stirring, in a medium-sized saucepan over moderately low heat just until the gelatin dissolves—about 3 minutes. Cool for 10 minutes, then stir in the cheese, almonds, pimiento, olives, and salt; chill, uncovered, until the mixture is tacky (about 1 hour). Remove from the refrigerator and fold in the whipped cream, then pour into a lightly oiled 6-cup ring mold and chill for several hours, until firm.

Unmold on a large plate, fill the center with cherry tomatoes, if you like, and garnish with ruffs of parsley or watercress.

BRAISED LAMB WITH BLACK OLIVES IN WINE GRAVY

4 to 6 servings

Not everyone likes to eat black olives out of hand, so if you should be left with some after a party or special dinner, you can use them to good advantage in this robust lamb stew. You may also, if you like, substitute pitted or pimiento-stuffed green olives for the black. Note that the recipe can also be used to rid your refrigerator of partial bottles of wine and almost-empty cans of beef or chicken broth.

Like most stews, this one can be frozen and enjoyed later (directions for freezing are included at the end of the recipe).

> 2 pounds boned lamb shoulder, cut in 1-inch cubes
> ½ cup unsifted all-purpose flour
> 1 teaspoon salt

¼ teaspoon freshly ground black pepper
¼ cup olive or vegetable oil
1 large yellow onion, peeled and chopped
1 large clove garlic, peeled and crushed
Juice of 1 lemon
¼ teaspoon crumbled leaf rosemary
½ to 1 cup coarsely chopped pitted black olives (or pitted or pimien-to-stuffed green olives)
½ to ¾ cup dry red or white wine
¼ to ½ cup beef or chicken broth or water

Dredge the lamb by shaking, a few cubes at a time, in a paper bag with the flour, salt, and pepper. Brown the lamb, again doing a few cubes at a time, in the oil in a large, heavy skillet over moderately high heat. Reduce the heat to moderate, add the onion and garlic, and sauté, stirring now and then, for about 10 minutes, or until limp and lightly browned. Add the remaining ingredients, cover, and simmer slowly for 1½ to 2 hours, or until the lamb is very tender.

Serve hot, with rice, buttered noodles, or boiled new potatoes.

To Freeze Cool the stew to room temperature, then ladle into freezer containers of a size appropriate to your needs. Fill each container to within ½ inch of the top; snap on the lids, label, and date, then place in a freezer set at 0° F. Keeping time: about 6 months.

When you are ready to serve the stew, dump solidly frozen into a heavy kettle or saucepan, set over low heat, and bring to serving temperature while stirring occasionally.

PICADINHO
(BRAZILIAN MINCED MEAT)

6 to 8 servings

Like so many quick skillet dishes, this Brazilian one becomes a savory catchall for a number of odds and ends—olives, tomato paste and sauce, nuts, even raisins and/or coconut, should you have any going begging. Improvise as you like, tasting each step of the way. *Picadinho* can be ladled over hamburger buns and served like sloppy Joes; it can be spooned over fluffy boiled rice, an omelet, or scrambled eggs. It can be enjoyed as is and it can be used to fill those wonderful Brazilian turnovers known as *empadas* (see the recipe variation that follows). You may also be pleased to know that *picadinho* freezes beautifully (instructions are included at the end of the recipe).

> 1 large Spanish onion, peeled and minced
> 2 medium cloves garlic, peeled and crushed
> 3 tablespoons olive or peanut oil
> 1 pound lean ground beef
> ½ teaspoon ground coriander
> ¼ teaspoon ground ginger
> ¼ teaspoon crumbled leaf thyme
> 2 medium vine-ripe tomatoes, peeled, cored, and coarsely chopped, or 1 tomato plus ½ to 1 cup leftover tomato sauce
> 2 to 4 tablespoons tomato paste
> 1 to 2 tablespoons honey or light brown sugar (to mellow the tartness of the tomatoes)
> ¼ cup minced fresh parsley
> ⅓ to ⅔ cup coarsely chopped pimiento-stuffed green or pitted ripe olives
> ½ to 1 cup seedless raisins (optional)
> ½ to 1 cup shredded or flaked coconut (optional)
> ½ to 1 cup chopped nuts (almonds, pignoli, peanuts, pecans, walnuts) (optional)
> ½ to 1 cup leftover dry white or red wine (optional)
> Salt and freshly ground black pepper to taste

Stir-fry the onion and garlic in the oil in a large, heavy skillet over moderate heat for 12 to 15 minutes, until soft and lightly browned. Push to one side of the skillet, add the beef, and brown well, breaking up large clumps with a fork. Stir in all the remaining ingredients (including all or some of the optionals) and cook, uncovered, over low heat for about 45 minutes, stirring occasionally, until the mixture is quite thick (slightly thicker than a spaghetti sauce) and the flavors are well blended.

Serve hot as suggested in the headnote, or cool and use to fill *empadas* (see recipe variation that follows).

To Freeze We suggest, first of all, freezing the *picadinho* in half-pint containers so you have a variety of options about using it—each container measures 1 cup, about the right amount for one omelet that will serve four persons, two sloppy Joes, or one portion when ladled over boiled rice. Cool the *picadinho* to room temperature, then spoon into half-pint containers, filling each to within ½ inch of the top. Snap on the lids, label, and date and place in a freezer set at 0° F. Keeping time: about 4 months at 0° F.

When ready to use, bring slowly to serving temperature in a small heavy skillet or saucepan set over low heat. Stir frequently to prevent sticking.

VARIATION

Empadas (*8 servings*)   Preheat the oven to moderately hot (375° F.). Prepare Flaky Egg Piecrust (page 145) as directed, or prepare your own favorite pastry recipe, making enough for a two-crust pie. Roll the pastry thin as for pie crust, then cut in 6-inch circles, using a saucer as a cutting guide. Spoon about ⅓ cup of *picadinho* across the center of each pastry circle, leaving ½-inch margins at both ends. Moisten the edges of the pastry circles, then fold in half to enclose the filling; crimp with a fork to seal. Bake the *empadas,* uncovered, on an ungreased baking sheet in the preheated oven for about 30 minutes, or until lightly browned. Serve hot or cold.

Parsley

Best Way to Store   Wash the parsley sprigs in cool water, discarding any that are yellowing or wilting, then stand the sprigs in a glass of cool water and pop a plastic bag loosely on top.

Be sure you check to see that the refrigerator control dial is in the medium range. If it is set too cold, the parsley may freeze (then go limp the instant it thaws).

To Freeze   To freeze leftover minced parsley, spoon 1 tablespoon minced parsley into each compartment of an ice-cube tray, add 2 to 3 tablespoons cold water to each compartment, then freeze until firm. Pop the "parsley cubes" into a plastic bag, twist the top into a gooseneck, and secure with a twist-band. You can keep the parsley cubes "on ice" for about 6 months. To use, simply add the frozen cubes to soups, stews, or sauces—each cube = 1 tablespoon minced parsley. The water will quickly evaporate, leaving the parsley "almost" fresh.

N O T E *For directions on how to freeze parsley sprigs, see the special note re freezing fresh herbs on page 173.*

Maximum Storage Time A week to 10 days in the refrigerator; see the section on freezing (above) for freezer storage time.
Roles in Cooking To flavor, color, and decorate food; also, sometimes, to thicken sauces (see the recipe for Pesto Sauce on page 177).
Recipe Uses More than mere cosmetics. A judicious use of parsley, for example, will improve the flavor of almost any savory dish—soups, sauces and sandwich spreads, stews, casseroles and vegetables, salads and salad dressings, scrambled eggs, breads, and stuffings.

N O T E *For additional recipes, included elsewhere in this book, that call for varying amounts of fresh parsley, see the Appendix.*

BEEF AND RICE WITH TOMATO AND SWEET PEPPER

6 servings

Stews, more than any other category of recipe, are perfect receptacles for an assortment of oddments because they are virtually fail-safe. This particular stew, for example, is a clean-up-your-refrigerator sort of recipe because it neatly uses small amounts of tomato sauce, minced parsley, and sweet pepper, chicken and/or beef broth, dry red or white wine—all ingredients you're apt to have on hand if you've made anything Italian, Spanish, or Mexican lately.

It freezes well, which means that you can parlay today's leftovers into next month's elegant meal.

> 5 tablespoons olive or vegetable oil
> 1 medium Spanish onion, peeled and coarsely chopped
> 1 large clove garlic, peeled and minced
> ¼ to ½ cup minced sweet green or red pepper
> 1 medium carrot, peeled and coarsely chopped

2 pounds boned beef chuck, cut in 1-inch cubes
2 to 4 tablespoons minced fresh parsley
1 bay leaf, crumbled
1½ cups beef or chicken broth or water or a combination of them
⅓ to ⅔ cup dry red or white wine
⅓ to ½ cup tomato sauce
1 cup uncooked rice
Salt and freshly ground black pepper to taste

Heat 3 tablespoons of the oil in a large, heavy kettle set over moderate heat, then add the onion, garlic, sweet pepper, and carrot and stir-fry for 10 minutes, or until the onion is limp and golden; remove the sautéed vegetables to a small bowl, using a slotted spoon.

Raise the heat under the kettle to high and brown the beef, a few cubes at a time, without adding any more oil to the kettle; as the beef browns, lift to paper toweling to drain. Return the sautéed vegetables and beef to the kettle; add all the remaining ingredients except the rice, salt, and pepper, then cover and simmer for about 1½ hours, stirring now and then, until the beef is very tender.

Meanwhile, sauté the rice in the remaining 2 tablespoons of oil in a saucepan over moderate heat for 2 to 3 minutes, or until rice is golden and translucent. Remove from the heat and reserve.

When the meat is tender, season to taste with salt and pepper. Stir the rice into the kettle, cover, and simmer for about 20 minutes, stirring occasionally, or until the rice is done. Serve at once.

To Freeze Cool the stew to room temperature, then ladle into freezer containers of a size that meets your particular needs (half-pints if you live alone, pints if there are two of you, quarts for families or for entertaining). Fill each container to within ½ inch of the top; snap on the lid, date, label, and place in a freezer set at 0° F. Keeping time: about 4 months at 0° F.

When ready to serve, dump the solidly frozen stew into a heavy kettle or saucepan, set over low heat, and bring to serving temperature, stirring frequently to prevent sticking. Thin the stew, if needed, with a little water.

BEEF-STUFFED EGGPLANT

6 to 8 servings

A perfectly delicious way to recycle leftover cooked rice and to put the last of a bunch of parsley and can of tomato sauce to good use.

This filling is good baked inside sweet green or red peppers (6 large ones should be enough to accommodate this amount of filling; steam the stuffed peppers exactly as the recipe directs for the eggplant). The filling is also good all by itself—a sort of skillet scramble that is hearty enough to serve as a main dish.

4 small to medium eggplants, cut in half lengthwise (do not peel)
¼ cup olive oil
¾ cup beef broth or water or a combination of the two (for steaming the eggplants)

STUFFING

1 pound lean ground beef chuck
2 medium yellow onions, peeled and chopped
2 cloves garlic, peeled and minced
½ teaspoon crumbled leaf basil
¼ teaspoon crumbled leaf marjoram
Pinch of crumbled leaf thyme
2 to 4 tablespoons minced fresh parsley
Pulp scooped from the eggplants above
¼ to ½ cup tomato sauce (whatever amount you have left over)
½ cup beef broth or water or a combination of the two
1 to 1½ cups leftover cooked rice
Salt and freshly ground black pepper to taste

Brush the cut surface of each eggplant half with 1½ teaspoons olive oil. Set the eggplant halves, cut sides up, on a broiler pan and broil about 5 inches from the flame for 3 to 5 minutes, or until richly browned. Remove the eggplants from the broiler and cool until easy to handle. With a sharp knife, scoop out the insides of each eggplant half, leaving shells ¼ inch thick. Chop the scooped-out pulp (you will use it in the stuffing).

To make the stuffing, stir-fry the beef, onions, garlic, basil, marjoram, and thyme in a very large, heavy skillet over moderate heat for 8 to 10 minutes, or until the beef is no longer pink. Mix in the parsley, chopped eggplant pulp, tomato sauce, and broth and simmer, uncovered, for 10 to 15 minutes, or until the mixture is about the consistency of pasta sauce and the flavors are well blended. Mix in the rice, season to taste with salt and pepper, then mound the mixture in the eggplant shells.

Place the stuffed eggplants on a rack in a large, heavy kettle; pour in the ¾ cup broth or water and bring to a simmer over moderately low heat. Cover the kettle and steam the eggplants for 1 hour.

To brown, run the stuffed eggplants quickly under the broiler.

BALTIC CREAMED BACON AND MUSHROOMS

4 to 6 servings

This perfectly elegant Finnish dish enables you to rid your refrigerator shelves of any oddments of parsley and cream (sour cream, light or heavy cream, half-and-half). It will also accommodate as much as ½ pound of bacon—a troublesome leftover, sometimes, for those who do not insist upon having it every morning for breakfast. (You may also be pleased to know that you can substitute ½ pound of dried, chipped beef for the bacon—simply sauté the mushrooms in ¼ cup [½ stick] of butter or margarine instead of in bacon drippings and add the chipped beef toward the end, just before you smooth in the sour cream.) This dish is hearty enough to serve as a main course and is equally delicious ladled over toast, rice, buttered noodles, kasha, or bulgur.

> ½ pound sliced bacon, cut crosswise into julienne strips
> 2 large yellow onions, peeled and coarsely chopped
> 2 pounds medium mushrooms, trimmed of coarse stem ends, wiped clean, and sliced thin
> 1 teaspoon dill weed
> ⅛ teaspoon freshly ground black pepper
> ⅛ teaspoon ground mace or grated nutmeg
> ½ teaspoon paprika

CONTINUED

1 cup cream (light, heavy, or half-and-half), at room temperature
¼ cup minced fresh parsley
½ to 1 cup sour cream, at room temperature
Salt to taste

In a large, heavy skillet set over moderately high heat, fry the bacon until crisp and brown. With a slotted spoon, scoop the browned bacon bits to paper toweling to drain.

Pour off and reserve the bacon drippings, then spoon 4 tablespoons of them back into the skillet. Add the onions and sauté over moderate heat for about 10 minutes, until lightly browned, then add the mushrooms and stir-fry for 10 minutes, or until their juices have cooked down. Add the dill weed, pepper, mace, paprika, and cream and simmer, uncovered, for 10 to 15 minutes, or until the cream has reduced by one-half.

Add the reserved bacon, parsley, sour cream, and salt to taste and warm just to serving temperature (do not boil or the cream may curdle).

P E P P E R S :   See **Green (Bell) Peppers (Also Sweet Red and Yellow).**

Pimiento

Few of us attribute much more than cosmetic value to these sweet, scarlet peppers, and yet they are surprisingly nutritious (concentrated sources of vitamins A and C), not to mention flavorful. Despite the fact that pimientos are packed in very small quantities (2-ounce jars for sliced pimientos and 4-ounce jars for the whole), they are nonetheless a problem leftover (in certain areas, they are canned in even larger quantities).

Best Way to Store   Keep pimientos in their own jar, tightly capped, in the refrigerator. If you have canned pimientos left over, transfer to a small jar (include all liquid), cover tight, and store in the refrigerator.

Maximum Storage Time   About 10 days.

Roles in Cooking   To add color, yes, but also to provide a mild, sweet pepper flavor.

Recipe Uses   All manner of casseroles and scalloped and creamed foods call for pimiento, as do molded vegetable salads, cheese dips, and spreads.

N O T E   *For additional recipes, included elsewhere in this book, that call for varying amounts of pimiento, see the Appendix.*

PIMIENTO-SALMON LOAF

4 servings

Pimiento and evaporated milk are two of those foods that invariably seem to be packaged in amounts too large to use in a single recipe— so you're stuck with a partial jar or can, which too often go bad before they can be used. Our solution—make this salmon loaf. It's an unusually good one, we think, full of flavor, moist, and yet firm enough to slice well.

2 cans (7¾ ounces each) salmon, drained well
2 eggs, beaten lightly
1½ cups soft bread crumbs (corn bread crumbs are especially good)
½ cup evaporated milk (or plain milk, cream—light, heavy, or sour
   —or any combination thereof)
1 small yellow onion, peeled and chopped
Juice of ½ lemon
2 tablespoons chopped pimiento
2 tablespoons chopped fresh parsley
2 tablespoons snipped fresh chives
2 slices bacon

Preheat the oven to moderate (350° F.).
Pick over the salmon to remove bits of skin and bone, then flake and

mix well with all the remaining ingredients except the bacon. Shape into a round or oval loaf and place on a lightly greased 8- or 9-inch pie pan. Drape the bacon slices over the loaf and bake, uncovered, in the preheated oven for 40 minutes, or until lightly browned.

Remove from the oven and let stand for 10 to 15 minutes before slicing.

N O T E   *The amounts of onion, pimiento, parsley, and chives can all be varied in accordance with both the amount you have on hand and with your personal preferences.*

P I M I E N T O - R O Q U E F O R T   P A S T A   R I N G

6 servings

This is the sort of recipe that cleans up a lot of leftovers: pimiento, snippets of Cheddar as well as Roquefort or blue cheese, bread crumbs, even evaporated milk and/or light or heavy cream.

> 3 eggs, separated
> 1½ cups any milk-cream combination (whatever it is you need to use up—evaporated milk, light or heavy cream, half-and-half)
> 1 cup soft bread crumbs (either white or whole-wheat)
> 2 to 4 tablespoons minced pimiento
> 2 tablespoons melted butter or margarine
> ¼ teaspoon crumbled leaf thyme
> ⅛ teaspoon crumbled leaf rosemary
> ½ teaspoon paprika
> ⅛ teaspoon freshly ground black pepper
> ¾ cup finely crumbled Roquefort or blue cheese
> ¾ cup coarsely grated sharp Cheddar cheese
> 1 cup elbow macaroni, cooked according to package directions and drained well

Preheat the oven to moderately slow (325° F.).

Beat the egg yolks lightly, then combine with the milk-cream mixture in a mixing bowl. Add the crumbs, pimiento, melted butter, herbs, paprika, pepper, Roquefort, and Cheddar and stir well to blend. Fold in the macaroni, then beat the egg whites to soft peaks and fold in also.

Pour the mixture into a well-greased 5-cup ring mold and set in a shallow baking pan on the center rack of the preheated oven. Pour water into the baking pan to a depth of 1½ inches, then bake the pasta mold, uncovered, in the water bath for about 1 hour, or until set.

Unmold at once on a round platter and serve as is, or topped with creamed chicken, turkey, ham, or chipped beef. This is also good with tomato sauce.

CONFETTI CORN

4 servings

This skillet scramble is as quick to make as it is colorful. The time to prepare it is when you have bits and pieces of pimiento, green pepper, and/or bacon on hand.

4 slices bacon, cut crosswise into julienne strips
1 large Spanish or Bermuda onion, peeled and coarsely chopped
⅓ to ⅔ cup minced sweet green pepper
1 package (10 ounces) frozen whole-kernel corn, thawed
1 teaspoon salt
Several grindings of black pepper
2 to 4 tablespoons minced pimiento

Brown the bacon in a large, heavy skillet over moderately high heat and drain on paper toweling; pour off all but 2 tablespoons of the drippings. Stir-fry the onion and green pepper in the drippings over moderate heat for 8 to 10 minutes, until the onion is limp and golden. Stir in the corn, salt, and black pepper; cover and simmer for 8 to 10 minutes, or until the corn is done.

Mix in the pimiento and reserved bacon crumbles and serve.

SWISS, PIMIENTO, AND BACON SPREAD

About 1½ cups

2½ cups finely grated Gruyère or, if you prefer, 1¼ cups each finely
  grated Gruyère and sharp Cheddar cheese, at room temperature
1 very small yellow onion, peeled and minced fine
4 to 6 tablespoons sour cream or mayonnaise (just enough to give the
  mixture a good spreading consistency)
1 teaspoon Dijon or spicy brown mustard
2 pimientos, drained and minced
4 slices lean bacon, fried until crisp, then crumbled fine

In a small mixing bowl or in a food processor equipped with the
metal chopping blade, cream the cheese, onion, 4 tablespoons of the
sour cream, and the mustard until smooth. If the mixture seems stiff,
blend in 1 to 2 additional tablespoons of sour cream.

Fold in the pimiento and bacon and use as a sandwich spread.

P R E S E R V E S : See **Jams, Jellies, Marmalades, and
Preserves.**

Prunes and Other Dried Fruits

(Apricots and Figs)

Drying is the oldest method of food preservation known to man and
for thousands of years sun-drying was the technique. Fully ripe plums,

for example, would be spread out under the sun and left until they shriveled and dried. Result? Prunes. Today plums, apricots, figs, and other fruits are dried under carefully controlled conditions; about 75 percent of their moisture is extracted, leaving sweet, compact, easily digested fruits that are excellent sources of iron, calcium, phosphorous, copper, vitamin A, thiamine (or B_1), riboflavin (or B_2), and niacin, another important vitamin of the B complex.

As for calories, dried fruits contain plenty—a medium-sized apricot averages about 30 calories, a fig about 60, and a prune approximately 20.

Apricots, dried only in halves, are available in 1-pound boxes and moistureproof pliofilm bags, also in 8-ounce bags. Dried figs are pressed into small blocks and wrapped in cellophane or plastic (8 ounces is the common size). With prunes, there is greater variety. First of all, there are four sizes of prunes: small (67 to 85 per pound), medium (53 to 67 per pound), large (43 to 53 per pound) and extra-large (36 to 43 per pound—these, by the way, are best for stuffing). Almost all dried prunes marketed today are "tenderized"; they can be bought whole or pitted in 1-pound boxes and in 1-pound and 8-ounce bags.

Best Ways to Store Opened packages of dried fruits should be tightly resealed (press out all air pockets) or, if necessary, overwrapped in plastic food wrap. They may be stored either in a dark, dry, cool, well-ventilated area or in the refrigerator.

Maximum Storage Time About 6 months at room temperature, 8 months in the refrigerator.

Roles in Cooking Dried fruits are used principally for flavor, color, texture, and nutritive value. When cooked and puréed, they can be used as fillings to bind cake layers, tortes, pastries, and pinwheel and bar cookies. Cooked, puréed dried apricots are traditionally used to seal the porous surface of *petits fours* before they are frosted. And when thinned with a little dry white wine, apricot purée makes a splendid glaze for roast ham or fowl, as well as for fruit tarts.

Recipe Uses Poultry stuffings, strudels, Danish pastries, quick breads, steamed puddings, fruit cakes, cookies, confections, and fruit compotes—all these commonly call for dried fruits. So do many Hungarian, Czech, Polish, and Balkan soups, stews, casseroles, and desserts.

Special Comments Here's a handy trick: use kitchen shears to chop or dice dried fruits, dipping the shears into warm water whenever they gum up.

N O R W E G I A N   F R U I T   S O U P

6 to 8 servings

Although the mixture is soupy, it isn't a soup per se. Usually it's served as dessert. The beauty of this particular recipe is that you can use almost any combination of dried fruits as long as the total amount is 3 cups. So improvise with the quantities suggested below to make best use of the leftover dried fruits you have on hand.

This keeps well in the refrigerator for about a week.

> 1 cup dried apricots
> ½ cup pitted prunes
> ½ cup dried peaches
> ½ cup seedless or sultana raisins
> ½ cup dried currants
> 6½ cups water
> 1 cup granulated sugar or firmly packed light or dark brown sugar
>   (or use some of each, again using up leftovers)
> 1 stick cinnamon, broken in several pieces
> 4 whole cloves
> ¼ cup quick-cooking tapioca
> ¼ cup sweet Madeira, Marsala, Port, or cream sherry
> Honey or light corn syrup to taste (optional)

Place the dried fruits, 4 cups of the water, ½ cup of the sugar, and the spices in a large, heavy saucepan; cover and simmer over low heat for 15 minutes. Remove from the heat, then cover and let cool to room temperature, discarding the cinnamon stick and cloves when the mixture has cooled.

In a separate saucepan, mix the remaining 2½ cups water, ½ cup sugar, and tapioca; let stand for 5 minutes, then set over moderate heat and bring to a full boil, stirring constantly. As soon as the tapioca turns transparent (this will happen almost as soon as the mixture boils), remove from the heat and cool for 20 minutes, stirring now and then.

Stir the tapioca mixture into the fruit, then mix in the wine. If the mixture is not sweet enough to suit you, add a little honey or light corn syrup.

Serve warm or cold as a dessert.

UNCOOKED SWEETMEATS

About 5 dozen small balls

Here's an uncooked confection from the Old South, this one made with a variety of dried fruits—dates, raisins, and figs, plus chopped nuts and just enough moisture to bind them all together. You may find these sticky fruits easier to weigh than to measure, so for your convenience we have noted the weights needed of each.

Stored airtight, these will keep for about a month.

⅔ cup diced, pitted dates (¼ pound)
⅔ cup diced dried figs (¼ pound)
½ cup seedless raisins (¼ pound)
½ cup finely minced pecans or walnuts
2 to 3 teaspoons bourbon, brandy, or orange or lemon juice
½ cup granulated sugar

Grind the fruits together in a meat grinder fitted with the fine blade. Combine thoroughly with the nuts and just enough bourbon or other liquid to form a stiff "dough." Pinch off bits of the "dough" and shape into small balls about ½ inch in diameter.

Roll the balls in the sugar, then store airtight and allow to mellow for a couple of days before serving.

QUICK WHOLE-WHEAT-APRICOT BREAD

One 8½ × 4½ × 2½-inch loaf

This fruit-nut bread freezes unusually well (see below) and is a handy one to have "on ice," so to speak, as insurance against drop-in guests.

    1 cup sifted all-purpose flour
    1 cup *unsifted* whole-wheat flour
    2 teaspoons baking powder
    ½ teaspoon salt
    ½ cup firmly packed light or dark brown sugar
    1 cup coarsely chopped dried apricots (or diced, pitted prunes or dates
        or whole seedless raisins or dried currants)
    1 egg, beaten lightly
    1 cup milk
    ¼ cup melted shortening or vegetable oil

Preheat the oven to moderate (350° F.).

Combine the flours, baking powder, and salt in a large mixing bowl. Work in the sugar, pressing out any lumps with your spoon, then stir in the chopped apricots. Combine the egg with the milk and shortening in a separate bowl or large measuring cup. Make a well in the center of the dry ingredients, then pour the combined liquids in all at once and stir briskly just enough to mix—no longer or the bread may be tough.

Spoon the mixture into a well-greased 8½ × 4½ × 2½-inch baking pan and let stand on the counter for 10 minutes before baking, then bake in the preheated oven for about 45 minutes, or until the loaf begins to pull from the sides of the pan and seems springy to the touch.

Remove from the oven and loosen the bread around the edges with a knife or thin-bladed spatula, then turn out on a wire rack and cool to room temperature before cutting.

To Freeze   If you live alone or if your family is small, you may want to divide the loaf in half before freezing. Wrap the cooled bread snugly in heavy-duty aluminum foil or in plastic freezer wrap; label, date, and place in a freezer set at 0° F. Keeping time: about 6 months at 0° F.

To use, slice off the amount of bread you need with a serrated knife, then rewrap the balance and return to the freezer.

Raisins and Dried Currants

The Egyptians, it's said, were the first to discover that sun-dried grapes (which we know as raisins) had an altogether different flavor from fresh grapes and that they kept far longer. Today, two varieties of grapes are commercially dried into raisins: muscats, which emerge as the familiar, dark seedless raisins, and the light sultanas, which become the golden raisins of the same name. Dried currants closely resemble dark seedless raisins in color and flavor, but they are only about a fourth as large. The two varieties of raisins and dried currants may be used interchangeably in recipes.

Best Way to Store In a tightly capped glass jar in the refrigerator. Raisins and currants do not require refrigeration, but left on the cupboard shelf in their own cartons they will soon dry and attract bugs. If you are not going to refrigerate them, at least transfer any leftovers to screw-top jars and set on a cool, dry shelf.

Maximum Storage Time Almost indefinitely in the refrigerator; about a year if stored in an airtight glass jar at room temperature, although both dried currants and raisins may dry further and become about as hard as BB shot. They must then be softened or plumped before they can be used (see Special Comments, below).

Roles in Cooking To add color, flavor, and a moist, chewy texture.

Recipe Uses Pies, puddings, cookies, cakes, yeast and quick breads —all often call for raisins. But so do a number of Latin American and Middle Eastern meat and seafood dishes; see the recipes for Picadinho and Macedonian Marinated Fish on pages 235 and 252.

Special Comments Whenever raisins or dried currants shrivel and harden, they must be plumped or softened before they can be used— otherwise they will remain bullet-hard. Here's the technique:

Mix raisins or dried currants measure for measure with water (or a combination of water and wine, brandy, or fruit juice), then simmer slowly for 5 to 10 minutes, until the fruits are plump and soft. Drain well before using.

Another technique that works well is to dump the dried currants or raisins into a large, fine, rustproof strainer, then to set the strainer à *la* double boiler over a pan of simmering water; cover and steam for 5 to 10 minutes, until the fruits are soft. Again, drain the fruits well before using.

Tip A problem commonly encountered when making cakes, puddings or pies with dried currants or raisins is that they sink to the bottom of the batter or filling. To prevent this, dredge the raisins or dried currants well with part of the flour called for in the recipe, then fold the dredged fruits (and any remaining dredging flour) into the recipe at the very end (the same technique should be used for chopped nuts and candied fruits).

N O T E *For additional recipes, included elsewhere in this book, that call for varying amounts of raisins or dried currants, see the Appendix.*

MACEDONIAN MARINATED FISH

4 to 6 servings

If you have hard, dry raisins on hand and/or a cup or so of leftover dry white wine, this recipe will put both to good use. Serve cold as a luncheon entrée or, if you prefer, as part of an antipasto.

1½ pounds flounder fillets, cut in 2-inch squares
½ cup unsifted flour
½ cup best-quality olive oil
¼ teaspoon freshly ground black pepper
3 medium yellow onions, peeled and sliced tissue thin
2 medium carrots, peeled and sliced tissue thin
⅔ to 1 cup dry white wine
⅓ cup white wine vinegar
¼ to ½ cup seedless or sultana raisins, soaked for 10 minutes in 1 cup boiling water, then drained well
¼ to ⅓ cup pignoli (pine nuts)

Dredge each piece of fish on both sides in the flour, then brown, a few pieces at a time, in ¼ cup of the oil in a large, heavy skillet over moderately high heat. As the fish browns, transfer to a 9 × 9 × 2-inch baking dish and sprinkle lightly with pepper. Continue browning the fish, adding more oil, if necessary, to keep the fish from sticking.

When all fish has been browned, pour any remaining oil into the skillet; add the onions and carrots and stir-fry for 12 to 15 minutes, until very limp. Add the wine and vinegar to the skillet and boil for 2 to 3 minutes; add the raisins and nuts.

Pour the skillet mixture over the fish; cool to room temperature, then cover and chill for several hours before serving.

APPLESAUCE REFRIGERATOR RELISH

About 2 cups

One of the quickest ways imaginable to utilize leftover raisins or dried currants. If they are hard and withered, plump them by soaking for about 10 minutes in hot water (drain well before mixing into the relish). This particular relish is a snappy accompaniment to baked ham, roast pork, chicken, turkey, goose, or duckling.

1 cup applesauce
⅓ cup seedless raisins or dried currants, plumped if necessary in hot
   water, then drained well
¼ cup finely minced celery
1 tablespoon prepared horseradish
¼ teaspoon ground cinnamon

Combine all the ingredients in a small mixing bowl; cover, then chill for about 2 hours. Stir well before serving.

CRANBERRY-RAISIN (MOCK CHERRY) PIE

One 8-inch pie

This tart pie is adapted from an old New England recipe. It's a great pie for the Christmas holidays and appeals to many who usually are not tempted by sweet desserts. If you prefer a sweeter pie, add ¼ to ⅓ cup white (granulated) sugar.

> 1 recipe of your favorite pastry (enough for a double-crust pie)
> 2 cups fresh cranberries, washed, stemmed, sorted, and coarsely chopped
> ¾ cup seedless raisins, coarsely chopped
> 1½ tablespoons grated lemon or orange rind
> ½ cup firmly packed light or dark brown sugar
> 2 tablespoons rum
> 1 tablespoon honey
> 1 tablespoon all-purpose flour
> 1 tablespoon butter

Preheat the oven to very hot (450° F.).

Prepare the pastry as your recipe directs and divide in half, then roll one-half into an 11-inch circle. Ease into an 8-inch pie pan and trim the overhang so that it measures 1 inch all around.

Dump the cranberries into the unbaked pie crust, then strew the raisins and grated rind over them. Combine the sugar, rum, honey, and flour and pour evenly over all (if your brown sugar is hard, the rum and honey will help dissolve it so you can beat out most of the lumps). Dot the butter over the filling.

Roll out the remaining pastry into a second 11-inch circle, cut into ½-inch strips, then weave a lattice top over the filling. Trim the overhanging strips so they are even with the bottom crust overhang. Roll the overhanging pastry up onto the rim of the pie pan and crimp with your fingers, making a high fluted edge.

Bake the pie in the very hot oven for 10 minutes, then reduce the heat to moderate (350° F.) and bake for 25 minutes longer. Let the pie cool for 25 to 30 minutes before cutting.

IRISH SODA BREAD

One 9-inch flat, round loaf

This is a quick, delicious breakfast bread that calls for from ¾ to 1¼ cups of raisins or dried currants. Serve oven-hot with plenty of butter. If you don't polish off the loaf at one sitting, reheat leftovers this way: Sprinkle the bread lightly with water, then wrap snugly in aluminum foil and set in a very slow (300° F.) oven for about 20 minutes, or until piping hot.

> 4 cups sifted all-purpose flour
> ¼ cup granulated sugar
> 2 teaspoons baking soda
> 2 teaspoons baking powder
> ½ teaspoon salt
> ¾ to 1¼ cups seedless raisins or dried currants
> 1 cup sour milk or buttermilk
> 2 eggs, beaten lightly
> ½ cup (1 stick) butter, melted

Preheat the oven to moderately hot (375° F.).

In a large mixing bowl combine the flour, sugar, baking soda, baking powder, and salt; stir in the raisins, then make a well in the center of the dry ingredients. Combine the milk, beaten eggs, and butter; pour all at once into the dry ingredients and stir lightly but briskly just enough to mix.

Shape the dough into a large, round loaf in a greased 9-inch pie pan, then make a deep X-cut in the top of the loaf. Bake in the preheated oven for 30 to 40 minutes, or until the loaf is nicely browned and sounds hollow when thumped with your fingers.

Cut into wedges and serve at once.

BANBURY TARTS

1 dozen

These little tarts are fine for lunch boxes and picnics. Or serve them with a sharp Cheddar and a glass of sherry or Madeira for a holiday snack. You can use one whole egg in place of the yolks.

> 1 cup seedless raisins, chopped
> ¼ cup firmly packed light or dark brown sugar
> 2 egg yolks, beaten lightly
> 3 tablespoons dry bread or cracker crumbs
> 1 tablespoon grated lemon or orange rind
> 1 recipe of your favorite pastry (enough for a double-crust pie)

CONTINUED

Preheat the oven to hot (400° F.).

Mix the raisins, sugar, egg yolks, crumbs, and grated rind; let stand while you attend to the pastry. Mix it as your recipe directs; divide in half, then roll each half out as for pie crust (about ⅛ inch thick). Cut the pastry into 3-inch squares, then place a heaping teaspoon of the filling in the center of each. Moisten the edges of the pastry squares with cool water. Fold half of each square over diagonally to enclose the filling and form a triangle; press the edges together, then crimp with a 3-tined fork.

Bake the tarts on an ungreased baking sheet in the preheated oven for 15 to 20 minutes, or until lightly browned.

Serve hot or cold.

Rice (Cooked)

(White, Brown, or Wild)

There's nothing particularly pressing or puzzling about using up raw rice (it keeps virtually forever), but dealing with leftover cooked rice (the white, brown, and wild) is something else again (have you ever cooked precisely the amount of rice you needed and never had any left over?). Few of us realize that leftover cooked rice can simply be reheated and served a second or third time around, or that it keeps well for several days in the refrigerator.

Brown rice, by the way, is simply rice that has not been completely husked and polished. But wild rice is something else again, technically not rice at all but a highly prized grass native to the Great Lakes states that is almost worth its weight in gold.

Best Way to Store   In a tightly covered bowl or storage carton in the refrigerator. As for raw rice, we like to store it in large preserving jars with the lids securely screwed down.

Maximum Storage Time   3 to 5 days for leftover cooked white, brown, or wild rice; indefinitely for uncooked rice.

Roles in Cooking   Brown and white rice are used to stretch expensive meats, poultry, and seafoods by providing a filling accompaniment or base; to offer a bland counterpoint to such piquant foods as curries; to help thicken and bind puddings, casseroles, croquettes, and stuffings; and to provide a quick, cheap, and satisfying source of carbohydrates (energy). Wild rice has considerably more character and crunch and a rich, nutlike flavor.

Recipe Uses   We tend to think of rice as a backdrop upon which other foods are presented, and yet all three varieties are integral to a variety of recipes: stuffings, egg and/or cheese recipes, pilaf, risotto, soups, quick breads (including pancakes), skillet dishes and casseroles, meat loaves and croquettes, desserts. For additional ideas on using white and brown rice, you might have a look at any Oriental recipes you may have, as well as any Middle Eastern, Italian (*northern* Italian), Spanish, Mexican, and South American recipes. Rice is a staple in most of these cuisines. As for wild rice, it is wholly North American and is most likely to appear in recipes from Minnesota and Wisconsin.

Special Comments   The best way we've found for reheating cold, leftover cooked rice (and this goes for brown and wild rice as well as white) is to dump it into a large, rustproof sieve and to set, double-boiler style, over a pan containing about 1½ inches of boiling water. Fork the rice up lightly, then cover the sieve (with the pan lid if it will fit or, failing that, with foil) and steam for about 5 minutes, or until the rice is fluffy and hot. Serve just as you would freshly cooked rice.

How to Use Very Small Amounts   Up to ½ cup of leftover cooked rice (wild rice is especially good) may be added to pancake or muffin batter (stir in at the last minute); it may be folded into an omelet or scrambled into eggs; it may be mixed into almost any casserole, skillet dish, stuffing, or hash.

N O T E   *For additional recipes, included elsewhere in this book, that call for varying amounts of cooked rice (white, brown, or wild), see the Appendix.*

SPANISH ONIONS STUFFED WITH PECANS, MUSHROOMS, AND RICE

6 servings

This is one of our favorite vegetable recipes, not only because it is delicious, but also because it puts leftover cooked rice to the best possible use. It's also a handy way to use up mushroom stems, if you should have any on hand.

> 6 Spanish onions, each about the size of a softball
> 1 cup cooked rice
> ⅔ to ¾ cup finely chopped pecans
> 1 egg, beaten lightly
> ½ cup minced mushroom stems or mushrooms that have been stir-fried for 5 minutes in 2 tablespoons butter
> ¼ teaspoon crumbled leaf thyme
> Pinch of ground mace or grated nutmeg
> Salt and freshly ground black pepper to taste

Preheat the oven to moderate (350° F.).

Cut 1 inch off the top of each onion; peel the onions, then parboil them in about 1½ inches of lightly salted water for about 20 minutes, or until nearly tender. Drain the onions well, then scoop out the insides, leaving onion shells about ⅜ inch (2 layers of onion) thick.

Chop the scooped-out onion and measure out 1 cup of it (the remainder can be used in soups or stews, hashes or hamburgers); mix in all the remaining ingredients and toss well. Taste for salt and pepper and add more, if needed. Stuff the hollowed-out onions with the mixture, packing it in lightly and piling it up on top.

Bake the stuffed onions, uncovered, in the preheated oven for 30 to 40 minutes, or until the stuffing is dappled with brown.

RICE AND ONION PIE

6 to 8 servings

A delicate, quichelike pie made with leftover cooked rice in which you can also use up odds and ends of Swiss or Cheddar cheese, evaporated milk, and/or light or heavy cream.

1 baked 9-inch pie shell

1 egg white, beaten until frothy

2 large yellow onions, peeled and coarsely chopped

3 tablespoons butter or margarine

2 large eggs, beaten lightly

1 cup milk (or any combination of milk and leftover evaporated milk, light or heavy cream, or half-and-half)

1 to 1¼ cups coarsely grated Gruyère, Swiss, or Cheddar cheese

1 to 1½ cups leftover cooked rice

1½ teaspoons salt

¼ teaspoon crumbled leaf thyme or rosemary

⅛ teaspoon grated nutmeg

⅛ teaspoon freshly ground black pepper

Preheat the oven to moderate (350° F.). Brush the bottom crust of the pie shell with beaten egg white and let air-dry for 10 minutes (to help keep the crust from going soggy).

Stir-fry the onions in the butter in a large, heavy skillet over moderate heat for 8 to 10 minutes, until golden; cool slightly.

In a large mixing bowl, combine the eggs and milk, then mix in all of the remaining ingredients. Pour into the pie shell and bake for 35 to 45 minutes, or until the filling is set like custard.

Remove from the oven and cool for about 15 minutes, then cut into wedges and serve as a light luncheon or supper entrée.

CURRIED CRAB AND RICE SALAD

6 servings

Here's a perfectly splendid way to utilize leftover cooked rice (as much as 2 cups of white, brown, *or* wild rice). You may also substitute another seafood for the crab, if you like—diced, cooked shrimp or lobster are especially good, as is flaked white fish. You can even use canned tuna or salmon (two 7 to 7¾-ounce cans), or diced, cooked ham, chicken, or turkey.

Tip   A nifty way to stretch the number of servings to 8 (and, at the same time, to add an exotic touch) is to add a diced ripe papaya or two large, diced ripe peaches.

CONTINUED

1 large yellow onion, peeled and chopped
2 tablespoons butter or margarine
2 teaspoons curry powder
1 cup diced celery
2 cups flaked, boned, cooked crab meat (about 1 pound)
1½ to 2 cups leftover cooked rice
2 hard-cooked eggs, peeled and coarsely chopped
2 tablespoons minced sweet pickle
1 ripe papaya or 2 large ripe peaches, halved, peeled, seeded, and cut
   in small dice (optional)
½ to ¾ cup mayonnaise
Juice of 1 lemon
2 to 4 tablespoons milk or light cream (as needed to moisten and help
   bind the salad)
Salt and freshly ground black pepper to taste

Stir-fry the onion in the butter in a heavy skillet over moderate heat for 8 to 10 minutes, or until golden; blend in the curry powder, then reduce the heat to low and let mellow for 2 to 3 minutes to remove the "raw" curry taste. Empty all into a large mixing bowl and add the celery, crab, rice, eggs, pickle, and papaya, if you like. Toss gently but thoroughly.

Combine ½ cup of the mayonnaise and the lemon juice, pour over the mixture, and toss again to mix. If the salad seems dry, add the remaining ¼ cup mayonnaise and, if necessary, 2 to 4 tablespoons of milk or cream. Season to taste with salt and pepper.

Chill for several hours before serving so the flavors have a chance to mellow and mingle.

MEXICAN BLACK BEANS AND RICE

4 to 6 servings

This is an uncommonly quick and good skillet dish that calls for from 2 to 2½ cups of cooked rice—a perfect way to use leftovers. This may seem like a lot of leftover cooked rice, but it isn't, really, if you've miscalculated (easy to do) or if your family wasn't as hungry as usual. This recipe also allows you to add chopped sweet pepper and parsley as optional ingredients (if you should have them left over, too).

2 medium yellow onions, peeled and chopped
1 large clove garlic, peeled and crushed
½ medium sweet green, red, or yellow pepper, cored, seeded, and
   chopped (optional)
2 tablespoons olive oil
¼ teaspoon ground coriander
¼ teaspoon ground cinnamon
⅛ teaspoon grated nutmeg or ground mace
2 to 2½ cups leftover cooked rice
2 to 3 tablespoons minced fresh parsley (optional)
1 can (1 pound) black beans, drained well
Salt and freshly ground black pepper to taste

Stir-fry the onions, garlic, and, if you like, the green pepper in the
oil in a large, heavy skillet over moderate heat for 8 to 10 minutes, until
the onions are limp and golden; do not brown. Mix in the coriander,
cinnamon, nutmeg, rice, and also the parsley, if you should have some
going begging. Stir-fry for about 5 minutes over moderate heat—just
until the rice is hot and each grain is lightly glazed with the oil. Mix
in the black beans and salt and pepper to taste and heat and stir for
about 5 minutes longer—just until the beans are good and hot.

Dish up and serve in place of potatoes or as a main dish. To accompany, serve a crisp green or a tart fruit salad.

ACORN SQUASH STUFFED WITH PEANUT AND PEPPER PILAF

4 servings

2 medium acorn squash
1 medium Spanish onion, peeled and chopped
1 small sweet green pepper, cored, seeded, and chopped
1 small sweet red pepper, cored, seeded, and chopped
3 tablespoons peanut or vegetable oil
1 cup coarsely chopped roasted peanuts
3 tablespoons cider vinegar
2 tablespoons light brown sugar, honey, or sweetened condensed
   milk
2 to 2½ cups leftover cooked rice

CONTINUED

1 to 1½ cups leftover diced, cooked meat (turkey, chicken, beef, pork, ham, or lamb) (optional)
Water or chicken or beef broth (if needed to moisten the stuffing)
¼ cup grated Parmesan cheese

Preheat the oven to moderate (350° F.).

Bake the squash whole (simply place them in a shallow, open baking pan) in the preheated oven for 45 minutes, or just until you can pierce them fairly easily with a fork (they should be firm-tender, not mushy-soft). Remove the squash from the oven and cool until easy to handle.

Meanwhile, stir-fry the onion and peppers in the oil in a large, heavy skillet over moderate heat for 10 to 12 minutes, or until limp and lightly browned. Turn the heat to low; add the peanuts, vinegar, and brown sugar and keep warm while you prepare the squash.

Halve each squash lengthwise and discard the stringy portions and seeds, then scoop out the flesh, leaving shells about ¼ inch thick; cut the squash flesh in ¼-inch cubes, add to the skillet, and toss to mix. Add the rice and, if you like, the meat and toss well again.

Set the lid on the skillet askew and heat slowly for 5 to 10 minutes —just until the squash seems tender and the mixture is piping hot. (If at any time it threatens to stick or to cook too dry, moisten with a little water or broth.) Meanwhile, preheat the broiler.

Stuff the mixture into the squash shells, scatter grated Parmesan on top of each, and broil 5 to 6 inches from the heat for 2 to 3 minutes, until dappled with brown.

Serve at once as a main course, accompanied, if you like, by a crisp green salad and chunks of crusty bread.

Sour Cream

Commercial or "dairy" sour cream, you'll be pleased to know, is made from light rather than heavy cream and averages only about 30 calories per tablespoon. It is nothing more than pasteurized sweet cream (or a combination of sweet cream and milk) that is soured under carefully controlled conditions (the souring agent is usually a lactic-acid-producing bacterium). Sometimes rennet (an extract obtained from the lining of calves' stomachs) is added to help curd the cream. The clotted sour cream is then homogenized so that it develops the thick, spoon-up smoothness we like.

Best Way to Store   In the refrigerator, in a tightly covered carton or container.

Maximum Storage Time   About 10 days, although much will depend upon the freshness of the sour cream (pay attention to the date stamped on the carton).

Roles in Cooking   Principally to impart a tartness of flavor and smoothness of consistency. When teamed with baking soda in cakes, cookies, or quick breads, sour cream produces carbon-dioxide gas, an effective leavener. Finally, because of its acidity, sour cream can help to tenderize the tougher cuts of meat, especially if the meat is cubed as for stew, then marinated several hours in the sour cream.

Recipe Uses   So many of the Russian and Middle European classics depend upon sour cream—beef Stroganoff, all manner of paprikashes, borschts, creamed vegetables, and fruit soups. It's a Scandinavian staple, too, drifted over pickled herring or smoked salmon. And, of course, sour cream is essential to the whole repertoire of cheesecakes and pies.

Special Comments   Always bring sour cream to room temperature before smoothing into a hot dish (soup, stew, sauce, gravy, etc.) because it will be less likely to curdle. Also, never allow a mixture containing sour cream to boil because it will curdle for certain.

How to Use up Small Amounts   Beat a tablespoon or two—or even up to ¼ cup—of sour cream into mashed potatoes; use to dress green beans or sliced or shredded beets instead of butter; stir into chopped or puréed spinach; mix up to ½ cup of sour cream into your favorite meat or fish loaf; add to scalloped potatoes; mix into hamburgers or spoon atop them as soon as they come off the grill or griddle.

N O T E   *For additional recipes, included elsewhere in this book, that call for varying amounts of sour (or soured) cream, see the Appendix.*

SOUR CREAM, CAPER, AND HORSERADISH SAUCE

About ¾ cup

This sauce and its easy variation are both ideal ways to use moderate amounts of leftover sour cream. Serve either with sliced tongue, boiled beef, or ham, or with poached or fried fish.

½ cup sour cream
2 tablespoons mayonnaise
2 tablespoons cream (light or heavy) or evaporated milk
2 tablespoons prepared horseradish
1 tablespoon capers
⅛ teaspoon white pepper

Mix all the ingredients, cover, and let stand at room temperature for 30 minutes before serving.

VARIATION

Mustard, Caper, and Horseradish Sauce   Prepare as directed, but blend in 1 to 2 tablespoons Dijon or spicy brown mustard.

COLD ASPARAGUS WITH SOUR CREAM– HORSERADISH DRESSING

4 to 6 servings

An elegant but effortless way to use leftover sour cream *and* heavy cream. This dish, by the way, is equally good made with cooked broccoli spears or artichoke hearts (use two bunches of broccoli or three 10-ounce packages of frozen artichoke hearts cooked according to package directions). Serve as a salad with cold salmon or ham.

2 pounds fresh asparagus or, if you prefer, 2 cans (15 ounces each) white asparagus spears

DRESSING

2 tablespoons best-quality olive oil
Juice of ½ lemon
1 tablespoon Dijon or spicy brown mustard

2 tablespoons dry white wine or vermouth
2 tablespoons prepared horseradish
½ to ¾ cup sour cream
½ to ¾ cup heavy cream, whipped to soft peaks

Trim the fresh asparagus, if you use it, of coarse stems, then wash, peel, and cook in lightly salted water just until tender (about 10 minutes); drain canned asparagus well. Arrange half of the asparagus spears in a 9 × 9 × 2-inch baking dish. Blend all the dressing ingredients until smooth and pour half over the asparagus. Arrange the remaining asparagus on top, then pour the remaining dressing evenly over all.

Cover and marinate for several hours in the refrigerator before serving.

BRAISED VEAL LOIN WITH LEMON-SOUR CREAM GRAVY

6 to 8 servings

An exquisite recipe—and one that will use up anywhere from ½ to 1 cup of sour cream, as well as ½ to 1 cup of chicken or beef broth or stock.

3½ to 4 pounds boned and rolled veal loin (in one piece)
¼ cup (½ stick) unsalted butter
4 medium carrots, peeled and coarsely chopped
2 medium ribs celery, trimmed, washed, and coarsely chopped
2 medium yellow onions, peeled and coarsely chopped
1 small clove garlic, peeled and minced
¼ teaspoon crumbled leaf thyme
¼ teaspoon crumbled leaf sage
½ to 1 cup chicken broth or stock (or substitute beef broth or stock, if that is what you have)
Juice and finely grated rind of 2 lemons
½ to 1 cup sour cream, at room temperature
Salt and freshly ground black pepper to taste

Brown the veal well in the butter in a large, heavy kettle over moderately high heat. Lift out and set aside for the time being. Add the carrots, celery, onions, garlic, thyme, and sage, then reduce the heat to moderate and stir-fry for 8 to 10 minutes, until the onions are limp and golden. Return the veal to the kettle and add the chicken broth and lemon juice and rind. Adjust the heat so the kettle liquid ripples gently, then cover and simmer for about 2½ hours, or until the veal is very tender.

Remove the veal from the kettle and keep warm; purée the kettle mixture, a little at a time, in a food processor fitted with the metal chopping blade or in an electric blender at high speed. Return to the kettle, then boil, uncovered, for 15 to 20 minutes, until the mixture is reduced by half. Turn the heat to low, smooth in the sour cream, and bring just to serving temperature (do not boil). Taste for salt and pepper and season as needed.

Slice the veal thin and serve with plenty of the gravy. Delicious with fluffy cooked rice.

SOUR CREAM–CUCUMBER SAUCE

About 1½ cups

1 medium cucumber, peeled, seeded, and cut in small dice
¾ cup sour cream
2 tablespoons white wine vinegar or tarragon vinegar
¼ teaspoon salt
⅛ teaspoon white pepper
1 tablespoon minced fresh dill or ¼ teaspoon dill weed

Mix all the ingredients, cover, and chill for several hours. Serve with baked or boiled ham, or poached, broiled, or fried fish.

CINNAMON-TOPPED SOUR CREAM COOKIES

About 5 dozen

3½ cups sifted all-purpose flour
½ teaspoon salt
½ teaspoon baking soda
½ teaspoon baking powder
1 cup (2 sticks) butter or margarine, at room temperature
1½ cups granulated sugar
¾ cup sour cream
1 teaspoon vanilla extract

TOPPING

¼ cup granulated sugar mixed with 1 teaspoon ground cinnamon

Preheat the oven to moderately hot (375° F.).

Sift the flour, salt, soda, and baking powder together onto a piece of wax paper and set aside for the time being. Cream the butter and sugar until fluffy-light; add the sour cream and vanilla and beat well. Slowly mix in the dry ingredients.

Drop the dough by rounded teaspoonfuls onto well-greased baking sheets, spacing the cookies 2 inches apart. Bake in the preheated oven for 8 minutes, then sprinkle the topping over the cookies and bake for 2 to 3 minutes longer, or until lightly ringed with brown and the tops feel springy to the touch.

Transfer at once to wire racks to cool.

VARIATIONS

Caraway–Sour Cream Cookies Prepare as directed, adding 1 tablespoon caraway seeds along with the dry ingredients.

Sour Cream–Nut Cookies Prepare the cookie dough as directed, then fold in 1 to 1½ cups coarsely chopped pecans, walnuts, blanched almonds, or filberts. Bake as directed.

CABBAGE SLAW WITH
SOUR CREAM DRESSING

4 to 6 servings

3 cups finely shredded cabbage
2 tablespoons finely grated yellow onion
1½ teaspoons salt
¼ teaspoon freshly ground black pepper
1 cup sour cream or soured heavy cream
⅓ cup cider vinegar
⅓ to ½ cup honey
1 tablespoon prepared mustard
1 teaspoon paprika

Place the cabbage, onion, 1 teaspoon of the salt, and the black pepper in a large mixing bowl and toss well. Combine the remaining ingredients, including the remaining ½ teaspoon of salt, blending until smooth. Pour over the cabbage mixture and toss well, then cover and let "season" for several hours in the refrigerator before serving.

Toss well again and serve.

SOUR MILK: See **Buttermilk and Sour Milk.**

SPICES: See **Herbs and Spices (Dried).**

SUGAR: See **Brown Sugar.**

SWEETENED CONDENSED MILK: See **Milk.**

Tomato Paste, Purée, and Sauce

(Plus Some Notes on Ketchup and Chili Sauce)

When we were researching this book, we asked a number of friends and relatives what one leftover they found the peskiest to use up. Their answers were immediate—and virtually unanimous: *tomato paste!* In our experience, tomato paste *is* a problem. Although it is packed in small quantities (6-ounce cans, each of which equals ¾ cup), few recipes call for more than a tablespoon or two of tomato paste at a time, so an almost full can is relegated to the refrigerator shelf. Usually it's forgotten or ignored until it spoils. And what of the other canned tomato products? Purée? Sauce? Ketchup and chili sauce? How does one differ from the other? Can they be used interchangeably? Let's discuss them one by one.

TOMATO PASTE

This is a thick, highly concentrated, unseasoned tomato purée—very strong of flavor and very acid, which is why it is called for in such small quantities.

Best Way to Store In a tightly covered glass jar in the refrigerator. You may, of course, cover the partly used can of tomato paste with foil or plastic food wrap and refrigerate it, but we think it develops a metallic taste.

To Freeze Friends told us that they had had good luck freezing tomato paste, so we tried their method and it worked for us, too. Here's how. Place a piece of heavy-duty aluminum foil in a small, shallow baking pan and smooth as flat as possible. Measure out level tablespoonfuls of tomato paste and drop, just as you would cookie dough, onto the foil. Set the pan, uncovered, directly on the freezing surface of a freezer set at 0° F. and quick-freeze the tomato paste—this should take about an hour. Peel the frozen "clumps" of tomato paste from the foil, wrap each individually and airtight in plastic food wrap or foil, then bundle the packets in a plastic bag so they don't get lost in the freezer. Label and date the bag, then twist the top into a gooseneck and

secure with a twist-band. Store in a freezer set at 0° F. (It is important, of course, that you freeze leftover tomato paste without delay, that is, as soon after opening the can as possible to minimize exposure to airborne microorganisms of spoilage. Don't decide to freeze tomato paste after it's been sitting, opened, on the refrigerator shelf for several days.) We prefer to use frozen tomato paste in cooked dishes—soups, sauces, skillet scrambles, casseroles, and the like. There is no need to thaw the frozen tomato paste before using it—just drop the solidly frozen clumps into saucepan or skillet. They will melt soon enough.
Maximum Storage Time   About 10 days if stored in a glass jar; about 5 to 7 days if stored in the original can; about 2 months if frozen.
Roles in Cooking   To flavor, color, and thicken; also to help bind ingredients together (as in a casserole or pasta sauce).

N O T E   *Because tomato paste is so tart (acid), it is sometimes necessary to mellow the recipes in which it's used by adding 1 to 2 tablespoons of honey or brown sugar.*

Recipe Uses   Tomato paste is integral to almost all tomato-based Italian dishes (pasta sauces, lasagne, manicotti, pizza, etc.). In addition, it figures prominently in a wide variety of Spanish, Mexican, and Latin American dishes and in such Tex-Mex classics as chili.
How to Use Very Small Amounts   A tablespoon or two of tomato paste will enrich the color and flavor of soups (especially the canned or dried "instant" soups), and by mixing about 1 tablespoon each of tomato paste and grated onion with 3 cups of beef consommé, you can improvise a jiffy madrilène. You can also smooth about 1 tablespoon of tomato paste into most gravies, as well as into such classic sauces as Newburg, Colbert, and curry with good results. Also try mixing 1 to 2 tablespoons of tomato paste into baked beans, creamy salad dressings, fish and poultry salads, cheese spreads, and, finally, into burgers or meat, chicken, or salmon loaves.

TOMATO PURÉE

Once available in small quantities, tomato purée is now packed almost altogether in large (30 ounces or more) institutional cans, which some supermarkets do stock. In certain areas of the country, it is also available in 15-ounce (2-cup) sizes. For small, family-sized recipes, however, it has been replaced by tomato sauce, packed in handy 8-ounce tins. What is tomato purée? How does it differ from tomato sauce? Tomato paste? Think of it as puréed, sieved whole tomatoes on their way to becoming tomato paste. They are boiled down to the consistency of a sauce—no more. Tomato paste is reduced further, to a spoon-thick concentrate. In consistency, tomato purée most resembles tomato sauce, but unlike tomato sauce it is *un*seasoned (save for the possible addition of salt).

Best Way to Store   Tightly covered in a glass jar in the refrigerator.

Maximum Storage Time   About 10 days.

Roles in Cooking   Like tomato paste, tomato purée is used principally to flavor, color, thicken, and bind ingredients. Because it is only half as thick as tomato paste, you must use about twice as much of it to achieve the same intensity of flavor. And you must cook the purée down to the desired consistency.

Recipe Uses   Many cooks use tomato purée for a variety of pasta sauces, adding their own pet seasonings. Tomato purée can also be turned into an almost instant tomato sauce (all you need do is season to taste and boil the mixture down slightly). It can be used as the liquid ingredient in meat loaves and burgers (in place of water or bouillon), thereby yielding a far more flavorful product. Tomato purée may be used interchangeably with tomato sauce—but taste the recipe and add oregano or marjoram, thyme, and basil as needed.

How to Use Very Small Amounts   Make instant mini-pizzas by spreading split English muffins with tomato purée (1 to 2 tablespoons of it per half muffin), sprinkle lightly with oregano and thyme, top with thinly sliced mozzarella, then broil just until bubbling and touched with brown. Add ½ cup or less of tomato purée to a tomato or vegetable soup, to a pasta sauce, to any casserole containing tomatoes, to baked beans, to chili, meat loaves, or burgers. Or make a quick tomato soup by combining 1 part tomato purée with 1½ parts each beef consommé and milk (do not allow the mixture to boil or it will curdle). Season to taste with salt and freshly ground pepper and, if you like, with marjoram and thyme, or tarragon and thyme, or rosemary and thyme.

TOMATO SAUCE

This amounts to little more than *seasoned* tomato purée, which it has virtually replaced on many supermarket shelves. Usually tomato sauce contains onion, sweet pepper, herbs, spices, sugar, and salt in addition to tomatoes. It's puréed and sieved so that it's uniformly smooth and satiny, and it's packed in 8- and 15-ounce cans (1 and 1⅞ cups).

Best Way to Store Tightly covered in its own can or in a glass jar in the refrigerator.

Maximum Storage Time About 7 to 10 days, with the sauce in the jar having the longer shelf life because it can be more tightly sealed and because glass is an inert material totally unaffected by the acid in the tomatoes (tomato sauce stored in its original can may develop a "tinny" taste).

Roles in Cooking Precisely the same as for tomato purée (which see).

Recipe Uses Once again, look to your collection of Italian, Spanish, and Latin American recipes for ideas on using up leftover tomato sauce.

How to Use Small Amounts See the suggestions given for tomato purée (tomato sauce may be used interchangeably with it, although if you substitute tomato sauce in a recipe that specifies tomato purée, you will have to reduce the seasonings slightly—tomato sauce, remember, is seasoned, tomato purée unseasoned).

Special Comments Here are some tomato equivalents and substitutions that may prove useful:

• 1 can (8 ounces) tomato sauce = 1 pound fresh tomatoes, peeled, chopped, sieved, and seasoned to taste (with salt, sugar, pepper, basil, marjoram or oregano, thyme, and, if you like, about 1 small minced onion and ½ small minced sweet pepper), then simmered until the thickness of sauce

• 1 cup tomato purée = 1 pound fresh tomatoes, peeled, chopped, sieved, and simmered until the consistency of sauce

• 1 cup tomato sauce = 1 cup tomato purée (seasoned to taste with onion salt, sugar, pepper, basil, marjoram or oregano, and thyme)

• ½ cup tomato sauce or purée + ½ cup water = 1 cup tomato juice (for recipe use, not for drinking)

• ½ cup tomato purée or sauce + ½ cup water = 1 cup canned tomatoes (solid pack)

• ½ can (6-ounce size) tomato paste + ½ cup water = 1 cup tomato purée, or if seasoned to taste with onion salt, pepper, oregano or marjoram, basil, and thyme, ½ can tomato paste combined with ½ cup water will approximate 1 can (8-ounce size) of tomato sauce.

• 1 can (8-ounce size) tomato sauce + ¼ cup water = 1 can (10¾-ounce size) condensed tomato soup (the soup just as it comes from the can, not as it is diluted with water)

SOME NOTES ON KETCHUP AND CHILI SAUCE

These two tomato sauces are highly spiced, sweet-sour condiments that should be used in small quantities only. Ketchup (also spelled "catsup") is the milder of the two, also the smoother because it has been puréed and sieved). Chili sauce is hotter (thanks to the chili peppers it contains), thicker, and lumpier. Ketchup and chili sauce may be used interchangeably with one another (and they may also be substituted for small amounts—from 1 to 3 tablespoons—of tomato paste). But they are far too spicy to be used in place of either tomato sauce or purée.

Best Way to Store   In the refrigerator, tightly capped, in their own bottles.

Maximum Storage Time   3 to 4 months (ketchup and chili sauce both begin to darken during prolonged storage, and although they are safe to eat, they have lost their dazzling red color and some of their sharp, lively flavor).

Roles in Cooking   To add flavor, piquancy, and color, primarily. But both ketchup and chili sauce can also be used to help bind together dips, spreads, and egg, fish, and chicken salads.

Recipe Uses   Sauces, salad dressings, cocktail dips, and sandwich spreads are where you'll find the most opportunities to use up the last of a bottle of ketchup or chili sauce.

How to Use Very Small Amounts   Stir into any tomato-based casserole or skillet dish (but no more than 2 to 3 tablespoons, and be sure to taste as you add); mix into chili or baked beans or meat loaves. Make a jiffy thousand island dressing by stirring about 2 tablespoons of ketchup or chili sauce into ¾ cup of mayonnaise, then folding in 2 to 3 tablespoons of sweet pickle relish. You may also safely add 1 to 2 tablespoons of ketchup or chili sauce to your favorite pasta sauce or pizza topping.

NOTE *For additional recipes, included elsewhere in this book, that call for varying amounts of the different tomato products, see the Appendix.*

Tomato Paste

TOMATO- AND ANCHOVY-STUFFED FLOUNDER ROLLS IN WINE SAUCE

4 servings

Because anchovy and tomato paste are two of the foods we usually have to buy in larger quantities than we need, you should make this recipe either when you are down to tag ends of each or when you have a definite idea as to how you'll use up the balance. The recipe should also be planned when you are left with a small amount of white wine in the bottom of the bottle.

4 small flounder fillets
¼ teaspoon freshly ground black pepper
2 tablespoons butter, at room temperature
2 teaspoons anchovy paste
2 teaspoons tomato paste

WINE SAUCE

¼ cup (½ stick) butter or margarine
3 tablespoons all-purpose flour
¼ to ½ teaspoon salt, or to taste
Pinch of freshly ground black pepper
¾ cup water
½ cup dry white wine

Preheat the oven to moderately hot (375° F.).

Sprinkle the fish fillets with pepper. Cream the butter with the anchovy and tomato pastes, then spread the mixture on one side of each fillet. Roll the fillets up jelly-roll style, place in a well-greased shallow baking dish, and set aside.

For the sauce, melt 3 tablespoons of the butter in a small, heavy saucepan; blend in the flour, salt, and pepper, then add the water and cook, stirring constantly over low heat, until thickened and smooth—about 3 minutes. Slowly add the wine, stirring all the while, then cook slowly, stirring frequently, for 10 minutes. Taste the sauce for salt and add a bit more, if needed.

Pour the wine sauce over the fish and dot with the remaining 1 tablespoon of butter, then bake, uncovered, in the preheated oven for 45 minutes.

BURGER STROGANOFF

6 servings

Tomato paste isn't the only commonly leftover food this recipe puts to good use. Another is sour cream. You could even add as much as 2 tablespoons spicy brown mustard and/or 1 tablespoon anchovy paste, but if you do omit all salt. True Stroganoffs, few people realize, contain very little sour cream, and, indeed, the quantity for this variation is flexible—from ⅓ to ¾ cup.

> 2 pounds lean ground beef chuck
> 2 tablespoons bacon drippings, butter, or margarine
> 1 large Spanish onion, peeled and moderately coarsely chopped
> 1 large clove garlic, peeled and minced
> 1 pound mushrooms, wiped clean, trimmed of coarse stem ends, and sliced thin
> 3 large, very ripe tomatoes, peeled, cored, and chopped (include juice)
> 1 to 3 tablespoons tomato paste
> 1 to 2 tablespoons spicy brown or Dijon mustard (optional)
> 1 tablespoon anchovy paste (optional)
> ⅛ teaspoon freshly ground black pepper
> Salt to taste
> ⅓ to ¾ cup sour cream, at room temperature

Brown the beef lightly in the bacon drippings, breaking up large clumps, in a large, heavy skillet over moderately high heat. Add the onion, garlic, and mushrooms and stir-fry along with the beef for about 10 minutes, or until limp and golden. Stir in the tomatoes and their juice, tomato paste, the mustard and/or anchovy paste (if you like), and the pepper.

Reduce the heat and simmer, covered, for 30 minutes, then uncover and simmer for 20 to 25 minutes longer, stirring often, until the mixture has reduced to a saucelike consistency (about like pasta sauce). Taste for salt and season as needed.

Smooth in the sour cream (do not allow to boil or the cream may curdle), then serve over buttered noodles or fluffy boiled rice.

PEPPERONI AND GARBANZO BAKE

4 servings

This casserole and the one for Pastichio, which follows, can each accommodate whatever amount of tomato paste you have left over—from 2 to 4 or 5 tablespoons.

> ½ pound pepperoni, sliced ¼ inch thick
> 1 tablespoon olive oil
> 1 large yellow onion, peeled and coarsely chopped
> 1 clove garlic, peeled and minced
> ¼ teaspoon crumbled leaf marjoram
> ¼ teaspoon crumbled leaf thyme
> ¼ teaspoon fennel seeds
> ¼ cup dry white wine (a good way to use up tag ends)
> 2 to 4 tablespoons tomato paste
> 1 can (1 pound) tomatoes (do not drain)
> 1 tablespoon light brown sugar (to mellow the tartness of the tomatoes)
> ½ teaspoon salt
> ⅛ teaspoon freshly ground black pepper
> 1 can (1 pound, 4 ounces) garbanzo beans (chick-peas), drained

Lightly brown the pepperoni in the olive oil in a large, heavy skillet over moderately high heat; using a slotted spoon, lift the pepperoni slices to paper toweling to drain. Drain all but 2 tablespoons of the drippings from the skillet, add the onion and garlic, and stir-fry for 10 minutes, until lightly browned. Mix in the marjoram, thyme, fennel seeds, and wine and simmer for 3 to 4 minutes. Smooth in the tomato paste, then add the tomatoes and brown sugar and simmer, uncovered, breaking up large clumps of tomatoes, for about 25 minutes, or until the mixture thickens slightly.

Meanwhile, preheat the oven to moderate (350° F.).

Add the salt and pepper to the mixture in the skillet, then the garbanzo beans and drained slices of pepperoni. Transfer all to a lightly greased 1½-quart casserole; set, uncovered, in the preheated oven and bake for about 1½ hours, stirring two to three times during baking, until bubbly and lightly browned, and the flavors seem well blended.

Serve with a rough peasant bread and a crisp green salad.

PASTICHIO

6 to 8 servings

In addition to using up leftover tomato paste, this Greek classic also takes care of any half-used, 1-pound boxes of elbow macaroni you may have stuck away on a cupboard shelf. It is a splendid entrée for an informal buffet or supper, and, best of all, it can be frozen (directions are given at the end of the recipe).

WHITE SAUCE

¼ cup (½ stick) butter
7 tablespoons all-purpose flour
2 cups milk
¾ teaspoon salt
⅛ teaspoon white pepper
⅛ teaspoon ground mace
1 large egg, beaten lightly

CONTINUED

MACARONI MIXTURE

½ pound elbow macaroni, cooked according to package directions
and drained well
½ cup of the white sauce (above)
1 large egg, beaten lightly
1 teaspoon salt

LAMB MIXTURE

1 large yellow onion, peeled and chopped fine
1 large clove garlic, peeled and minced
2 tablespoons olive oil
1 pound lean ground lamb shoulder
2 to 5 tablespoons tomato paste
1½ teaspoons crumbled mint flakes
¼ teaspoon ground cinnamon
¼ teaspoon crumbled leaf rosemary
¼ teaspoon crumbled leaf thyme
½ teaspoon salt
⅛ teaspoon freshly ground black pepper

TOPPING

⅔ cup grated Parmesan cheese

Prepare the white sauce first. In a medium-sized heavy saucepan, melt the butter over moderate heat; blend in the flour to make a smooth paste, then add the milk and heat, whisking briskly, until thickened and smooth—about 3 minutes. Turn the heat to the lowest point; add the salt, white pepper, and mace and allow the sauce to mellow for about 10 minutes, or until no raw, starchy flavor remains. Remove from the heat and measure out ½ cup of sauce to use in the macaroni mixture. Blend a little of the remaining sauce into the beaten egg, then stir back into the pan. Let the sauce stand off the heat until you are ready for it, whisking from time to time to prevent a "skin" from forming on the surface.

To make the macaroni mixture, pour the macaroni into a large mixing bowl. Whisk the ½ cup of white sauce with the egg and salt, pour over the macaroni, and toss well to mix. Set aside while you prepare the lamb mixture.

Sauté the onion and garlic in the olive oil in a large, heavy skillet set over moderate heat for 8 to 10 minutes, just until limp and golden. Add the lamb, breaking up large clumps, and fry for 3 to 5 minutes, just until no longer pink. Smooth in all the remaining ingredients and heat, stirring now and then, for about 15 minutes, until slightly thickened and the flavors are well blended.

Preheat the oven to moderate (350° F.) while you assemble the pastichio.

Butter a 9 × 9 × 2-inch ovenproof glass baking dish, then layer the ingredients into it this way: one-half of the macaroni mixture, a generous sprinkling of grated Parmesan cheese (2 to 3 tablespoons), all of the lamb mixture (press this layer firmly into the macaroni one underneath), another generous sprinkling of Parmesan, the remaining macaroni mixture, and still more Parmesan. Top with the remaining white sauce and scatter the remaining grated Parmesan evenly on top.

Set the *pastichio,* uncovered, in the preheated oven and bake for 45 minutes to 1 hour, or until bubbling and lightly browned. Remove from the oven and let stand for 25 to 30 minutes, then cut into squares and serve.

To Freeze Assemble the *pastichio* in a lightly buttered 9 × 9 × 2-inch freezer-to-oven casserole. Do not bake. Overwrap the *pastichio* snugly in heavy-duty aluminum foil, and quick-freeze by setting directly on the freezing surface of a freezer set at 0° F. When the *pastichio* is frozen brick-hard, unwrap, lift from the casserole (this is so that you can use the casserole dish in the meantime and save freezer space), then rewrap the solidly frozen *pastichio* in heavy-duty foil, pressing out all air pockets. Label and date and store at 0° F. Keeping time: about 3 months.

If you live alone or if your family is small, you can assemble the *pastichio* in small aluminum-foil containers—like those in which many frozen foods are packed (you can buy these in most housewares stores). Simply layer the *pastichio* into the aluminum containers in the order the recipe suggests, dividing the total amount evenly; overwrap in heavy-duty foil, label, date, and quick-freeze.

When you are ready to bake the *pastichio,* set it, solidly frozen, in a moderate oven (350°) and bake as directed above, but keep the container covered with foil for the first 30 minutes of baking. You may also need to increase the total baking time by 15 to 20 minutes. The smaller or individual-sized containers will, of course, need less time—perhaps 45 minutes from the solidly frozen state to piping hot.

If you've frozen the *pastichio* in a freezer-to-oven casserole, then removed it once it was solidly frozen, simply unwrap the solidly frozen block and slip it into the same casserole—it will fit like a glove. Cover loosely with foil for the first 30 minutes of baking, then proceed as directed above.

Tomato Sauce and Purée

CREOLE SQUASH PUDDING

6 servings

As you read the ingredient list below, consider all the options you have for using up leftovers: green pepper, mushroom stems, tomato sauce, chicken or beef broth, and cracker meal or bread crumbs.

> 2 medium yellow onions, peeled and coarsely chopped
> ½ cup minced sweet green pepper
> 1 clove garlic, peeled and crushed
> 1 to 1½ cups chopped mushrooms or mushroom stems
> 3 tablespoons olive oil
> ½ to ¾ cup tomato sauce or 1 large, ripe tomato, peeled, cored, seeded, and coarsely chopped
> ½ teaspoon fennel seeds, crushed
> ¼ teaspoon crumbled leaf basil
> Pinch of crumbled leaf thyme
> 2 tablespoons butter or margarine
> 3 tablespoons all-purpose flour
> 1½ cups chicken or beef broth or a half-and-half mixture of broth and water or dry white wine
> ¼ teaspoon cayenne pepper
> ½ teaspoon salt
> ½ cup cracker meal or soft bread crumbs
> 2 pounds yellow squash or zucchini, sliced ½ inch thick, parboiled just until crisp-tender, then drained well

Preheat the oven to moderately hot (375° F.)
Stir-fry the onions, green pepper, garlic, and mushrooms in the oil

in a large, heavy skillet for 10 to 15 minutes, until lightly browned. Mix in the tomato sauce, fennel seeds, basil, and thyme and cook, stirring, for 5 minutes.

Melt the butter in a small saucepan over moderate heat and blend in the flour. Add the broth, cayenne, and salt and heat, stirring constantly, until thickened and smooth—3 to 4 minutes. Blend in the crumbs.

Combine the sauce, squash, and sautéed mixture; spoon into a buttered shallow 2-quart casserole and bake, uncovered, in the preheated oven for 1 hour. Cool for 10 minutes and serve.

RICE MALAGA

6 servings

Here is another splendid way to utilize leftover tomato sauce (or purée), as well as between ⅓ and ½ cup of minced green pepper—not to mention 2 cups of almost any leftover meat.

> 1 medium Spanish onion, peeled and chopped
> 2 cloves garlic, peeled and minced
> ⅓ to ½ cup minced sweet green pepper
> ⅓ cup olive oil
> ½ pound mushrooms, wiped clean and sliced thin
> 2 cups cubed, cooked ham, chicken, or turkey or leftover beef, lamb, or pork roast
> 1¼ cups uncooked rice
> 1½ teaspoons salt
> ¼ teaspoon freshly ground black pepper
> ¼ teaspoon paprika
> ⅛ teaspoon powdered saffron
> ½ to ¾ cup tomato sauce or purée
> 2 cans (10½ ounces each) chicken broth
> 1½ cups fresh or frozen green peas

Preheat the oven to moderately slow (325° F.).

Stir-fry the onion, garlic, and green pepper in the oil in a shallow, flameproof 2-quart casserole over moderate heat for 5 to 8 minutes, or until the onion is limp and golden. Add the mushrooms and sauté for 5 minutes, until lightly browned.

Mix in all the remaining ingredients except the peas; cover, set in the preheated oven, and bake for 35 minutes. Stir in the peas, re-cover, and bake for 10 to 15 minutes longer, or until the peas are tender and the rice has absorbed almost all of the liquid.

Serve with chunks of hot, crusty bread and a crisp green salad.

CHILI-BURGER OMELET

6 servings

This is an unusually flexible recipe that enables you to put a variety of different leftovers to good use: tomato sauce and/or juice, evaporated milk or cream, snippets of Cheddar, Swiss, or Parmesan cheese. You needn't, of course, have all of the above leftovers in order to make the recipe (alternate ingredients are given for each).

N O T E   *You may add up to 1 cup of cooked leftover vegetables to the burger mixture —green peas, whole-kernel corn, baked beans, diced carrots—again, use whatever you have on hand. You may also add 1 to 2 tablespoons tomato paste if you should have some of that left over. And you may even substitute 1 large ripe tomato, peeled, cored, and chopped, for the tomato sauce or juice.*

> 2 medium yellow onions, peeled and moderately coarsely chopped
> 1 medium sweet green pepper, cored, seeded and moderately coarsely chopped (or if you should have half a large green pepper on hand or scraps of red, yellow, and green pepper left over, use those)
> 4 tablespoons (½ stick) butter or margarine
> ¾ pound lean ground beef chuck
> ½ teaspoon crumbled leaf marjoram
> ¼ teaspoon crumbled leaf thyme
> ¼ teaspoon crumbled leaf basil
> 4 to 6 teaspoons chili powder (depending upon how "hot" you like things)
> 1½ teaspoons salt
> ⅔ to 1⅓ cups tomato sauce or juice (or a combination of the two)
> 6 eggs

⅓ cup evaporated milk, milk, or cream (light, heavy, half-and-half) or any combination of these as long as the total amount of liquid is ⅓ cup

⅛ teaspoon freshly ground black pepper

1 to 1½ cups coarsely grated Cheddar and/or Swiss cheese or ½ cup grated Parmesan cheese

In a large, heavy skillet set over moderate heat, stir-fry the onions and pepper in 2 tablespoons of the butter for about 10 minutes, until limp and touched with brown; scrape onto a large plate and reserve. Shape the beef into one large, flat burger and brown well on both sides in the skillet; break the burger into small clumps, then return the sautéed onions and pepper to the skillet and mix well. Stir in the marjoram, thyme, basil, chili powder, and ½ teaspoon of the salt and let mellow for 2 to 3 minutes over moderate heat. Add the tomato sauce or juice (or the chopped tomato); turn the heat to its lowest point and simmer very slowly, stirring occasionally, for 25 to 30 minutes, or until quite thick and the flavors are well blended.

In a heavy 10-inch skillet with a flameproof handle, melt the remaining 2 tablespoons of butter over moderate heat; tip the skillet in a circular motion so that the sides and bottom are well coated with butter. Quickly beat the eggs with the milk, remaining teaspoon of salt, and the pepper and pour into the skillet. Cook without stirring for about 2 minutes, or until the eggs begin to solidify around the edges of the skillet. Very gently spoon the chili mixture on top, distributing it as evenly as possible over the surface of the eggs. Cook, uncovered and without stirring, for 2 to 3 minutes longer, or until the eggs begin to set underneath the chili (simply push a bit of the chili in the center of the omelet aside and take a look).

Meanwhile, preheat the broiler.

Scatter the cheese evenly over the chili mixture, then broil 5 to 6 inches from the heat for 2 to 3 minutes, or until bubbling and touched with brown.

To serve, cut in wedges as you would a pizza. Particularly good accompaniments are buttery chunks of garlic bread and a tartly dressed green salad.

Ketchup and Chili Sauce

OYSTERS KIRKPATRICK

6 appetizer servings, 4 entrée servings

One wouldn't think that this elegant oyster dish would be compounded of leftovers, but it indeed can be, using as it does ¼ cup ketchup or chili sauce, ¼ cup minced green pepper, ½ cup finely grated Cheddar, and 6 bacon slices.

> 2 quarts rock salt
> 6 slices bacon, cut crosswise into 4 equal pieces
> 2 dozen oysters on the half shell
> ¼ cup ketchup or chili sauce
> ¼ cup finely minced sweet green pepper
> ½ cup finely grated sharp Cheddar cheese

Preheat the oven to very hot (450° F.).

Make beds of rock salt in four pie pans; dampen the salt slightly with cold water and heat, uncovered, in the preheated oven for 5 minutes. Meanwhile, stir-fry the bacon in a medium-sized skillet over moderate heat until limp; drain the bacon on paper toweling and reserve.

Arrange 6 oysters on the half shell in each pan of salt, pushing firmly into the salt to anchor. Blend the ketchup and green pepper and ladle a heaping teaspoonful over each oyster. Top each with a piece of bacon and a sprinkling of cheese. Bake, uncovered, in the 450° oven for 5 to 7 minutes, or until the bacon is crisp.

Serve piping hot, as an appetizer or entrée.

VANILLA WAFER CRUMBS : See **Crumbs.**

Vegetable Shortening

Although we do not consider this a troublesome leftover (and for that reason have not devoted a full section to it), we *have* made some notes and observations about the storage and recycling of vegetable shortening in the section on Cooking Oils (see page 81).

Vinegar

Here's another staple that we assume—wrongly—to be nonperishable. It's true that an unopened bottle of vinegar will last almost indefinitely. But once it is exposed to airborne yeasts and molds, vinegar may in time cloud, mold, throw a sediment, or grow a jellylike layer known as a "mother." Wine, rice, malt, and herbal vinegars, by the way, spoil more easily than the cider (brown) or distilled (white) because they are less acid and often less pure as well.

Best Way to Store   All vinegars should be stored in their own bottles, tightly capped, on a cool, dark, dry shelf.

Maximum Storage Time   About 6 months for cider and distilled vinegars (or until they cloud or dregs appear in the bottom of the bottle); about 2 to 3 months for wine and herbal vinegars. Once a vinegar clouds or shows sediment, use it up promptly, or if badly clouded discard it. Although the jellylike "mother" is unsightly, it is harmless. To remove it, pour the vinegar through a fine sieve lined with several thicknesses of clean, dry cheesecloth, then transfer the vinegar to a clean, sterilized bottle and screw the cap down tight. Store on a cool, dark, dry shelf.

Roles in Cooking   Vinegar is used as a preservative in pickles and relishes, as a marinade (tenderizer) for sinewy meats (the vinegar's acid helps convert tough connective tissue into gelatin), as an agent for quick-souring milk or cream. Vinegar also has the power to "cook" (coagulate) the flesh of delicate fish or shellfish, which is the principle used in preparing the South American *ceviche* (a tart, raw seafood appetizer steeped in vinegar and/or lime juice) and the Japanese *sushi* (raw cubes of fish marinated in rice wine). And, of course, vinegar is prized for its tart, almost lemonlike flavor. Indeed, in covered-wagon days when fresh lemons were unavailable, pioneer women made a mock lemon pie out of vinegar (see the recipe that follows).

Recipe Uses   The best places to look for recipes containing vinegar? Among your collections of pickles and relishes; barbecued meats, fish, and fowl; salads and salad dressings. And have a look, too, at Oriental cookbooks—the sweet-sour recipes depend upon vinegar. So do many German recipes (we've included one of the best known—Old German Sauerbraten—on page 288), to say nothing of many Scandinavian classics (pickled herring, to name one).

Special Comments   Do not attempt to make pickles or relishes with less than the freshest, clearest vinegar (molded or clouded vinegar will, in all probability, spoil the pickles or relishes). It's also important that the vinegar be from 4 to 6 percent acid strength (the strength should be clearly marked on the label) because it is acidity that inhibits the growth of the microorganisms of spoilage.

Can the different vinegars be used interchangeably in most recipes? Not really. Distilled (white) vinegar is best reserved for pickling; it is far too acid for everyday cooking. Cider (brown) vinegar is the best all-around choice because it is not too tart. Rice vinegar is more delicate—perfect for *sushi* and *sashimi,* for cold marinated vegetables and tossed salads. Wine and herb vinegars are preferred for green salads and often for marinades, too, because they are less likely to impart a strong vinegary flavor.

N O T E   *For additional recipes, included elsewhere in this book, that call for varying amounts of vinegar, see the Appendix.*

MOCK LEMON (VINEGAR) PIE

One 9-inch pie

It's astonishing how much this vinegar pie (an American frontier favorite) tastes like lemon custard pie. Make it with whole eggs, or if you should have egg yolks left over, substitute two of them for each whole egg. This is a perfectly splendid way to get rid of that last inch or so of vinegar in the bottle.

    1 cup granulated sugar
    ⅓ cup firmly packed light brown sugar
    ¼ cup unsifted all-purpose flour
    ⅛ teaspoon grated nutmeg
    ⅛ teaspoon ground cardamom
    1 cup water
    ¼ cup cider vinegar
    ½ cup (1 stick) butter, melted
    3 large eggs (or 6 large egg yolks)
    1 unbaked 9-inch pie shell

Preheat the oven to moderate (350° F.).

In a mixing bowl, combine the sugars, flour, and spices, pressing out any brown sugar lumps. Mix in the water, vinegar, and melted butter, then the eggs. Pour into the unbaked pie shell and bake in the preheated oven for about 1 hour, or until the filling is puffed and touched with brown.

Cool the pie to room temperature before cutting.

PEPPERY PICKLED NEW POTATOES

6 to 8 appetizer servings

This unusual appetizer appears to be an Acapulco specialty; at least it is served at a number of that resort's better restaurants. It's also a delicious way to use up cloudy vinegar (as much as 1½ cups of it), as well as bay leaves that may be browning and losing their pungency. For best results, use the smallest round new potatoes you can find, those measuring no more than one inch in diameter and preferably less than that—in other words, they should be about the size of a large grape.

N O T E: *These pickled potatoes will keep well in the refrigerator for a week to 10 days.*

> 36 (about 1½ pounds) small, round new potatoes (from ½ to 1 inch in diameter or, if unavailable, 1½ pounds somewhat larger potatoes, halved)
> 1½ cups cider vinegar
> 1½ cups water
> 3 large cloves garlic, peeled and halved lengthwise
> 4 bay leaves
> 1 teaspoon dill weed
> ¼ to ½ teaspoon crushed dried red chili peppers (depending upon how "hot" you like things)

Scrub the potatoes well under cool water, then cook in their jackets in just enough water to cover until firm-tender—about 15 to 20 minutes. Drain well, cool until easy to handle, then peel.

In a small saucepan, bring the vinegar, water, garlic, bay leaves, dill weed, and chili peppers just to a boil. Arrange the potatoes in a sterilized 1-quart preserving jar and pour in the vinegar mixture. Cool to room temperature, screw on the lid, and store in the refrigerator.

Serve with wooden picks as a cocktail snack.

OLD GERMAN SAUERBRATEN

6 to 8 servings

We first tasted this sauerbraten at the home of Carol Zaiser, a friend and highly respected travel writer who is, in private life, Mrs. Ewen Gillies. We thought the sauerbraten and accompanying *Kartoffel Kloesse* (potato dumplings) the best we'd ever eaten, so we asked Carol about both recipes. They are old German favorites with which she grew up in Philadelphia, recipes that her mother learned from her mother, Mrs. Bertha Reichelt, who emigrated from Germany to America in the late nineteenth century. Carol shared the recipes with us and graciously consented to our reprinting them here.

The sauerbraten enables you to use up any vinegar that may be beginning to cloud (or a red jug wine that is starting to turn), and it's a dandy way to get rid of half a dozen bay leaves of questionable age. The potato dumplings (recipe follows) are the classic accompaniment to sauerbraten, but they also provide an outlet for a couple of slices of stale bread and the last of a box of farina.

> 1 boned and rolled beef rump roast (4 to 4½ pounds), with some fat covering
> 2 cups cider vinegar mixed with 2 cups cold water (or 3 cups dry red wine of the claret type mixed with 1½ cups cold water)
> 2 tablespoons granulated sugar
> 1 tablespoon salt
> 12 whole cloves
> 6 bay leaves
> 6 peppercorns
> 2 medium yellow onions, peeled and sliced thin
> ½ lemon, sliced thin
> 2 tablespoons butter or bacon drippings
> 6 gingersnaps
> ¾ cup sifted all-purpose flour
> 1 cup cold water

Place the meat in a large, deep bowl (preferably a ceramic one), then pour in the vinegar or wine mixture. Add the sugar, salt, cloves, bay leaves, peppercorns, and onion and lemon slices. Cover with plastic food wrap and marinate in the refrigerator for 3 days. Twice a day, turn the beef in the marinade.

When you are ready to cook the sauerbraten, lift the roast from the marinade and pat it dry on paper toweling; reserve the marinade. Brown the roast well on all sides in the butter or bacon drippings in a large, heavy kettle (one with a snug-fitting lid) over moderately high heat. Reduce the heat to low and gradually pour in the marinade (including onions, lemon, and all spices); add the gingersnaps and adjust the heat so the kettle liquid bubbles very gently, then cover and simmer slowly for about 3 hours, or until the roast is fork tender. Turn the roast in the kettle liquid three to four times as it cooks so it will be more evenly flavored.

About 30 minutes before the meat is done, spread the flour out on a pie pan, then set, uncovered, in a moderate oven (350° F.) to brown lightly (this will take about 30 minutes). Remove the flour from the oven, then add it gradually to the 1 cup cold water, whisking briskly to make a smooth paste. Set aside for the moment.

Lift the roast from the kettle to a large plate. Pour the kettle mixture through a fine sieve set over a large heatproof bowl, then return the strained cooking liquid to the kettle. Discard the strained-out herbs, spices, and onion and lemon slices. Set the kettle over moderately low heat, then gradually pour in the flour paste, whisking vigorously all the while. Heat and stir until thickened and smooth and no raw, starchy taste remains—about 3 minutes. Return the roast to the gravy, cover, and heat slowly for 10 minutes.

To serve, lift the roast from the gravy, remove the strings, and slice fairly thin. Arrange slices of sauerbraten on a large, heated platter, wreathe with *Kartoffel Kloesse,* and spoon some of the gravy on top of the meat and dumplings. Pass the remainder in a gravy boat.

KARTOFFEL KLOESSE (POTATO DUMPLINGS)

6 to 8 servings

These dumplings are the traditional accompaniment for Old German Sauerbraten (see preceding recipe). They provide an excellent way to utilize one to two slices of stale bread, as well as odds and ends of farina and fresh parsley.

N O T E *Do not make these dumplings more than a few hours ahead of time because they will absorb moisture in the refrigerator and soften so much that they will be difficult to handle. And when cooking the dumplings, boil for 3 minutes only after the cooking water returns to a boil; otherwise they may disintegrate.*

> 5 medium baking potatoes, scrubbed but not peeled
> 3 slices bacon, cut crosswise into julienne strips
> 2 teaspoons salt
> 3 large eggs
> 1 cup plus 2 tablespoons sifted all-purpose flour
> ½ cup farina
> 1 to 2 slices stale bread, cut in ¼-inch cubes

¼ teaspoon grated nutmeg
⅛ teaspoon ground cinnamon
½ teaspoon granulated sugar
2 tablespoons minced fresh parsley
Lightly salted water for cooking the dumplings (about 2 gallons)

Boil the potatoes in their jackets in a large, covered saucepan for 35 to 40 minutes, or just until a fork will pierce them easily. Drain very dry and cool until easy to handle, then peel and rice or mash. Spread the riced potatoes out on a clean, dry dishtowel and allow to stand, uncovered, for 20 minutes (this is so the towel will absorb as much potato moisture as possible and keep the dumplings from being soggy).

Meanwhile, fry the bacon in a small, heavy skillet over moderate heat until crisp and brown; drain off all drippings, then crumble the bacon as fine as possible and let stand on a piece of paper toweling until needed.

Empty the drained riced potatoes into a large mixing bowl and make a well in the center. Add the salt and the eggs, breaking them one by one into the well. Sift the flour on top, then add the reserved bacon and all remaining ingredients (except the lightly salted cooking water) and knead together with your hands until uniformly mixed. Shape into balls just slightly larger than golf balls and arrange one layer deep on a wax paper-lined tray or baking sheet. Refrigerate, *uncovered,* until ready to cook (but for no longer than 4 hours).

When ready to cook, heat the lightly salted water to the boiling point in a very large kettle—the kind you would cook pasta in (about 3- or 4-gallon capacity); at the same time, preheat the oven to very slow (250° F.). Drop about half of the dumplings into the water, spacing them as evenly as possible so they will not stick to one another. When the cooking water returns to a boil, adjust the heat so it ripples gently, then cover the kettle and cook the dumplings for 3 minutes *exactly.*

Lift the dumplings from the water with a slotted spoon and arrange one layer deep on a large, heatproof plate; set a large colander upside down over them, so it acts like a perforated lid, and set in the preheated oven to keep warm while you cook the remaining dumplings. Boil them just as you did the first batch.

Serve hot with Old German Sauerbraten, including plenty of its rich, spicy gravy.

Wheat Germ

What is it exactly? The most nutritious part of the wheat kernel, the heart, the part that will germinate and grow, hence the name wheat germ.

Best Way to Store   Tightly capped in its own jar in the refrigerator. If you are short of refrigerator space, the wheat germ can be kept on a cool, dry shelf, but it will not last nearly so long.

Maximum Storage Time   About 6 months if refrigerated, 1 month if not refrigerated.

Roles in Cooking   To provide flavor, texture, color, and, most of all, nutritive value. Wheat germ is packed with protein, vitamins, and minerals. It is, alas, also fairly high in calories—about 110 per ounce (¼ cup).

Recipe Uses   Breads—particularly whole-grain or health breads— often call for wheat germ, as do cookies and quick breads. We like to use wheat germ for "crumbing" chicken and as toppings for meat and vegetable casseroles. We also like to mix it into meat loaves and burgers (about ½ cup of wheat germ per pound of meat is a good average).

How to Use Very Small Amounts   Try tossing a couple of tablespoons of wheat germ into a crisp green salad, or sprinkling over fresh fruits, or layering into fruit pies or cobblers. Or team small amounts of wheat germ with your favorite breakfast cereal.

SOY AND GINGER CHICKEN BREASTS CRUMBED WITH WHEAT GERM

4 servings

Wheat germ for crumbing chicken? It's terrific—crunchy and nut-flavored.

> ½ cup wheat germ
> ¼ cup freshly grated Parmesan cheese
> ¼ teaspoon freshly ground black pepper

½ cup (1 stick) unsalted butter, melted
1 (1 inch) cube peeled fresh gingerroot, crushed in a garlic press
1 small garlic clove, peeled and crushed
¼ cup soy sauce
2 tablespoons dry sherry, Port, or Madeira
2 whole chicken breasts, halved

Preheat the oven to moderate (350° F.).

On a piece of wax paper, combine the wheat germ, cheese, and pepper; in a small bowl, mix well the butter, ginger, garlic, soy sauce, and sherry. Dip the chicken breasts first into the soy mixture, then into the wheat germ so each piece is well coated on all sides.

Lay the chicken breasts one layer deep in a small, shallow roasting pan and bake, uncovered, in the preheated oven for about 45 minutes, or until nicely browned and tender. Baste the chicken from time to time with the remaining soy mixture, and if toward the end of baking the chicken seems to be browning too fast, cover with foil.

HEALTH COOKIES

4 to 4½ dozen

We call these "health" cookies because they contain ¾ cup of wheat germ, 1 cup of raisins, and 1½ cups of freshly grated carrots. Best of all, they're good and spicy.

2 cups *unsifted* all-purpose flour
¾ cup wheat germ
1 teaspoon baking powder
1 teaspoon ground cinnamon
½ teaspoon grated nutmeg
½ teaspoon ground ginger
Pinch of salt
1 cup vegetable shortening
1¼ cups firmly packed light brown sugar
2 eggs
1½ cups coarsely grated carrots
1 cup seedless raisins

Preheat the oven to moderately hot (375° F.).
Combine the flour, wheat germ, baking powder, spices, and salt on

a piece of wax paper and set aside for the time being. Cream the shortening and sugar until light and fluffy, then beat in the eggs; add the reserved flour mixture alternately with the grated carrots, beginning and ending with the flour mixture. Stir in the raisins.

Drop the dough from rounded teaspoonfuls onto lightly greased baking sheets, spacing them about 1½ inches apart and flattening each slightly. Bake in the preheated oven for 10 to 12 minutes, or until lightly browned.

Transfer at once to wire racks to cool.

CRUNCHY-CRUSTED WHEAT GERM MUFFINS

1 dozen

1½ cups *unsifted* all-purpose flour
1 cup wheat germ
¼ cup freshly grated Parmesan cheese
1 tablespoon granulated sugar or light brown sugar
1 tablespoon (3 teaspoons) baking powder
½ teaspoon salt
¼ teaspoon crumbled leaf oregano
¼ teaspoon crumbled leaf basil
¼ teaspoon crumbled leaf rosemary
1 cup milk
¼ cup vegetable oil
1 egg, beaten lightly

CRUNCHY TOPPING

3 tablespoons wheat germ
1 tablespoon freshly grated Parmesan cheese
1 tablespoon melted butter
2 teaspoons granulated sugar or light brown sugar

Preheat the oven to hot (400° F.).

In a large mixing bowl combine the flour, wheat germ, cheese, sugar, baking powder, salt, and herbs; in a smaller bowl, combine the milk, oil, and egg. Make a well in the center of the dry ingredients, pour the liquid mixture in all at once and mix briskly but lightly—no matter if there are a few lumps. Quickly combine all the ingredients for the topping.

Spoon the batter into muffin-pan cups lined with paper cupcake liners (if you have no liners, simply grease the pans well), filling each cup no more than two-thirds full. Sprinkle each muffin lightly with topping and bake in the preheated oven for about 15 minutes, or until lightly browned.

Serve at once, with plenty of butter.

W H O L E - G R A I N F L O U R S : See **Flours (Whole-Grain).**

Wine

Table wines . . . sherry . . . Port . . . Madeira. How often are you left with an inch or two in the bottom of the bottle? And how often do the almost-empty bottles appropriate valuable refrigerator and cupboard space? Wines cost far too much simply to be poured down the drain (even if you've less than a cup left over). And remembering all the cracks about the chef being into the sherry, we hesitate to drink the leftovers. *Every* time, at least. So what can be done about them? Here are a few ideas.

Best Way to Store Keep the wines in their original bottles, tightly corked or capped, and standing upright. Table wines (dry reds, whites, and rosés) should be refrigerated. Fortified wines (sherries, Ports,

Madeiras, Marsalas, and the like) should be kept on a cool, dark, dry shelf.

Maximum Storage Time   A week to 10 days for refrigerated table wines (but it varies from wine to wine), about 2 months for fortified wines if kept in a truly cool spot. Some may keep longer, some not so long, so many variables must be considered—the age, condition, and purity of the wine in the first place, the weather, the storage conditions. The best practice is to examine the wine from time to time, to taste it, and the minute it begins to sharpen in flavor or sour (turn to vinegar), to use it straightaway.

Roles in Cooking   Wines are used principally for flavor and color, although the more acid table wines (robust reds and whites) can be used as marinades to help tenderize meats. And if the wines are not heated or cooked—as when making a trifle or wine jelly—they add considerable "kick" (Tipsy Parson wasn't named Tipsy Parson for nothing). Finally, wines—particularly fortified wines—are used for steeping and aging fruit cakes and plum puddings. They are, in fact, a mild preservative.

Recipe Uses   Whenever you have wine left over, think French. So many French classics—both the sweets and the savories—rely upon wines. So do many favorite Italian recipes, not to mention German, Swiss, Austrian, Spanish, Portuguese, and English. Wines are integral to dozens of sauces and gravies, to soups and stews, to casseroles, cakes, and puddings.

Special Comments   A few words about an absurdity called "cooking sherry." It is nothing more than sherry liberally salted, an abomination dreamed up during Prohibition to discourage people from drinking sherry that was intended for cooking. It is still possible to buy "cooking sherry," but foolhardy to do so (the wine is both inferior and expensive). The best sherry (or any other wine for that matter) to use for cooking is the wine that you would buy to drink.

How to Use Very Small Amounts   You can add a splash or two of wine to almost any soup, sauce, stew, or fruit compote with good results—add slowly and taste as you go. Dribs of table wine that are souring can be added to the vinegar bottle (either to cider or to wine vinegar), they can be mixed into hamburger or stirred into chili or spaghetti sauce. They make dandy seasoners for glazed carrots, parsnips, and beets, as well as for slaws and potato, tuna, and chicken salads. As for sweet wines, stir 1 to 2 tablespoons into custards and cobblers, even more (¼ to ⅓ cup) into fruit pies. Sprinkle sherry or Port, Madeira or Marsala over cake layers before you frost them, blend into fillings and frostings, add to a ham glaze, or use in candying sweet potatoes. Or substitute ¼ to ⅓ cup of a sweet wine for ¼ to ⅓ cup of the liquid called for in a fruit gelatin.

N O T E *For additional recipes, included elsewhere in this book, that call for varying amounts of wine, see the Appendix.*

WHITE WINE SAUCE FOR VEGETABLES

About 1½ cups

This quick sauce, which calls for an amount of dry white wine that's often left over, will also use up 1 egg yolk. It's equally delicious on cooked asparagus, broccoli, Brussels sprouts, cabbage, or green beans.

    3 tablespoons butter or margarine
    3 tablespoons all-purpose flour
    ½ teaspoon salt
    ⅛ teaspoon freshly ground black pepper
    Pinch of ground mace or grated nutmeg
    1 cup milk
    ⅓ to ½ cup dry white wine
    1 egg yolk, beaten lightly

Melt the butter in a medium-sized saucepan over moderate heat; blend in the flour, salt, pepper and mace. Add the milk and wine and heat slowly, stirring constantly, until thickened and smooth—3 to 5 minutes. Blend a little of the hot sauce into the egg yolk, then stir back into the pan and cook over lowest heat, stirring constantly, for another 3 to 5 minutes.

Serve at once over boiled or steamed vegetables.

ITALIAN WINE CAKE

One 9-inch round cake

The liquid in this unusual cake is *dry white wine*— ½ cup of it. So if you should have an almost-empty bottle, don't pitch it out (or merely drink it to get rid of it); try this crunchy-crusted cake. Its texture is not the cottony-soft one we're accustomed to in American cakes, rather it is dense—sort of a cross between steamed pudding and fresh-baked bread. The cake is best when topped with crushed fresh berries, *zabaglione,* or simply drizzled with light cream.

    2 cups sifted all-purpose flour
    1 cup granulated sugar
    1½ teaspoons baking powder
    ½ teaspoon baking soda
    Pinch of salt
    1 teaspoon finely grated lemon or orange rind
    2 eggs, beaten until frothy
    ½ cup dry white wine
    ⅓ cup corn or peanut oil

Preheat the oven to moderate (350° F.).

Combine the flour, sugar, baking powder, soda, salt, and rind in a mixing bowl. Make a well in the center, add the eggs, and stir just until crumbly. Now combine the wine and oil and add, one-third of the total amount at a time, beating lightly after each addition.

Pour the batter into a well-greased and -floured 9-inch layer cake pan and bake in the preheated oven for 30 to 35 minutes, or until the cake has pulled from the sides of the pan and is springy-firm to the touch. Cool the cake upright in its pan for 10 minutes, then loosen around the edges and turn out.

Cool completely before cutting into wedges and serving, either plain or topped as described above.

SAVORY LIMA BEANS WITH WINE

6 to 8 servings

This is one of those simple French country dishes that is both filling
and frugal.

- 1 pound dried large lima beans, washed and soaked overnight in
  enough cold water to cover
- Soaking water plus enough chicken and/or beef broth and/or water
  to total 3 cups
- 1 pork hock or meaty ham bone
- 3 medium yellow onions, peeled and each stuck with 2 cloves
- 1 bay leaf, crumbled
- ¼ teaspoon crumbled leaf thyme
- Pinch of crumbled leaf rosemary
- 1 tablespoon salt
- ⅛ teaspoon freshly ground black pepper
- ¾ to 1¼ cups dry white wine
- ¼ cup minced parsley (optional)

Put the beans and the 3 cups of liquid in a large kettle; add the pork
hock, onions, bay leaf, thyme, and rosemary and simmer, covered, for
1 hour. Add the salt, pepper, and wine and simmer, still covered, for
45 minutes longer.

Lift the onions and the pork hock from the kettle with a slotted
spoon; remove the cloves from the onions and discard, then coarsely
chop the onions and return to the kettle. Cut the meat from the pork
hock and stir into the kettle.

Mix in the parsley, if you like, and serve as a main dish.

Yogurt

Plain yogurt is what concerns us here—not the fruited varieties that
can be eaten like soft ice cream. Because yogurt has emerged recently

as a popular health and diet food, more and more recipes are calling for it, but too frequently, alas, in less than full-container (1-cup) quantities. And what happens to the balance? More often than not, it sits unused in the refrigerator until it spoils. Many people find yogurt too acid to stomach agreeably; others simply don't like it *au naturel*. Fortunately, there are a number of *easy* ways to use up small amounts of leftover yogurt, and our purpose here is to pass them along.

Best Way to Store Tightly covered, in the coldest part of the refrigerator.

Maximum Storage Time 5 to 7 days.

Roles in Cooking Because of its acidity, yogurt can be used to marinate (and tenderize) meats (and it often is in India and the Middle East). It imparts a refreshingly tart flavor, and as a concentrated, fermented milk akin to clabber, it is highly nutritious. Faddists, of course, believe yogurt to be imbued with magical, life-giving properties. In truth, the nutritive value of yogurt is essentially the same as the milk from which it is made—except that it is far more acid, so much so that it may aggravate ulcers (either actual or incipient) or other problems associated with stomach hyperacidity. Finally, yogurt can be used to bind ingredients loosely together—as in a sauce or salad dressing.

Recipe Uses Recipes that most often call for yogurt are East Indian, Balkan, Russian, and Middle Eastern in origin. Cooks in these areas employ yogurt in marinades and sauces; they team it with cooked vegetables and raw greens and top desserts with it. Yogurt also makes a dandy low-calorie substitute for sour cream (see that section in this book, pages 262–68) or mayonnaise in cole slaws, tuna and chicken salads, Stroganoffs and paprikashes, fruit soups or purées (1 tablespoon of plain yogurt contains approximately 8 calories vs. 30 for sour cream and 100 for mayonnaise).

Special Comments Some yogurts are made of whole milk, others from skim milk, so the calorie counts vary significantly—anywhere from about 80 to 160 calories per cup. Yogurts produced in this country are made of cow's milk, although those of India and the Middle East are more likely to be made of the richer goat, sheep, or yak milk.

How to Use Very Small Amounts Try spooning fresh yogurt over fresh berries or sliced peaches in place of cream or sour cream; serve it instead of sour cream with borscht; blend it into cooked green beans, beets, or cabbage; add it to any cream soup or to vichyssoise (but do not allow any mixture containing yogurt to boil or it will curdle); mix small amounts of plain yogurt with applesauce or stir into stewed prunes, or apricots; add small amounts to omelets or scrambled eggs; spread on pancakes, English muffins, or toast along with jam; smooth into hot chocolate, mix into dips and spreads (yogurt is particularly good with those containing soft cheeses); beat into mashed potatoes or use to top baked potatoes in place of sour cream. In short, give your imagination free rein.

N O T E   *For additional recipes, included elsewhere in this book, that call for varying amounts of yogurt, see the Appendix.*

SHREDDED ZUCCHINI WITH ONION AND YOGURT

4 servings

A perfectly delicious way to put ½ cup of leftover plain yogurt to good use. If you should have a food processor, equip it with the metal chopping blade and coarsely chop the zucchini (cut in 1-inch cubes). Or grate the squash on the second coarsest side of a four-sided grater.

- 1 medium Spanish or Bermuda onion, peeled and moderately coarsely chopped
- 2 tablespoons butter or margarine
- 3 medium zucchini, washed, trimmed, and moderately coarsely grated or chopped
- ¼ teaspoon crumbled leaf rosemary
- ¼ teaspoon salt, or to taste
- ⅛ teaspoon freshly ground black pepper
- ½ cup plain yogurt, at room temperature

Stir-fry the onion in the butter in a large, heavy skillet over moderate heat for about 10 minutes or until lightly browned; add the zucchini and stir-fry for 8 to 10 minutes longer, or until golden. Stir in the rosemary, salt, and pepper; turn the heat to its lowest point and allow the mixture to mellow, uncovered, for about 20 minutes, stirring now and then.

Smooth in the yogurt and warm for about 2 minutes longer (but do not boil lest the yogurt curdle), then dish up and serve.

CURRIED COLE SLAW WITH YOGURT

6 to 8 servings

1 medium cabbage, trimmed of coarse outer leaves, quartered, cored, and shredded moderately fine
1 medium yellow onion, peeled and minced

DRESSING

½ cup mayonnaise
½ cup plain yogurt (or sour cream)
¼ to ⅓ cup evaporated milk or milk
1 tablespoon spicy brown prepared mustard
2 teaspoons curry powder
2 tablespoons drained capers (optional)
2 tablespoons ketchup
½ teaspoon salt
⅛ teaspoon freshly ground black pepper

Place the cabbage and onion in a large mixing bowl. Place all the dressing ingredients in an electric blender or food processor fitted with the metal chopping blade and buzz for about 10 seconds nonstop, until uniformly creamy. (If you have neither blender nor processor, simply whisk the ingredients together briskly.)

Pour the dressing over the slaw and toss well to mix. If slaw seems a little dry, drizzle in enough milk to give it a nice creamy consistency. Cover and chill for several hours before serving.

VEAL PAPRIKASH WITH YOGURT

4 servings

Here's an elegant, low-calorie entrée that neatly uses up ½ to ¾ cup of leftover plain yogurt. Approximate number of calories per serving? A slimming 260.

1 pound mushrooms, stemmed, wiped clean, and sliced thin (for recipes that call for mushroom stems, see the Appendix)
2 tablespoons butter or margarine

1 pound veal round, sliced and pounded thin as for scaloppine, then
   cut in finger-sized strips
¾ teaspoon salt
⅛ teaspoon freshly ground black pepper
⅛ teaspoon grated nutmeg or ground mace
2 tablespoons dry white wine or vermouth
1 tablespoon paprika
½ to ¾ cup plain yogurt, at room temperature

Stir-fry the mushrooms in the butter in a large, heavy skillet over moderately high heat for 8 to 10 minutes, or until the mushrooms have released their juices and the juices have cooked away. Push the mushrooms to one side of skillet and raise the heat to high; add the veal and stir-fry quickly—just until no longer pink and the juices have once again boiled away. Lower the heat to moderate, then add the salt, pepper, nutmeg, and wine and continue stirring until the liquids have cooked down for a third time.

Smooth in the paprika, then the yogurt. Bring just to serving temperature and ladle over boiled noodles or fluffy cooked rice (do not allow to boil or the yogurt will curdle).

CHICKEN IN YOGURT WITH CORIANDER, CUMIN, AND CARDAMOM

4 servings

In the north of India where this dish is a specialty, the chicken would be baked in a clay oven called a *tandoor*. We use a combination of broiling and baking, which produces similar, if not identical, results.

2 tablespoons minced fresh gingerroot or 1 teaspoon ground ginger
¼ teaspoon coriander seeds
¼ teaspoon cumin seeds
¼ teaspoon crushed dried red chili peppers
⅛ teaspoon freshly ground black pepper
⅛ teaspoon ground cardamom
Pinch of ground cloves

CONTINUED

Pinch of ground cinnamon
½ teaspoon salt
½ to ¾ cup yogurt, plus enough milk, chicken broth, or water to total
   1 cup
Juice of ½ lime or ½ small lemon
2 tablespoons peanut oil
2 tablespoons tomato paste or ketchup
1 to 2 tablespoons honey (use 2 tablespoons if you use tomato paste)
1 clove garlic, peeled and crushed
1 broiler-fryer (3 to 3½ pounds), disjointed

Purée all the ingredients but chicken in an electric blender or in a food processor fitted with the metal chopping blade. If you have neither blender nor processor, pulverize the ginger, spices, and salt with a mortar and pestle, then blend with all the remaining ingredients except the chicken.

Arrange the chicken one layer deep in a shallow casserole; pour in the puréed mixture, then cover and marinate in the refrigerator for at least 12 hours but preferably for 24. No need to turn the chicken in the marinade.

Preheat the broiler; preheat the oven (if separate from the broiler) to moderately slow (325° F.).

Remove the chicken from the marinade and arrange, skin side up and one layer deep, in a small, shallow baking pan. Scrape excess marinade from the skin side of the chicken and add to the remaining marinade; reserve. Broil chicken about 5 inches from the heat for 8 to 10 minutes to brown the skin side. Remove the chicken from the broiler, cover the pan with foil, and bake in the preheated oven for 40 to 45 minutes, or until the chicken is tender. Strain and reserve the pan drippings. Raise the oven temperature to moderately hot (375° F.).

Blend the strained pan drippings with the reserved marinade and pour over the chicken. Bake, uncovered, for 15 minutes, or until bubbling hot.

Serve the chicken topped with some of the hot marinade on a bed of fluffy boiled rice. Any remaining marinade may be passed as sauce.

BOSNIAN LAMB BALLS IN CARAWAY-YOGURT SAUCE

4 servings

LAMB BALLS

1 pound ground lamb shoulder
½ cup *unsifted* all-purpose flour
2 tablespoons finely minced yellow onion
3 large eggs
½ teaspoon salt
⅛ teaspoon freshly ground black pepper
Pinch of crumbled leaf rosemary
Pinch of crumbled leaf thyme
Pinch of ground mace

SAUCE

1 tablespoon caraway seeds
¾ to 1 cup plain yogurt, at room temperature
¼ cup milk, buttermilk, or sour cream, at room temperature
2 tablespoons minced fresh mint or parsley

Preheat the oven to moderately hot (375° F.).

Mix all the lamb ball ingredients together and shape into 1-inch balls. Arrange one layer deep in a well-greased and -floured 9 × 9 × 2-inch baking dish and bake, uncovered, in the preheated oven for 30 to 35 minutes, or until lamb balls are cooked through.

Meanwhile, pulverize the caraway seeds with a mortar and pestle, then combine with all the remaining sauce ingredients and let stand until ready to use.

Remove the lamb balls from the oven for 10 minutes; reduce the oven temperature to moderately slow (325° F.). Pour the sauce over the lamb balls and stir gently to combine with the drippings, then return to the oven and bake, uncovered, for 15 to 20 minutes—just long enough to heat the sauce.

Serve as is, or with cooked rice.

APPENDIX

A List of Recipes Categorized
According to the Leftovers They Use

(SEE INDEX FOR RECIPE PAGE NUMBERS)

ANCHOVIES

Anchovy Fillets
Anchovy Butter (3 to 5)
Green Goddess Dressing (3 to 4)

Anchovy Paste
Jansson's Temptation (1 to 3 tablespoons)
Visby Fish Pudding (1 to 3 tablespoons)
Spinach-Buttermilk Soup with Veal and Pork Balls (up to 3 tablespoons)
Burger Stroganoff (1 tablespoon)
Anchovy Butter (3 to 4 teaspoons)
Green Goddess Dressing (2 to 4 teaspoons)
Anchovy-Stuffed Eggs (1 to 3 teaspoons)
Tomato- and Anchovy-Stuffed Flounder Rolls in Wine Sauce (2 teaspoons)
Salsa Verde (Green Sauce) (½ to 2 teaspoons)

BANANAS (RIPE)

Frozen Banana Cream (3 to 4)
Banana Yogurt (2)
Banana-Oatmeal Cookies (1 cup mashed)
Oatmeal-Banana Muffins (1)

BOUILLONS, BROTHS, AND CONSOMMÉS (CANNED)

NOTE   *You may use these three interchangeably, although when using the stronger consommé, you may need to reduce the amount of salt called for in a recipe.*
Nut-Cream Soup (3½ to 4 cups chicken or beef)
Austrian Veal Stew (up to 3½ cups chicken and/or beef)
Curried Apple Soup (up to 3 cups chicken or beef)
Cajun Rice Dressing (3 cups chicken or beef)

Plantation Peanut Soup (2 cups beef or chicken)
Golden Cheddar and Carrot Soup (2 cups beef or chicken)
Vegetable-Bulgur Pilaf (up to 1¾ cups beef or chicken)
Beef and Rice with Tomato and Sweet Pepper (1½ cups beef or chicken)
Creole Squash Pudding (up to 1½ cups beef or chicken)
Savory Lima Beans with Wine (up to 1½ cups beef or chicken)
Kotleti (Russian Meatballs Smothered in Cream Gravy) (1½ cups beef)
Beef-Stuffed Eggplant (up to 1¼ cups beef)
Beef and Bulgur Loaf (1 cup beef or chicken)
Open-Face Meat Pie (1 cup beef or chicken)
Baked Squash and Tomato Strata (1 cup beef or chicken)
Curried Tuna Mousse (1 cup beef or chicken)
Currant-Glazed Chunks of Veal (up to 1 cup chicken or beef)
Baked Potatoes Stuffed the Portuguese Way with Creamed Salt Cod (up to 1
    cup beef or chicken)
Creamed Diced Carrots with Green Pepper (1 cup chicken)
Bifes Enrolados (Brazilian Beef Rolls Stuffed with Hard-Cooked Eggs and
    Olives) (¾ to 1 cup beef)
Sagey Meatball Casserole with Apples (½ to 1 cup beef or chicken)
Onion-Smothered Round Steak (½ to 1 cup beef or chicken)
Braised Veal Loin with Lemon–Sour Cream Gravy (½ to 1 cup chicken or beef)
Parmesan-Crumbed Chicken in Cognac-Cream Sauce (½ to 1 cup chicken)
Chicken in Yogurt with Coriander, Cumin, and Cardamom (¼ to ½ cup
    chicken)
Braised Lamb with Black Olives in Wine Gravy (¼ to ½ cup beef or chicken)
Cabbage and Walnuts in Sour Cream (¼ cup beef or chicken)

BREAD (STALE)

Hootsla (Bread Cube Omelet) (10 to 12 slices)
Kotleti (Russian Meatballs Smothered in Cream Gravy) (8 slices)
Buttery Bread and Berry Pudding (8 slices)
Cheese, Bread, and Oyster Bake (6 slices)
Old South Shrimp and Cheese Pudding (6 slices)
Buttermilk Ham Loaf (4 slices)
Soufflé-Light Salmon Patties (3 slices)
Visby Fish Pudding (2 slices)
Anatolian Cheese-Stuffed Peppers (2 slices)
Tuna, Almond, and Egg Casserole (2 slices)
Kartoffel Kloesse (Potato Dumplings) (1 to 2 slices)
Salsa Verde (Green Sauce) (1 slice)

BROWN SUGAR (LIGHT OR DARK)

Fresh Fruit Pudding-Cobbler (up to 1½ cups light or dark)
Health Cookies (1¼ cups light)
The Very Best Devil's Food Cake (1 cup light)
Sesame Crisps (1 cup light)
Banana-Oatmeal Cookies (1 cup light)
Cornstarch Seafoam Frosting (1 cup light or dark)
Spicy Date-Oatmeal Clusters (1 cup light or dark)
Over-the-Top Cookies (1 cup light or dark)
Easy Date-Filled Cookies (1 cup light or dark)
Norwegian Fruit Soup (1 cup light or dark)
Pear-Pecan Pudding-Cake (¾ cup light)
Buttermilk Spice Cake (¾ cup light or dark)
Orange-Almond Lace Cookies (⅔ cup light)
Kauai Sweet-Sour Spareribs (½ cup dark or light)
Chunks of Chicken in Sweet-Sour Sauce (½ cup light or dark)
Quick Whole-Wheat–Apricot Bread (½ cup light or dark)
'Lasses Bread (½ cup light or dark)
Parkin (½ cup dark)
Cranberry-Raisin (Mock Cherry) Pie (½ cup light or dark)
Buttermilk-Ham Loaf (⅓ to ½ cup light or dark)
Swedish Brown Beans (⅓ cup light)
Mock Lemon (Vinegar) Pie (⅓ cup light)
Oatmeal-Banana Muffins (⅓ cup light or dark)
Frosted Coffee-Bran Bars (⅓ cup light or dark)
Honey-Whole Wheat Rolls (¼ cup light or dark)
Banbury Tarts (¼ cup light or dark)
Anise Cookies (¼ cup dark or light)
Maple-Nut Sauce (¼ cup light or dark)
Bulgarian Sweet-Sour Bean Soup (2 to 4 tablespoons light or dark)
Plantation Peanut Soup (2 tablespoons light)
Vanilla-Wafer Crumb Crust (2 tablespoons light or dark)
Chocolate-Wafer Crust (2 tablespoons light or dark)
Acorn Squash Stuffed with Peanut and Pepper Pilaf (2 tablespoons light
    brown sugar)

BULGUR AND KASHA

Beef and Bulgur Loaf (1 cup bulgur)
Vegetable-Bulgur Pilaf (¾ to 1 cup bulgur or kasha)
Tabbouleh (Arabic Salad of Kasha, Tomato, Onion, and Mint) (¾ to 1 cup
    kasha or bulgur)

BUTTERMILK AND SOUR MILK

Spinach-Buttermilk Soup with Veal and Pork Balls (2 to 3 cups
    buttermilk)
Indonesian Chicken with Coconut and Peanut Sauce (2½ cups buttermilk)
Lime-Pineapple-Buttermilk Sherbet (2 to 2½ cups buttermilk)
Steamed Brown Bread (2 cups buttermilk or sour milk)
Angel Biscuits (2 cups buttermilk or sour milk)
Orange Buttermilk Pie (2 cups buttermilk)
Buttermilk Fudge (1½ cups buttermilk)
Buttermilk Gazpacho (1 to 1½ cups buttermilk)
Buttermilk-Ham Loaf (1 cup buttermilk or sour milk)
Irish Soda Bread (1 cup sour milk or buttermilk)
Buttermilk Pound Cake (1 cup buttermilk or sour milk)
Buttermilk Spice Cake (1 cup buttermilk or sour milk)
The Very Best Devil's Food Cake (1 cup sour milk or buttermilk)
Norwegian Nutmeg-Buttermilk Cookies (1 cup buttermilk)
Easiest Ever Strawberry Ice Cream (up to 1 cup buttermilk)
Tarragon-Buttermilk Dressing (¾ to 1 cup buttermilk)
Spinach-Endive Salad with Coconut-Buttermilk Dressing (½ to 1 cup
    buttermilk)
Low-Calorie Cottage Cheese-Chive Salad Dressing (½ cup buttermilk)
'Lasses Bread (½ cup buttermilk or sour milk)
Fresh Fruit Pudding-Cobbler (½ cup sour milk or buttermilk)
Crusty-Crumbed Oven-Fried Chicken (⅓ cup buttermilk or sour milk)
Bosnian Lamb Balls in Caraway-Yogurt Sauce (¼ cup buttermilk)

CANDIED (GLACÉED) FRUITS

Blue Grass Chess Pie (½ to 1 cup chopped, mixed candied or glacéed
    fruits)
Bolo Rei (King's Cake) (¾ cup finely chopped, mixed glacéed fruits)
Simnel Cake (½ cup coarsely chopped, mixed candied fruits)

CHEESES (SOFT, SEMIHARD, AND HARD)

Soft (Cottage, Ricotta, Cream Cheese, Processed Cheeses, etc.)
Chinese Cheese Pancakes (¾ cup cottage)
Low-Calorie Cottage Cheese–Chive Salad Dressing (⅔ to ¾ cup cottage)
Cottage Potatoes (⅓ to ¾ cup cottage or ricotta)
Classic Cream Cheese Frosting (half to three-quarter 8-ounce package cream
    cheese)

Coffee–Cream Cheese Frosting (half to three-quarter 8-ounce package cream cheese)

Chocolate–Cream Cheese Frosting (half to three-quarter 8-ounce package cream cheese)

Orange– or Lemon–Cream Cheese Frosting (half to three-quarter 8-ounce package cream cheese)

Processor Pâté with Cognac (half 8-ounce package cream cheese)

Deviled Ham Dip with Dill (half 8-ounce package cream cheese)

Cream Cheese and Almond Pinwheels (half 8-ounce package cream cheese)

Semihard (Cheddar, Swiss, Gruyère, Roquefort, Blue, Jack, etc.)

Swiss, Pimiento and Bacon Spread (2½ cups grated Gruyère or 1 ¼ cups each grated Gruyère and Cheddar)

Golden Cheddar and Carrot Soup (1½ to 2 cups grated Cheddar)

Old South Shrimp and Cheese Pudding (1½ to 2 cups grated Cheddar, Swiss, or jack)

Chili-Burger Omelet (1 to 1½ cups grated Cheddar and/or Swiss)

Grits and Cheddar Casserole (½ pound Cheddar, grated, or ½ pound mixed Cheddar, Swiss, and jack)

Ham and Grits au Gratin (½ pound Cheddar, grated, or ½ pound mixed Cheddar, Swiss, and jack)

Cheese, Bread, and Oyster Bake (6 sandwich-size slices Cheddar or Swiss)

Crisp Cheddar, Olive, and Onion Canapés (1⅓ cups grated Cheddar)

Rice and Onion Pie (1 to 1¼ cups grated Gruyère, Swiss, or Cheddar)

Cottage Potatoes (1 cup grated Cheddar, Swiss, or jack)

Cheese and Spinach Custard (1 cup grated Cheddar)

Wales Salad (1 cup grated Cheddar)

Corn and Pimiento Pudding (1 cup grated Cheddar or American)

Pimiento-Roquefort Pasta Ring (¾ cup crumbled Roquefort or blue plus ¾ cup grated Cheddar)

Oysters Kirkpatrick (½ cup grated Cheddar)

Visby Fish Pudding (½ cup grated Gruyère or Cheddar)

Mustard-Cheese Glaze for Broiled Burgers, Chops, and Chicken (3 ounces Gruyère or Cheddar, grated)

Baked Squash and Tomato Strata (¼ cup grated Cheddar)

Potato Puff (¼ cup grated Gruyère or Cheddar)

Roquefort-Horseradish Spread (¼ cup crumbled Roquefort or blue)

Hard (Parmesan, Romano, etc.)

Parmesan-Crumbed Chicken in Cognac-Cream Sauce (½ to 1 cup grated Parmesan)

Pastichio (⅔ cup grated Parmesan)

Chili-Burger Omelet (½ cup grated Parmesan)

Cheese-Crumb Topping (¼ to ½ cup grated Parmesan)

Crusty-Crumbed Oven-Fried Chicken (¼ to ½ cup grated Parmesan)

Anatolian Cheese-Stuffed Peppers (¼ to ½ cup grated Parmesan)

Crunchy-Crusted Wheat Germ Muffins (¼ cup plus 1 tablespoon grated Parmesan)

Soy and Ginger Chicken Breasts Crumbed with Wheat Germ (¼ cup grated Parmesan)

Visby Fish Pudding (¼ cup grated Parmesan)

Baked Squash and Tomato Strata (¼ cup grated Parmesan)

Potato Puff (¼ cup grated Parmesan)

Acorn Squash Stuffed with Peanut and Pepper Pilaf (¼ cup grated Parmesan)

Spinach-Buttermilk Soup with Veal and Pork Balls (up to ¼ cup grated Parmesan)

Tarragon-Buttermilk Dressing (1 to 3 tablespoons grated Parmesan)

COCONUT (FLAKED OR SHREDDED)

Coconut-Almond Cookies (1 cup)

Curried Coconut and Cabbage (½ to 1 cup)

Indonesian Chicken with Coconut and Peanut Sauce (½ to 1 cup)

Picadinho (Brazilian Minced Meat) (½ to 1 cup)

Empadas (Brazilian Meat Turnovers) (½ to 1 cup)

Coffee-Coconut Softies (½ cup)

Spinach-Endive Salad with Coconut-Buttermilk Dressing (¼ to ½ cup)

COFFEE

Coffee-Orange Granité (2 to 2½ cups)

Roast Lamb Basted with Coffee (1½ to 3 cups)

The Very Best Devil's Food Cake (1 cup)

Coffee-Coconut Softies (1 cup)

Swedish Brown Beans (½ to ¾ cup)

Grandmama's Soft Molasses Cookies (⅔ cup)

Frosted Coffee-Bran Bars (½ cup)

Mocha Ice Cream Sauce (2 tablespoons)

COOKING OILS

N O T E   *Although there are many recipes in this book that call for one kind of cooking oil or another, we include in this list only those recipes that are strongly flavored enough to allow you to use less than the freshest oil successfully.*

Salsa Verde (Green Sauce) (½ cup olive oil)

Oatmeal-Banana Muffins (½ cup vegetable oil)

Rice Malaga ($\frac{1}{3}$ cup olive oil)
Chunks of Chicken in Sweet-Sour Sauce (6 tablespoons peanut or vegetable oil)
Beef and Rice with Tomato and Sweet Pepper (5 tablespoons olive or vegetable oil)
Braised Lamb with Black Olives in Wine Gravy ($\frac{1}{4}$ cup olive or vegetable oil)
Gingery Sweet-Sour Beef Stew with Molasses ($\frac{1}{4}$ cup peanut or vegetable oil)
Currant-Glazed Chunks of Veal ($\frac{1}{4}$ cup vegetable oil)
Vitello All'Uccelletto (Veal Scaloppine with Bay Leaves) ($\frac{1}{4}$ cup olive oil)
Beef-Stuffed Eggplant ($\frac{1}{4}$ cup olive oil)
Parmesan-Crumbed Chicken in Cognac-Cream Sauce ($\frac{1}{4}$ cup olive oil)
Bulgarian Sweet-Sour Bean Soup ($\frac{1}{4}$ cup olive oil)
Pesto Sauce ($\frac{1}{4}$ cup olive oil)

CORN MEAL AND GRITS

Rhode Island Jonnycakes ($1\frac{1}{2}$ cups stone- or water-ground corn meal)
Old Southern Batter Bread (1 cup corn meal)
Rice Batter Bread (1 cup corn meal)
Pepper Bread (1 cup corn meal)
Grits and Cheddar Casserole (1 cup grits)
Ham and Grits au Gratin (1 cup grits)
Owendaw ($\frac{3}{4}$ cup corn meal, $\frac{1}{2}$ cup grits)
Crisp Cheddar, Olive, and Onion Canapés ($\frac{3}{4}$ cup corn meal)
Corn Dogs ($\frac{1}{2}$ cup corn meal)
Steamed Applesauce Bread ($\frac{1}{2}$ cup corn meal)
Steamed Brown Bread ($\frac{1}{2}$ cup corn meal)
Blue Grass Chess Pie (2 tablespoons corn meal)

CORNSTARCH

Melting Moments (1 cup)
Chunks of Chicken in Sweet-Sour Sauce ($\frac{3}{4}$ cup plus 1 tablespoon)
Super-Crispy Fried Chicken ($\frac{3}{4}$ cup)
Highlands Shortbread ($\frac{1}{2}$ cup)
Chocolate Crispies ($\frac{1}{2}$ cup)
Coconut-Almond Cookies ($\frac{1}{3}$ cup)
Creamy Cornstarch Frosting ($\frac{1}{4}$ cup)
Cornstarch Seafoam Frosting ($\frac{1}{4}$ cup)
Swedish Brown Beans (2 tablespoons)
Orange and Ginger Sauce (2 tablespoons)

CORN SYRUP (LIGHT OR DARK)

Easiest Ever Strawberry Ice Cream (1 cup light)
Peanut-Maple Pie (1 cup dark)
Chocolate Brownie Pie (¾ cup dark)
Cranberry Glaze (½ cup light or dark)
Frozen Banana Cream (½ cup light or dark)
Lime-Pineapple Buttermilk Sherbet (½ cup light)
Orange-Almond Lace Cookies (½ cup light)
Fresh Blackberry-Strawberry Ice Cream (¼ to ¾ cup light)
Pineapple-Apricot Pie (¼ cup light)

CREAM (LIGHT, HEAVY, AND HALF-AND-HALF)

Tuna, Almond, and Egg Casserole (up to 2¾ cup any combination of milk and cream)
Cheese and Spinach Custard (up to 2 cups light or half-and-half)
Golden Cheddar and Carrot Soup (up to 2 cups any combination of milk and cream)
Baked Potatoes Stuffed the Portuguese Way with Creamed Salt Cod (up to 2 cups any combination of milk or cream)
Owendaw (up to 2 cups any combination of milk and cream)
Cheese, Bread, and Oyster Bake (up to 1½ cups of milk and cream)
Creamed Diced Carrots with Green Pepper (up to 1½ cups light or half-and-half)
Cherokee Chowder (1½ cups light or half-and-half or a combination)
Plantation Peanut Soup (up to 1½ cups light, heavy, or half-and-half)
Maple-Nut Sauce (1 to 1½ cups light or heavy)
Pimiento-Roquefort Pasta Ring (up to 1½ cups any combination of milk and cream)
Old Southern Batter Bread (up to 1¼ cups light)
Rice Batter Bread (up to 1¼ cups light)
Rice and Onion Pie (1 cup any combination of milk and cream)
Tuna, Almond, and Egg Casserole (up to 1 cup light or heavy)
Baltic Creamed Bacon and Mushrooms (1 cup light or heavy)
Blue Grass Chess Pie (1 cup light)
Curried Tuna Mousse (1 cup light, plus ½ cup heavy)
Hootsla (Bread-Cube Omelet) (1 cup any combination of milk and cream)
Old South Shrimp and Cheese Pudding (up to 1 cup light)
Easiest Ever Strawberry Ice Cream (up to 1 cup light or half-and-half milk and light cream combined)

Creamy Cornstarch Frosting (up to 1 cup)

Cornstarch Seafoam Frosting (up to 1 cup milk and light cream combined)

Cottage Potatoes (¾ to 1 cup light or heavy)

Corn and Pimiento Pudding (¾ cup light or heavy)

Boiled Dressing (¾ cup light or half-and-half plus ½ cup heavy)

Rhode Island Jonnycakes (up to ¾ cup light)

Frozen Banana Cream (¾ cup heavy)

Curried Apple Soup (½ to ¾ cup light or heavy)

Cold Asparagus with Sour Cream–Horseradish Dressing (½ to ¾ cup
   heavy)

Apple-Ginger Parfait (½ to ¾ cup heavy)

Mock Clotted Cream (½ to ¾ cup heavy)

Parmesan-Crumbed Chicken in Cognac-Cream Sauce (⅓ to ⅔ cup light or
   heavy)

Pimiento-Salmon Loaf (½ cup light or heavy)

Soufflé-Light Salmon Patties (½ cup heavy, light, or half-and-half)

Potato Puff (½ cup light or heavy)

Scalloped Eggplant (½ cup light or heavy)

Macaroni and Turkey Salad with Sweet Mustard Dressing (½ cup light or
   heavy)

Corn Dogs (½ cup light or heavy)

Grits and Cheddar Casserole (½ cup light or heavy)

Ham and Grits au Gratin (½ cup light or heavy)

Orange Fritters (½ cup heavy or light)

Easy Breakfast Waffles (½ cup light)

Paprika-Rolled Flounder Fillets in Dill-Wine Sauce (½ cup light or
   half-and-half)

Chili-Burger Omelet (⅓ cup light, heavy, or half-and-half)

Norwegian-Style Breaded Ham Patties (⅓ cup heavy, light, or
   half-and-half)

Kalvekarbonader (Norwegian Veal Patties) (⅓ cup light, heavy, or
   half-and-half)

Tuna- and Olive-Stuffed Potatoes (⅓ cup light)

Kotleti (Russian Meatballs Smothered in Cream Gravy) (¼ to ½ cup)

Onion-Smothered Round Steak (¼ to ½ cup light or heavy)

Mustard-Cheese Glaze for Broiled Burgers, Chops and Chicken (4 to 5
   tablespoons heavy or light)

Spinach-Endive Salad with Coconut-Buttermilk Dressing (¼ cup light,
   heavy, or half-and-half)

Lemon-Cardamom Pillows (¼ cup light or heavy)

Anatolian Cheese-Stuffed Peppers (3 to 6 tablespoons light or heavy)

Curried Crab and Rice Salad (2 to 4 tablespoons light cream)

Classic Cream Cheese Frosting (2 to 3 tablespoons light or heavy)

Coffee–Cream Cheese Frosting (2 to 3 tablespoons light or heavy)

Chocolate–Cream Cheese Frosting (2 to 3 tablespoons light or heavy)

Orange– or Lemon–Cream Cheese Frosting (2 to 3 tablespoons light or heavy)

Sour Cream, Caper, and Horseradish Sauce (2 tablespoons light or heavy)

Parkin (2 tablespoons light or heavy)

Mustard, Caper, and Horseradish Sauce (2 tablespoons light or heavy)

CRUMBS (BREAD, CRACKER, COOKIE, AND CAKE)

Soft Bread Crumbs

Mushroom Crust (4 cups)

Kotleti (Russian Meatballs Smothered in Cream Gravy) (4 cups)

Chicken Sesame (3 cups)

Scalloped Eggplant (2½ cups)

Date-Nut Pudding (2 cups)

Pimiento-Salmon Loaf (1½ cups)

Pork Chops with Peanut Stuffing (1 cup)

Pimiento-Roquefort Pasta Ring (1 cup)

Grits and Cheddar Casserole (1 cup)

Ham and Grits au Gratin (1 cup)

Spinach-Buttermilk Soup with Veal and Pork Balls (1 cup)

Corn and Pimiento Pudding (1 cup)

Lemon-Pecan Torte (1 cup)

Mother's Chocolate Bread Pudding (1 cup)

Soft Crumb Topping for Casseroles (1 cup)

Cheese-Crumb Topping (1 cup)

Parsley-Crumb Topping (1 cup)

Herbed Crumb Topping (1 cup)

Nut-Crumb Topping (1 cup)

Spicy Butter-Crumb Topping for Desserts (1 cup)

Parmesan-Crumbed Chicken in Cognac-Cream Sauce (½ to 1 cup)

Creole Squash Pudding (½ cup)

Maple-Apple-Yam Casserole (½ cup)

Dry Bread Crumbs

Fresh Fruit Pudding-Cobbler (2½ to 3 cups)

Crusty-Crumbed Oven-Fried Chicken (1½ to 2 cups)

Veal Milanese (1 cup)

Norwegian-Style Breaded Ham Patties (¾ to 1 cup)

Kalvekarbonader (Norwegian Veal Patties) (¾ to 1 cup)

Breaded Lamb Chops (¾ cup)

Sagey Meatball Casserole with Apples (½ cup)
Grits and Cheddar Casserole (½ cup)
Ham and Grits au Gratin (½ cup)
Äbblekage (Norwegian Apple Cake) (¼ to ⅓ cup)
Baked Squash and Tomato Strata (¼ cup)
Banbury Tarts (3 tablespoons)

Soda-Cracker (Saltine) Crumbs and Cracker Meal
Corn and Pimiento Pudding (1 cup cracker crumbs)
Veal Milanese (1 cup cracker meal)
Breaded Lamb Chops (¾ cup cracker meal)
Creole Squash Pudding (½ cup cracker meal)
Baked Squash and Tomato Strata (¼ cup cracker crumbs)
Banbury Tarts (3 tablespoons cracker crumbs)

Graham-Cracker, Cookie, and Cake Crumbs
Fresh Fruit Pudding-Cobbler (2½ to 3 cups graham-cracker, gingersnap, vanil-
   la- or lemon-wafer, or cake)
Classic Graham-Cracker Crust (1⅔ cups)
Athenian Honey-Cinnamon Cheesecake (crumbs from 20 graham crackers,
   about 1⅔ cups)
Vanilla-Wafer Crumb Crust (1⅔ cups)
Lemon-Wafer Crust (1⅔ cups)
Chocolate-Wafer Crust (1⅔ cups)
Gingersnap Crumb Crust (1⅔ cups)
Bourbon Balls (1¼ cups vanilla-wafer)
Scottish Ginger Torte (⅓ cup gingersnap, cake, or other cookie)

DATES (PITTED)

Date-Nut Pudding (1 cup chopped)
Easy Date-Filled Cookies (1 cup chopped)
Spicy Date-Oatmeal Clusters (1 cup chopped)
Quick Whole-Wheat–Apricot Bread (1 cup chopped)
Uncooked Sweetmeats (⅔ cup diced)
Date Scones (⅓ to ½ cup diced)

EGGS (WHITES, YOLKS, HARD-COOKED)

Whites
Upside-Down Nut Cake (⅔ cup)
Tutti-Frutti Meringues (4)
Almond Tuiles (Tiles) (4)
Cocoa-Cinnamon Ripple Coffee Cake (3)
Cream Cheese and Almond Pinwheels (2)

Coconut-Almond Cookies (2)
Mushroom Crust (1)
Anise Cookies (1)
Over-the-Top Cookies (1)
Rice and Onion Pie (1)

Yolks
Zabaglione alla Marsala (8)
Pytt i Panna (Swedish Hash) (6)
Mock Lemon (Vinegar) Pie (2 to 6)
Walnut Shortcakes (3)
Mocha Ice Cream Sauce (3)
Sablés (3)
Almond Sablés (3)
Potato Puff (2 to 4)
Boiled Dressing (2 to 3)
Flaky Egg Pie Crust (2)
Banbury Tarts (2)
Anise Cookies (2)
Fresh Fruit Pudding-Cobbler (1 to 2)
Nut-Cream Soup (1)
White Wine Sauce for Vegetables (1)
Orange and Ginger Sauce (1)

Hard-Cooked
Bifes Enrolados (Brazilian Beef Rolls Stuffed with Hard-Cooked Eggs and
    Olives (3)
Tuna, Almond, and Egg Casserole (2 to 4)
Curried Eggs (2 to 4)
Curried Crab and Rice Salad (2)
Buttermilk Gazpacho (2)
Open-Face Meat Pie (1 to 3)
Cheese and Spinach Custard (1 to 2)

FLOURS (WHOLE-GRAIN)

Steamed Applesauce Bread (1½ cups graham or whole-wheat)
Steamed Brown Bread (1½ cups graham or whole-wheat)
Oatmeal-Banana Muffins (1¼ cups whole-wheat or graham)
Rye Muffins (1 cup rye flour)
Honey-Whole Wheat Rolls (1 cup whole-wheat or graham)
Quick Whole-Wheat–Apricot Bread (1 cup whole-wheat)
Kartoffel Kloesse (Potato Dumplings) (½ cup farina)

GINGER (FRESH, CANDIED, AND PRESERVED)

Spinach-Endive Salad with Coconut-Buttermilk Dressing (2 to 3 tablespoons minced fresh)

Chicken in Yogurt with Coriander, Cumin, and Cardamom (2 tablespoons minced fresh)

Gingery Sweet-Sour Beef Stew with Molasses (2 tablespoons minced fresh, candied, or preserved)

Indonesian Chicken with Coconut and Peanut Sauce (two 1-inch cubes fresh, minced)

Szechuan Dry-Sautéed Broccoli (one 1- to 1½-inch cube fresh, minced)

Dry-Sautéed Green Beans (one 1- to 1½-inch cube fresh, minced)

Ginger-Glazed Carrots (one 1-inch cube fresh, minced)

Soy and Ginger Chicken Breasts Crumbed with Wheat Germ (one 1-inch cube fresh, crushed)

Kauai Sweet-Sour Spareribs (1 tablespoon minced fresh)

Curried Eggs (1 tablespoon minced fresh)

Honey-Soy Glaze (1 tablespoon minced fresh, candied, or preserved)

Quaker "Crackers" (48 thin slivers candied or preserved)

Ginger Ice Cream (½ to 1 cup chopped preserved or candied)

Orange and Ginger Sauce (¼ to ⅓ cup chopped candied or preserved)

GREEN (BELL) PEPPERS (ALSO SWEET RED AND YELLOW)

Pepper Bread (½ to ¾ cup chopped)

Creole Squash Pudding (½ cup minced)

Chili-Burger Omelet (½ large pepper, chopped)

Beef and Bulgur Loaf (½ medium pepper, chopped)

Buttermilk Gazpacho (½ cup diced)

Mexican Black Beans and Rice (½ cup chopped)

Macaroni and Turkey Salad with Sweet Mustard Dressing (½ cup minced)

Confetti Corn (⅓ to ⅔ cup minced)

Cajun Rice Dressing (⅓ to ½ cup chopped)

Rice Malaga (⅓ to ½ cup minced)

Beef and Rice with Tomato and Sweet Pepper (¼ to ½ cup minced)

Cherokee Chowder (¼ to ⅓ cup chopped)

Creamed Diced Carrots with Green Pepper (¼ to ⅓ cup chopped)

Curried Coconut and Cabbage (¼ cup chopped)

Oysters Kirkpatrick (¼ cup minced)

HERBS (FRESH)

Pesto Sauce (2 cups basil leaves)

Fresh Basil Jelly (2 cups basil sprigs)

Fresh Mint Jelly (2 cups mint sprigs)

Fresh Rosemary, Thyme, or Sage Jelly (2 cups rosemary, thyme, or sage sprigs)

Herbal Vinegars (1½ cups tarragon, chervil, thyme, dill, marjoram, or oregano sprigs)

Fines Herbes Vinegar (½ cup each chervil and tarragon sprigs)

Chunks of Veal Braised with Wine and Fresh Basil (⅓ to ½ cup chopped basil)

Green Goddess Dressing (¼ cup *each* minced tarragon and chives)

Cottage Potatoes (¼ cup minced chives)

Tabbouleh (Arabic Salad of Kasha, Tomato, Onion and Mint) (2 to 4 tablespoons minced mint)

Bosnian Lamb Balls in Caraway-Yogurt Sauce (2 tablespoons minced mint)

Plantation Peanut Soup (2 tablespoons minced chives)

Pimiento-Salmon Loaf (2 tablespoons snipped chives)

Tarragon–Buttermilk Dressing (2 tablespoons minced chives)

Low-Calorie Cottage Cheese–Chive Salad Dressing (2 tablespoons minced chives)

Bifes Enrolados (Brazilian Beef Rolls Stuffed with Hard-Cooked Eggs and Olives) (1 tablespoon minced chives)

Sour Cream–Mustard Sauce (2 tablespoons minced dill)

Sour Cream–Cucumber Sauce (1 tablespoon minced dill)

Paprika-Rolled Flounder Fillets in Dill-Wine Sauce (1 tablespoon minced dill)

Buttermilk Gazpacho (1 tablespoon minced dill)

HERBS AND SPICES (DRIED)

Chicken Sesame (⅓ cup sesame seeds)

Sesame Crisps (¼ to ½ cup sesame seeds)

Poppy Seed Sauerkraut (2 tablespoons poppy seeds)

Curried Apple Soup (2 tablespoons curry powder)

Vitello All' Uccelletto (Veal Scaloppine with Bay Leaves) (6 to 8 bay leaves)

Old German Sauerbraten (6 bay leaves, 12 whole cloves)

Peppery Pickled New Potatoes (4 bay leaves)

Chili-Burger Omelet (4 to 6 teaspoons chili powder)

Bosnian Lamb Balls in Caraway-Yogurt Sauce (1 tablespoon caraway seeds)

Caraway–Sour Cream Cookies (1 tablespoon caraway seeds)
Curried Coconut and Cabbage (1 tablespoon mustard seeds)
Boiled Dressing (2 to 3 teaspoons celery seeds)
Honey French Dressing (1 tablespoon paprika)
Paprika-Rolled Flounder Fillets in Dill-Wine Sauce (1 tablespoon paprika)
Super-Crispy Fried Chicken (1 tablespoon paprika)
'Lasses Bread (1 tablespoon ground ginger)
Grandmama's Soft Molasses Cookies (1 tablespoon ground ginger, 2
    teaspoons ground cinnamon, and 1 teaspoon ground cloves)
Anise Cookies (2 teaspoons each ground cardamom and anise, 1 teaspoon
    grated nutmeg)
Lemon-Cardamom Pillows (2 teaspoons ground cardamom)

HONEY

Honeyed Apple Chutney (1 cup)
Herbed Honey Glaze for Poultry, Pork, or Ham (¾ to 1 cup)
Athenian Honey-Cinnamon Cheesecake (¾ cup)
Honey-Hazelnut Bread (½ cup)
Cranberry Glaze (½ cup)
Honey–Chocolate Chip Cookies (½ cup)
Frozen Banana Cream (½ cup)
Cabbage Slaw with Sour Cream Dressing (⅓ to ½ cup)
Chunks of Chicken in Sweet-Sour Sauce (⅓ cup)
Honey-Glazed Beets and Sweets (¼ to ⅓ cup)
Honey French Dressing (¼ to ⅓ cup)
Fresh Blackberry-Strawberry Ice Cream (¼ to ¾ cup)
Honey–Whole Wheat Rolls (¼ cup)
Steamed Applesauce Bread (¼ cup)
Honey-Soy Glaze (¼ cup)
Acorn Squash Stuffed with Peanut and Pepper Pilaf (2 tablespoons)
Strawberry Butter (2 tablespoons)
Steamed Brown Bread (2 tablespoons)
All-Purpose Barbecue Sauce (1 to 4 tablespoons)
Boiled Dressing (1 to 3 tablespoons)
Chicken in Yogurt with Coriander, Cumin, and Cardamom (1 to 2
    tablespoons)
Picadinho (Brazilian Minced Meat) (1 to 2 tablespoons)
Curried Apple Soup (1 to 2 tablespoons)
Empadas (Brazilian Meat Turnovers) (1 to 2 tablespoons)
Cranberry-Raisin (Mock Cherry) Pie (1 tablespoon)
Low-Calorie Cottage Cheese–Chive Salad Dressing (1 tablespoon)

Spinach-Endive Salad with Coconut-Buttermilk Dressing (1 tablespoon)
Plantation Peanut Soup (1 tablespoon)

JAMS, JELLIES, MARMALADES, AND PRESERVES

Cranberry Glaze (1 cup cranberry jelly)
Buttermilk-Ham Loaf (½ to 1 cup tart red jelly)
Currant-Glazed Chunks of Veal (½ to ¾ cup currant or other tart jelly)
Äbblekage (Norwegian Apple Cake) (half 10-ounce jar raspberry or other berry jam)
Over-the-Top Cookies (half 10-ounce jar orange marmalade or raspberry jam)
Maple-Orange Glaze for Poultry and Pork (½ cup orange or ginger marmalade or any tart fruit jelly)
Ginger-Glazed Carrots (3 tablespoons orange marmalade or tart fruit jelly)

MAPLE SYRUP

Maple-Apple-Yam Casserole (1 cup)
Maple Sponge Cake (¾ cup)
Maple-Nut Sauce (½ to 1 cup)
Cranberry Glaze (½ cup)
Maple-Orange Glaze for Poultry and Pork (½ cup)
Peanut-Maple Pie (½ cup)
Date Scones (1 tablespoon)

MILK (EVAPORATED AND SWEETENED CONDENSED)

Evaporated

Golden Cheddar and Carrot Soup (up to 2 cups or in combination with milk or cream)
Cheese and Spinach Custard (up to 2 cups or in combination with milk or cream)
Baked Potatoes Stuffed the Portuguese Way with Creamed Salt Cod (up to 2 cups or in combination with milk or cream)
Cheese, Bread, and Oyster Bake (up to 1½ cups, or in combination with milk or cream)
Pimiento-Roquefort Pasta Ring (up to 1½ cups)
Maple-Nut Sauce (1 to 1½ cups)
Plantation Peanut Soup (up to 1½ cups)
Old Southern Batter Bread (up to 1¼ cups)
Rice Batter Bread (1¼ cups)

Pineapple-Apricot Pie (1 cup)
Curried Tuna Mousse (1 cup)
Easiest Ever Strawberry Ice Cream (1 cup)
Creamy Cornstarch Frosting (up to 1 cup)
Cornstarch Seafoam Frosting (up to 1 cup)
Hootsla (Bread-Cube Omelet) (up to 1 cup)
Rice and Onion Pie (up to 1 cup)
Old South Shrimp and Cheese Pudding (up to 1 cup)
Cottage Potatoes (¾ to 1 cup)
Rhode Island Jonnycakes (up to ¾ cup)
Boiled Dressing (¾ cup)
Corn and Pimiento Pudding (¾ cup)
Frozen Banana Cream (¾ cup)
Whipped Topping (½ to ¾ cup)
Crofter's Oat, Apple, and Lamb Loaf (½ cup)
Pimiento-Salmon Loaf (½ cup)
Macaroni and Turkey Salad with Sweet Mustard Dressing (½ cup)
Paprika-Rolled Flounder Fillets in Dill-Wine Sauce (½ cup)
Soufflé-Light Salmon Patties (½ cup)
Corn Dogs (½ cup)
Grits and Cheddar Casserole (½ cup)
Ham and Grits au Gratin (½ cup)
Potato Puff (½ cup)
Scalloped Eggplant (½ cup)
Easy Breakfast Waffles (½ cup)
Nut Waffles (½ cup)
Orange Fritters (½ cup)
Pork Chops with Peanut Stuffing (⅓ to ⅔ cup)
Chili-Burger Omelet (⅓ cup)
Norwegian-Style Breaded Ham Patties (⅓ cup)
Kalvekarbonader (Norwegian Veal Patties) (⅓ cup)
Tuna- and Olive-Stuffed Potatoes (⅓ cup)
Kotleti (Russian Meatballs Smothered in Cream Gravy) (¼ to ½ cup)
Curried Cole Slaw with Yogurt (¼ to ⅓ cup)
Mustard-Cheese Glaze for Broiled Burgers, Chops, and Chicken (4 to 5 table-
    spoons)
Spinach-Endive Salad with Coconut-Buttermilk Dressing (¼ cup)
Lemon-Cardamom Pillows (¼ cup)

Sweetened Condensed
Macaroni and Turkey Salad with Sweet Mustard Dressing (⅓ to ½ cup)
Plantation Peanut Soup (3 to 4 tablespoons)
Acorn Squash Stuffed with Peanut and Pepper Pilaf (2 tablespoons)

MOLASSES

Grandmama's Soft Molasses Cookies (1 cup)
All-Purpose Barbecue Sauce (1 cup)
Steamed Applesauce Bread (¾ cup)
Steamed Brown Bread (¾ cup)
'Lasses Bread (½ cup)
Frosted Coffee-Bran Bars (½ cup)
Anise Cookies (½ cup)
Gingery Sweet-Sour Beef Stew with Molasses (¼ to ⅓ cup)
Parkin (¼ cup)
Swedish Brown Beans (3 tablespoons)

MUSHROOM STEMS

Duxelles (Mushroom Paste) (minced, from 1 pound of mushrooms)
Skillet Veal in Mushroom and Wine Sauce (chopped, from ¾ to 1 pound of mushrooms)
Mushroom Crust (1¼ to 1½ cups minced)
Creole Squash Pudding (1 to 1½ cups chopped)
Spanish Onions Stuffed with Pecans, Mushrooms, and Rice (½ cup minced)

NUTS

Lemon-Pecan Torte (2 cups finely ground pecans)
Nut-Cream Soup (1½ cups finely ground blanched almonds or almonds and walnuts)
Cream Cheese and Almond Pinwheels (1½ cups ground almonds)
Lemon-Nut Bundt Cake (1½ cups chopped walnuts or pecans)
Sour Cream–Nut Cookies (1 to 1½ cups chopped pecans, walnuts, blanched almonds, or filberts)
Indonesian Chicken with Coconut and Peanut Sauce (1 to 1½ cups chopped peanuts)
Acorn Squash Stuffed with Peanut and Pepper Pilaf (1 cup chopped peanuts)
Plantation Peanut Soup (1 cup chopped peanuts)
Honey-Hazelnut Bread (1 cup chopped hazelnuts, pecans, or walnuts)
Peanut-Maple Pie (1 cup chopped peanuts)
Date-Nut Pudding (1 cup chopped pecans or walnuts)
Upside-Down Nut Cake (1 cup chopped walnuts, pecans, or other nuts)
Spicy Date-Oatmeal Clusters (1 cup chopped pecans, walnuts, or other nuts

Orange-Almond Lace Cookies (1 cup minced blanched almonds)
Almond Tuiles (Tiles) (1 cup finely ground blanched almonds)
Simnel Cake (1 cup finely ground almonds)
Coffee-Coconut Softies (1 cup chopped black walnuts, walnuts, or pecans)
Buttermilk Fudge (1 cup chopped walnuts or pecans)
Lemon-Nut Bundt Cake (¾ to 1½ cups chopped walnuts or pecans)
Pear-Pecan Pudding-Cake (¾ to 1 cup chopped pecans or walnuts)
Cabbage and Walnuts in Sour Cream (¾ to 1 cup chopped walnuts or
    pecans)
Honey-Whole Wheat Rolls (¾ cup chopped pecans, walnuts, peanuts, or
    almonds)
Chocolate Brownie Pie (¾ cup chopped pecans, walnuts, or other nuts)
Spanish Onions Stuffed with Pecans, Mushrooms, and Rice (⅔ to ¾ cup
    chopped pecans)
Bourbon Balls (⅔ cup minced pecans, black walnuts, or walnuts)
Honey–Chocolate Chip Cookies (⅔ cup chopped pecans or walnuts)
Picadinho (Brazilian Minced Meat) (½ to 1 cup chopped almonds, pignoli,
    peanuts, pecans, or walnuts)
Empadas (Brazilian Meat Turnovers) (½ to 1 cup chopped almonds,
    pignoli, peanuts, pecans, or walnuts)
Pork Chops with Peanut Stuffing (½ cup minced peanuts)
Wales Salad (½ cup slivered almonds)
Bolo Rei (King's Cake) (½ cup chopped pecans, walnuts, filberts, or
    almonds, plus ¼ cup chopped pignoli)
Walnut Shortcakes (½ cup finely ground walnuts)
Tutti-Frutti Meringues (½ cup chopped walnuts or pecans)
Banana-Oatmeal Cookies (½ cup chopped pecans, walnuts, or other
    nuts)
Uncooked Sweetmeats (½ cup finely minced pecans or walnuts)
Sesame Crisps (up to ½ cup chopped walnuts or pecans)
Scottish Ginger Torte (⅓ cup ground blanched almonds)
Coconut-Almond Cookies (⅓ cup chopped toasted blanched almonds)
Chocolate Crispies (⅓ cup ground walnuts)
Tuna, Almond, and Egg Casserole (¼ to ¾ cup chopped almonds, pecans,
    peanuts, or other nuts)
Nut-Crumb Topping (¼ to ½ cup minced pecans, walnuts, blanched
    almonds, or hazelnuts)
Maple-Nut Sauce (¼ to ½ cup chopped walnuts or pecans)
Macedonian Marinated Fish (¼ to ⅓ cup pignoli)
Bifes Enrolados (Brazilian Beef Rolls Stuffed with Hard-Cooked Eggs and
    Olives) (¼ cup minced almonds, peanuts, or pignoli)
Nut Waffles (¼ cup minced walnuts, pecans, or other nuts)

Cocoa-Cinnamon Ripple Coffee Cake (¼ cup minced pecans, walnuts, or blanched almonds)

Over-the-Top Cookies (¼ cup chopped walnuts)

Easy Date-Filled Cookies (¼ cup chopped walnuts, pecans, or blanched almonds)

Almond Sablés (¼ cup finely ground blanched almonds)

Pesto Sauce (3 to 4 tablespoons pignoli)

OATMEAL (ROLLED OATS)

Spicy Date-Oatmeal Clusters (2 cups)

Banana-Oatmeal Cookies (1¾ cups)

Oatmeal-Banana Muffins (1¼ cups)

Crofter's Oat, Apple, and Lamb Loaf (1 cup)

Parkin (1 cup)

OLIVES (GREEN OR RIPE)

Braised Lamb with Black Olives in Wine Gravy (½ to 1 cup coarsely chopped black, green, or pimiento-stuffed green)

Wales Salad (½ cup sliced pimiento-stuffed green)

Picadinho (Brazilian Minced Meat) (⅓ to ⅔ cup coarsely chopped pimiento-stuffed green or ripe)

Empadas (Brazilian Meat Turnovers) (⅓ to ⅔ cup coarsely chopped pimiento-stuffed green or ripe)

Tuna- and Olive-Stuffed Potatoes (¼ to ⅓ cup minced pimiento-stuffed green or ripe)

Crisp Cheddar, Olive, and Onion Canapés (¼ to ⅓ cup minced pimiento-stuffed green)

Salsa Verde (Green Sauce) (¼ cup minced ripe or pimiento-stuffed green)

Bifes Enrolados (Brazilian Beef Rolls Stuffed with Hard-Cooked Eggs and Olives) (3 to 5 tablespoons minced ripe or pimiento-stuffed green)

PARSLEY

Fresh Parsley Jelly (2 cups sprigs)

Fines Herbes Vinegar (½ cup sprigs)

Pesto Sauce (½ cup sprigs)

Salsa Verde (Green Sauce) (½ cup minced)

Bulgarian Sweet-Sour Bean Soup (⅓ cup minced)

Tabbouleh (Arabic Salad of Kasha, Tomato, Onion, and Mint) (¼ to ⅓ cup minced)

Parsley-Crumb Topping (¼ to ⅓ cup minced)

Tuna, Almond and Egg Casserole (¼ cup minced)
Chicken Sesame (¼ cup minced)
Picadinho (Brazilian Minced Meat) (¼ cup minced)
Empadas (Brazilian Meat Turnovers) (¼ cup minced)
Buttermilk-Ham Loaf (¼ cup minced)
Norwegian-Style Breaded Ham Patties (¼ cup finely chopped)
Kalvekarbonader (Norwegian Veal Patties) (¼ cup finely chopped)
Savory Lima Beans with Wine (¼ cup minced)
Tuna, Almond, and Egg Casserole (¼ cup minced)
Baltic Creamed Bacon and Mushrooms (¼ cup minced)
Green Goddess Dressing (¼ cup minced)
Beef and Rice with Tomato and Sweet Pepper (2 to 4 tablespoons minced)
Beef-Stuffed Eggplant (2 to 4 tablespoons minced)
Crusty-Crumbed Oven-Fried Chicken (2 to 4 tablespoons minced)
Mexican Black Beans and Rice (2 to 3 tablespoons minced)
Cherokee Chowder (2 tablespoons minced)
Tuna- and Olive-Stuffed Potatoes (2 tablespoons minced)
Pimiento-Salmon Loaf (2 tablespoons minced)
Bosnian Lamb Balls in Caraway-Yogurt Sauce (2 tablespoons minced)
Cajun Rice Dressing (2 tablespoons minced)
Pytt i Panna (Swedish Hash) (2 tablespoons minced)
Kartoffel Kloesse (Potato Dumplings) (2 tablespoons minced)
Veal Milanese (1 to 3 tablespoons minced)
Anchovy-Stuffed Eggs (1 tablespoon minced)
Bifes Enrolados (Brazilian Beef Rolls Stuffed with Hard-Cooked Eggs and
    Olives (1 tablespoon minced)

PIMIENTO

Wales Salad (½ cup chopped)
Swiss, Pimiento, and Bacon Spread (2 whole, minced)
Corn and Pimiento Pudding (3 to 4 tablespoons chopped)
Confetti Corn (2 to 4 tablespoons minced)
Pimiento-Roquefort Pasta Ring (2 to 4 tablespoons minced)
Pimiento-Salmon Loaf (2 tablespoons chopped)
Open-Face Meat Pie (1 to 2 tablespoons strips)

PRUNES AND OTHER DRIED FRUITS (APRICOTS AND FIGS)

Norwegian Fruit Soup (up to 2 cups mixed dried fruits—prunes, apricots,
    peaches, etc.)

Quick Whole-Wheat–Apricot Bread (1 cup chopped apricots or prunes)
Uncooked Sweetmeats (²⁄₃ cup diced figs)

RAISINS AND DRIED CURRANTS

Honeyed Apple Chutney (1 to 1½ cups dried currants or raisins)
Quick Whole-Wheat–Apricot Bread (1 cup raisins or dried currants)
Spicy Date-Oatmeal Clusters (1 cup)
Steamed Applesauce Bread (1 cup raisins or dried currants)
Steamed Brown Bread (1 cup raisins)
Banbury Tarts (1 cup raisins)
Coffee-Coconut Softies (1 cup raisins)
Health Cookies (1 cup raisins)
Irish Soda Bread (¾ to 1¼ cups raisins or dried currants)
Cranberry-Raisin (Mock Cherry) Pie (¾ cup raisins)
Simnel Cake (¾ cup raisins)
Lemon-Nut Bundt Cake (¾ cup raisins or dried currants)
Picadinho (Brazilian Minced Meat) (½ to 1 cup raisins)
Empadas (Brazilian Meat Turnovers) (½ to 1 cup raisins)
Norwegian Fruit Soup (½ cup each raisins and dried currants)
Tutti-Frutti Meringues (½ cup raisins)
Uncooked Sweetmeats (½ cup raisins)
Gingery Sweet-Sour Beef Stew with Molasses (⅓ to 1 cup raisins)
Bolo Rei (King's Cake) (⅓ cup raisins)
Applesauce Refrigerator Relish (⅓ cup raisins or dried currants)
Macedonian Marinated Fish (¼ to ½ cup raisins)

RICE (COOKED) (WHITE, BROWN, OR WILD)

Acorn Squash Stuffed with Peanut and Pepper Pilaf (2 to 2½ cups)
Mexican Black Beans and Rice (2 to 2½ cups)
Curried Crab and Rice Salad (1½ to 2 cups)
Beef-Stuffed Eggplant (1 to 1½ cups)
Rice and Onion Pie (1 to 1½ cups)
Rice Batter Bread (1 to 1½ cups)
Spanish Onions Stuffed with Pecans, Mushrooms, and Rice (1 cup)

SOUR CREAM

Plantation Peanut Soup (up to 1½ cups or in combination with milk and sweet cream)
Green Goddess Dressing (1 cup)

Buttermilk-Ham Loaf (1 cup)

Cabbage Slaw with Sour Cream Dressing (1 cup or 1 cup soured heavy cream)

Easiest Ever Strawberry Ice Cream (up to 1 cup)

Cabbage and Walnuts in Sour Cream (¾ to 1 cup)

Cottage Potatoes (¾ to 1 cup)

Sour Cream–Cucumber Sauce (¾ cup)

Lemon-Nut Bundt Cake (¾ cup)

Sour Cream–Nut Cookies (¾ cup)

Caraway–Sour Cream Cookies (¾ cup)

Cinnamon-Topped Sour Cream Cookies (¾ cup)

Baltic Creamed Bacon and Mushrooms (½ to 1 cup)

Braised Veal Loin with Lemon–Sour Cream Gravy (½ to 1 cup)

Austrian Veal Stew (½ to 1 cup)

Curried Apple Soup (½ to ¾ cup)

Mock Clotted Cream (½ to ¾ cup)

Cold Asparagus with Sour Cream–Horseradish Dressing (½ to ¾ cup)

Pimiento-Salmon Loaf (½ cup)

Curried Cole Slaw with Yogurt (½ cup)

Crisp Cheddar, Olive, and Onion Canapés (½ cup)

Deviled Ham Dip with Dill (½ cup)

Macaroni and Turkey Salad with Sweet Mustard Dressing (½ cup)

Soufflé-Light Salmon Patties (½ cup)

'Lasses Bread (½ cup)

Sour Cream, Caper, and Horseradish Sauce (½ cup)

Mustard, Caper, and Horseradish Sauce (½ cup)

Burger Stroganoff (⅓ to ¾ cup)

Norwegian-Style Breaded Ham Patties (⅓ cup)

Kalvekarbonader (Norwegian Veal Patties) (⅓ cup)

Onion-Smothered Round Steak (¼ to ½ cup)

Kotleti (Russian Meatballs Smothered in Cream Gravy) (¼ to ½ cup)

Spinach-Endive Salad with Coconut-Buttermilk Dressing (¼ cup)

Bosnian Lamb Balls in Caraway-Yogurt Sauce (¼ cup)

Swiss, Pimiento and Bacon Spread (4 to 6 tablespoons)

Anatolian Cheese-Stuffed Peppers (3 to 6 tablespoons)

Nut-Cream Soup (3 to 4 tablespoons, or up to ½ cup)

Classic Cream Cheese Frosting (2 to 3 tablespoons)

Coffee–Cream Cheese Frosting (2 to 3 tablespoons)

Chocolate–Cream Cheese Frosting (2 to 3 tablespoons)

Orange– or Lemon–Cream Cheese Frosting (2 to 3 tablespoons)

Parkin (2 tablespoons)

TOMATO PASTE, PURÉE, AND SAUCE (PLUS KETCHUP AND CHILI SAUCE)

Tomato Paste, Ketchup, and Chili Sauce

Pastichio (2 to 5 tablespoons tomato paste)

Pepperoni and Garbanzo Bake (2 to 4 tablespoons tomato paste)

Picadinho (Brazilian Minced Meat) (2 to 4 tablespoons tomato paste)

Empadas (Brazilian Meat Turnovers) (2 to 4 tablespoons tomato paste)

Bulgarian Sweet-Sour Bean Soup (2 to 4 tablespoons tomato paste)

Anatolian Cheese-Stuffed Peppers (2 to 3 tablespoons tomato paste)

Chicken in Yogurt with Coriander, Cumin, and Cardamom (2 tablespoons tomato paste or ketchup)

Burger Stroganoff (1 to 3 tablespoons tomato paste)

Gingery Sweet-Sour Beef Stew with Molasses (1 to 3 tablespoons tomato paste)

Bifes Enrolados (Brazilian Beef Rolls Stuffed with Hard-Cooked Eggs and Olives) (1 to 2 tablespoons tomato paste)

Chili-Burger Omelet (1 to 2 tablespoons tomato paste)

Roquefort-Horseradish Spread (1 to 2 tablespoons tomato paste, chili sauce, or ketchup)

Tomato- and Anchovy-Stuffed Flounder Rolls in Wine Sauce (2 teaspoons tomato paste)

All-Purpose Barbecue Sauce (½ cup ketchup or chili sauce)

Beef and Bulgur Loaf (¼ cup ketchup or tomato paste)

Oysters Kirkpatrick (¼ cup ketchup or chili sauce)

Curried Cole Slaw with Yogurt (2 tablespoons ketchup)

Chunks of Chicken in Sweet-Sour Sauce (2 tablespoons ketchup)

Buttermilk-Ham Loaf (1 to 2 tablespoons ketchup or tomato paste)

Tomato Sauce and Purée

Chili-Burger Omelet (⅔ to 1⅓ cups sauce)

Picadinho (Brazilian Minced Meat) (½ to 1 cup sauce)

Empadas (Brazilian Meat Turnovers) (½ to 1 cup sauce)

Rice Malaga (½ to ¾ cup sauce or purée)

Creole Squash Pudding (½ to ¾ cup sauce)

Plantation Peanut Soup (½ cup sauce)

Curried Tuna Mousse (up to ½ cup sauce or purée)

Beef and Rice with Tomato and Sweet Pepper (⅓ to ½ cup sauce)

Chunks of Veal Braised with Wine and Fresh Basil (⅓ to ½ cup sauce or purée)

Beef-Stuffed Eggplant (¼ to ½ cup sauce)

Beef and Bulgur Loaf (¼ cup sauce)

V I N E G A R

Old German Sauerbraten (2 cups cider vinegar)
Peppery Pickled New Potatoes (1½ cups cider vinegar)
All-Purpose Barbecue Sauce (1 cup cider or wine vinegar)
Boiled Dressing (¾ cup cider vinegar)
Honey French Dressing (⅔ cup cider, wine, or tarragon vinegar)
Kauai Sweet-Sour Spareribs (½ cup cider vinegar)
Bulgarian Sweet-Sour Bean Soup (½ cup cider vinegar)
Chunks of Chicken in Sweet-Sour Sauce (½ cup cider or rice vinegar)
Tarragon-Buttermilk Dressing (½ cup tarragon vinegar)
Macedonian Marinated Fish (⅓ cup white wine vinegar)
Gingery Sweet-Sour Beef Stew with Molasses (⅓ cup cider vinegar)
Cabbage Slaw with Sour Cream Dressing (⅓ cup cider vinegar)
Salsa Verde (Green Sauce) (¼ cup red wine vinegar)
Green Goddess Dressing (¼ cup tarragon vinegar)
Spinach-Endive Salad with Coconut-Buttermilk Dressing (¼ cup tarragon
    vinegar)
Mock Lemon (Vinegar) Pie (¼ cup cider vinegar)

W H E A T   G E R M

Crunchy-Crusted Wheat Germ Muffins (1 cup plus 3 tablespoons)
Health Cookies (¾ cup)
Soy and Ginger Chicken Breasts Crumbed with Wheat Germ (½ cup)

W I N E

Old German Sauerbraten (3 cups dry red, a not improbable amount to be
    left over now that better wines are being bottled by the gallon and
    half-gallon jug)
Austrian Veal Stew (up to 1½ cups dry red or white)
Bulgarian Sweet-Sour Bean Soup (1 cup dry white)
Savory Lima Beans with Wine (¾ to 1¼ cups dry white)
Creole Squash Pudding (up to ¾ cup dry white)
Macedonian Marinated Fish (⅔ to 1 cup dry white)
Vitello All'Uccelletto (Veal Scaloppine with Bay Leaves) (⅔ cup dry white
    or vermouth)
Chunks of Veal Braised with Wine and Fresh Basil (⅔ cup dry white)
Parmesan-Crumbed Chicken in Cognac-Cream Sauce (½ to 1 cup dry
    white)
Picadinho (Brazilian Minced Meat) (½ to 1 cup dry white or red)

Empadas (Brazilian Meat Turnovers) (½ to 1 cup dry white or red)

Braised Lamb with Black Olives in Wine Gravy (½ to ¾ cup dry red or white)

Currant-Glazed Chunks of Veal (½ cup dry white or red)

Tomato- and Anchovy-Stuffed Flounder Rolls in Wine Sauce (½ cup dry white)

Bifes Enrolados (Brazilian Beef Rolls Stuffed with Hard-Cooked Eggs and Olives) (½ cup Madeira or Port)

Italian Wine Cake (½ cup dry white)

Beef and Rice with Tomato and Sweet Pepper (⅓ to ⅔ cup dry red or white)

White Wine Sauce for Vegetables (⅓ to ½ cup dry white)

Skillet Veal in Mushroom and Wine Sauce (⅓ cup dry white wine)

Gingery Sweet-Sour Beef Stew with Molasses (¼ to ⅔ cup dry red or white)

Paprika-Rolled Flounder Fillets in Dill-Wine Sauce (¼ cup dry white or vermouth)

Cheese, Bread, and Oyster Bake (¼ cup dry white or sherry)

Pepperoni and Garbanzo Bake (¼ cup dry white)

Chunks of Chicken in Sweet-Sour Sauce (¼ cup dry white or vermouth)

Honey-Soy Glaze (¼ cup dry sherry, Madeira, or Port)

Norwegian Fruit Soup (¼ cup Madeira, Marsala, Port, or sherry)

Zabaglione alla Marsala (¼ cup Marsala)

Plantation Peanut Soup (3 tablespoons Port or sherry)

Nut-Cream Soup (2 to 3 tablespoons dry sherry)

Soy and Ginger Chicken Breasts Crumbed with Wheat Germ (2 tablespoons sherry, Port, or Madeira)

YOGURT

Bosnian Lamb Balls in Caraway-Yogurt Sauce (¾ to 1 cup)

Cottage Potatoes (¾ to 1 cup)

Easiest Ever Strawberry Ice Cream (up to 1 cup)

Veal Paprikash with Yogurt (½ to ¾ cup)

Chicken in Yogurt with Coriander, Cumin, and Cardamom (½ to ¾ cup)

Shredded Zucchini with Onion and Yogurt (½ cup)

Deviled Ham Dip with Dill (½ cup)

Low-Calorie Cottage Cheese-Chive Salad Dressing (½ cup)

Curried Cole Slaw with Yogurt (½ cup)

INDEX

ABOUT METRIC MEASURES

Going metric does not mean that you must abandon your favorite cookbooks, your measuring spoons, or even that antique copper mold that once belonged to your great-great-grandmother. But it does mean you must learn to relate that system of measuring to the one now coming into use. To help ease the transition, here are handy tables of Metric-American equivalents, as well as formulas for converting Fahrenheit to Celsius and vice versa.

NOTE: *For simplicity's sake, we have rounded the metric equivalents out to the nearest whole number wherever practical.*

VOLUME

American Measure		Approx. Metric Equivalent
1/4 cup	=	62 ml (milliliters)
1/3 cup	=	75 ml
1/2 cup	=	125 ml
2/3 cup	=	150 ml
3/4 cup	=	185 ml
1 cup	=	250 ml
1 quart	=	990 ml

NOTE: *Small amounts, more than likely, will continue to be measured with the standard measuring spoons.*

WEIGHTS

American Measure		Metric Equivalent
1 ounce	=	28.35 g (grams)
1 pound	=	453.59 g (about 1/2 kg)
2.2 pounds	=	1 kg (kilo, kilogram)

LINEAR MEASURES

American Measure		Metric Equivalent
1 inch	=	2.54 cm (centimeters)
1 foot (12 inches)	=	30.5 cm
1 yard (3 feet)	=	91 cm (0.9 m)
1 yard + 3½ inches (39½ inches)	=	1 m (meter)

TEMPERATURES

General	F°		C°
Normal body temperature	98.6	=	37
Water boils	212	=	100
Water simmers	180	=	82
Water freezes	32	=	0

Oven Heats
(to the nearest round deg. C.)

	F°		C°
Very slow	275	=	135
Slow	300	=	150
Moderately slow	325	=	165
Moderate	350	=	175
Moderately hot	375	=	190
Hot	400	=	205
Very hot	425–450	=	220–230
Extremely hot	500 or more	=	260 or more

Candy Tests

	F°		C°
Thread stage	230–234	=	110–112
Soft ball	234–240	=	112–116
Firm ball	244–248	=	118–120
Hard ball	250–266	=	121–130
Soft crack	270–290	=	132–143
Hard crack	300–310	=	149–154

Meat Doneness Test
(meat thermometer reading)

	F°		C°
Very rare	120	=	49
Rare	125–130	=	52–54
Medium rare	135–145	=	57–63
Medium	150–160	=	66–71
Well done (beef, veal, lamb, pork)	160–170	=	71–77
Well done (poultry)	180–185	=	82–85

TO CONVERT FAHRENHEIT TO CELSIUS	Subtract 32 from the Fahrenheit temperature, then divide by 1.8—e.g., 212° F. − 32 = 180 ÷ 1.8 = 100° C.
TO CONVERT CELSIUS TO FAHRENHEIT	Multiply the degrees Celsius by 1.8, then add 32—e.g., 100° C. × 1.8 = 180 + 32 = 212° F.